Nov 20, 199?

The Great Irish Famine

To Jim Rogers,

Thanking you for all the work you put in to making this tour such a success.

I am deeply indebted to you.

God wishes,

Don Mullan

Canon John O'Rourke

The Great Irish Famine

VERITAS

First published 1874
Second and third editions by
James Duffy and Co Ltd, Dublin

This abridged edition published 1989 by
Veritas Publications
7/8 Lower Abbey Street
Dublin 1

ISBN 1 85390 049 4 Hardback
ISBN 1 85390 130 X Paperback

Cover illustration by Darina Roche BA (after Käthe Collwitz, 1867-1945)
Cover design by Philip Melly
Illustrations from the *Illustrated London News* and *Pictorial Times*, courtesy
National Library of Ireland
Typesetting by Printset & Design Ltd, Dublin
Printed in the Republic of Ireland by Mount Salus Press Ltd

Contents

Introduction

During the Great 'Famine' of 1845-1849, Thomas Willis MD served the Bantry region of West Cork. He struggled heroically to bring what little comfort he could to the multitudes of sick and starving peasants. Dr Willis was a caring and sensitive physician who felt desperately inadequate in the face of an artificial hunger, for which food was the only real medicine. He was shocked by the avalanche of disease and deaths which overwhelmed Bantry, especially in 1847. What horrified him most was the use of a single hinged coffin to convey the dead to one mass grave. He estimated that this one coffin alone had, in a short period, carried several hundred men, women and children to the local pit, into which their remains were thrown.

When the 'Famine' later abated, rather than see the coffin burned or buried, Dr Willis felt it somehow symbolised the Golgotha of Ireland's poorest and most vulnerable and should, therefore, be preserved. He had three crosses fashioned from its wood. In 1870 he gave one of these crosses to Canon John O'Rourke, who later placed it in the safe keeping of the Presentation Sisters, Maynooth. It is, I believe, one of the most precious and moving relics of the Great 'Famine' which exists today in Ireland.

In February 1984, a full two years before I knew anything about Dr Willis' 'Famine' cross, I too was horrified to discover a similar coffin being widely used throughout north-east Brazil. It was my wife Margaret who first spotted it, tucked away in the rafters of the little church of Santa Victoria in the parish of Iguatu Ceara. It too had been invented to cope with the deluge of death which descended upon the region from 1979-1984, during which some three to four million Brazilian peasants died. All the while, food was being exported to richer markets, while arable land was producing cash-crops for foreign consumption. It is perhaps not surprising, therefore, that this Great 'Famine' in Brazil was referred to in a recent book title as 'O genocidio do Nordeste'.

In Brazil, Ethiopia, Sudan, South Africa, the Philippines, to name but a few, the cry of the poor is deafening if only we are prepared momentarily to halt our feverish pursuit of wealth and material comfort. The holocaust of poverty and hunger consumes 40,000 innocent human beings a day! Ireland too has its poor, and their poverty and suffering, like that of all 'Third World' people, is directly attributable to the unfair distribution of wealth and resources at national and international level. However, to those who have made power, profit and privilege their burning ambition, the poor do not count.

Thomas Willis and Canon John O'Rourke were moved to preserve the memory of the Great Irish 'Famine' of 1845-1849. Perhaps they foresaw the day when future generations of Irish people, at home and abroad, might help to redeem the appalling suffering and injustice they themselves witnessed, through making the politics of compassion a guiding principle in our national and foreign policies. Indeed, arising out of this heritage of hunger, the Irish could and should be the leading moral force in the Western World, working for a more humane and caring global society. Our continual failure to reach the UN target of just .7% of GNP diminishes Ireland's credibility as a country motivated by deep spiritual values and a sense of justice for all.

It is to be hoped that the republication of Canon O'Rourke's *History of the Great Irish Famine* will contribute to a broadly based political re-think on the issue of our Official Development Assistance, with renewed commitment at Cabinet level to see Ireland reach the United Nations target in time for the new millennium! Such a commitment would, we believe, have the popular support of the Irish electorate.

On behalf of AFrI, I wish to thank both Fr Martin Tierney and Veritas Publications for re-publishing this important work, as a contribution to our Great 'Famine' Project.

Royalties from the sales of the book will be graciously donated to AFrI's Great 'Famine' Project. The aim of the project is to help Irish people everywhere understand more clearly the cause and effect of this immense human catastrophe and its many parallels throughout the world today — a world where the poor need justice, far in excess of charity.

Far from wishing to trade in bitterness and hatred, the motto of the Great 'Famine' Project captures the essence of our hope:
'Let us not do unto others
the wrong that was done to our own'.

Don Mullan
Co-ordinator
The Great 'Famine' Project

2 June 1989

Further information on AFrI's Great 'Famine' Project can be obtained by writing to P.O. Box 1522, Dublin 1, Ireland.

Foreword

When invited to write the foreword to this new abridged edition of *The Great Irish Famine* I was about to set out on an African journey. The journey took me to projects mounted from Ireland for the poor, the famished and the dispossessed. The projects I visited dot the map of East Africa from Mozambique in the far south through Tanzania, Ethiopia and Sudan. I thought it would not be inappropriate to look back down the years from this trail and view Ireland's famine, dire poverty and dispossession of the 1840s against the backdrop of Africa's famines of the 1980s. The skeletal spectres and statistics of nearly a century and a half ago recalled in this book are thus thrown into stark relief. The haunting figures of our starving ancestors are seen alive and dying again in wasted black bodies.

At dusk in Nampula, a town in the more northerly parts of Mozambique, I met a small tattered band of people — a frightened old man, two older and a few young women. All were of pathetic appearance. There were but few children. One of the younger women held, perched on her hip the way African women often carry their babies, a wasted handful of a child. The child unbelievably was two years old. She had been able to walk but had lost the power, or perhaps just the will, to walk any more. They had struggled to the office of the relief officer. They were helpless and hopeless. For Nampula 1989 read Skibbereen 1846.

Wollaita, in the more southerly part of Ethiopia, was ravaged by famine in 1984 and again in 1985. This is a poor and over-populated area of Ethiopia. God knows these people suffered more than enough in two recent years of famine. Every poor family contributed its corpse or two to the charnel pile. But a new terror stalked the area from Christmas 1988 through the Spring months of 1989. Then fever struck. It was another echo of the Irish famine years when fever claimed as many lives as hunger. Meningitis in wild epidemic proportions took a toll of young and not so young in Ethiopia. The fever struck with savage speed and spared no families, not even the somewhat better off.. Fifteen thousand died in this one area in a few short months. The fever instilled fear. It was not easy to bury the dead or carry the dying victims across the hills on litters in search of life-saving medication. The more healthy feared the contagion. Was it Westport? Was it densely populated Mayo in 1846?

I sat down to write in Muglad in South Kordofan, Sudan. From the beginning of March to yesterday 9,377 Dinka tribespeople arrived by truck, by train, on foot from starving areas further south to seek refuge and succour in Muglad camp.

The camp is a discreet distance from the edge of the town. Now the numbers of desolate Dinka sheltering here match the town's own population of more than 18,000. Here a few months ago I saw starving people literally crawl the last yards and collapse in the camp. Every day took its toll. Bodies were carried outside the camp perimeters and buried in unmarked shallow graves, or scarcely covered at all. The vultures hovered overhead. There were reports of the scavenger wild dogs eating the sparse flesh of the victims of starvation and dispossession. These were once proud, cattle-owning, nomadic people. The last few years have robbed them of their herds or forced them to sell their remaining animals to raise the fares to flee their own land. They live the pages of this book.

Is this camp in South Kordofan a reflection through the years of the crowded workhouses of Ireland's 1840s or the crowded holds of the coffin ships, or the delousing reception centres across the Atlantic? Last year, according to conservative estimates, 250,000 people starved to death in Southern Sudan. This year greater efforts are being made to avert a repeat of the disaster. The Muglad town stores now hold nearly 2,000 tons of food. More than 12,000 tons have been processed through since February. Today the two-weekly distribution of family rations was completed in Muglad. Thirty-two truckloads of supplies arrived to add to stocks for the months ahead.

Irony of ironies, much of the food arriving in Muglad comes from the same source as the replacement food that fed the starving Irish robbed of their corn as payment to absentee landlords. It is American grain! It has earned the nickname 'Reagan' in Africa's recent famines. Grown as animal feed on the plains of America it replaces the milk, blood and meat from their herds that helped make up the traditional diet of these tall people from the South before they were robbed of their herds.

Too much of our history records wars and heroes of battles fought long ago. Not nearly enough is taught to new generations of the social struggles and battles for survival that were fought by countless thousands of our more humble forebears. Their monuments are there to be seen in every corner of our land but all too often they go unseen. I grew up outside the walls of what was Limerick's workhouse. In the 1840s it was a respectable distance from the outskirts of Limerick city as is Muglad camp today. I heard old people call our crossroads on the now fashionable Ennis Road, 'the Workhouse Cross'. A mile down the road was the paupers' graveyard with its lone naked cross and unmarked graves. I remember our fear of 'the fever' when we played on the road as children if a lonely pauper's funeral passed.

I have walked the famine roads of North Clare with their stunning views of Galway Bay, views scarcely appreciated by those who toiled to build these meaningless roadways. The signposts politely shelter today's people from the harsh memories. 'Bóithrin an Gorta' is translated softly into 'The Green Road' and so attracts few down these memory lanes laid by our starving ancestors in often pointless famine work schemes. The schemes were too often designed to protect the feckless Irish from becoming even more feckless, a danger to which they would undoubtedly have been exposed if given 'handouts'!

Like today's poor and dispossessed they were all too frequently blamed for their condition. Their monuments are everywhere in our land. This book, written in Maynooth in 1874 when memories were still green, passed on to another generation the story of harder times. It is healthy that we carry the memory forward. Let us tell our children. The folk memory is entrusted to us. We must carry it forward. I believe that folk memory is the source of much of the compassion which has fired the extraordinary generosity which has marked the reaching out of the people of Ireland to the famine victims of our time. I have just travelled the map of East Africa. Responses emanating from Ireland and going out to the poor and dispossessed stand out like beads in a rosary.

They link us with our own starving ancestors recalled in these pages and seen again in the African child tugging its mother's withered milkless breasts, in the exhausted Dinka herdsman crawling on all fours in cruel parody of his lost animals across the threshold of Muglad camp and then carried by scarcely less weak neighbours.

It was Margaret Meade, the great anthropologist, who said that a westerner who had not savoured the poverty of his or her native land should not presume to address the problems of another country. And Chesterton said that those who have not learned to respect the past have little to contribute to the future. The road through *The Great Irish Famine* is a *via dolorosa* but the book will help give a better understanding of the people from whom we have sprung. Read in the context of famine today this book will strengthen in us feelings of unity and solidarity that will fuel our compassion and readiness to share with those whose lot is the pangs of hunger in our world of plenty.

Aengus Finucane CSSp
Muglad
Sudan

25 May 1989

Preface

The author of this volume has, for a considerable time, been of the opinion that the leading facts of the Great Irish Famine of 1847 ought to be put together without unnecessary delay. Several reasons occurred to him why such a work should be done: the magnitude of the Famine itself; the peculiarity of its immediate cause; its influence on the destiny of the Irish race. That there should be no unnecessary delay in performing the task was sufficiently proved, he thought, by the fact that testimony of the most valuable kind, namely, contemporary testimony, was silently but rapidly passing away with the generation that had witnessed the scourge.

Having made up his mind to undertake such a work, the author's first preparation for it was to send query sheets to such persons as were supposed to be in possession of information on the subject. And he has here to express his gratitude and thanks to his numerous correspondents for the kindness and promptness with which his queries were answered. He cannot recall even one case in which this was not done. But there is a dark side to the picture too. In looking over the query sheets now, it is sad to find how many of those whose signatures they bear have already passed from amongst us.

Other materials of great importance lay scattered over the public journals of the period; were buried and stowed away in Parliamentary Blue Books and Parliamentary debates; were to be sought for in pamphlets, in periodicals, and more especially in the reports of the various societies and associations which were appointed for dispensing the alms given with such free hand, to aid in saving the lives of the famishing people. Those records will be found quoted and referred to in the course of the work.

Amongst them, it is but just to acknowledge how much the author owes to the report of the census commissioners for 1851; to the 'Transactions' of the Society of Friends; and to *Irish Crisis*, by Sir Charles E. Trevelyan, Bart, which originally appeared as an article in the *Edinburgh Review* for January 1848, but was reprinted in a small volume of 200 pages. Although far from agreeing with many of Sir Charles' conclusions (he was Secretary to the Treasury during the Famine), still the author cheerfully acknowledges that the statistical information in *Irish Crisis* is very valuable to a student of the history of the Famine period.

It was to be expected that the alarm about the potato blight and the Famine would be first raised through the public press. This was done by letters from various localities and by special reporters and commissioners, who travelled through the country to examine the state of the people as well as that of the potato crop. There was a commissioner from the London *Times* in Ireland at this period. His letters written to that journal were afterwards collected and they made an octavo volume of nearly 800 pages.

The English people, and many in Ireland, long adhered to the opinion that there was much exaggeration in the Irish newspapers regarding both the blight and the Famine; but subsequent investigation showed that there was very little, if any, exaggeration; nay, that the real facts were often understated. As to the Famine, several of the gentlemen sent by the charitable societies to make reports wrote back that there was no exaggeration whatever and for a very sufficient reason, namely, that in their opinion it was impossible to exaggerate the dreadful condition in which they found the people.

Another mode of acquiring information adopted by the author was to visit those parts of the country in which the Famine had raged with the greatest severity. On such occasions he not only had the advantage of examining the localities, but of conversing with persons whose knowledge of that awful calamity made them valuable and interesting guides.

As to the rest, it is left to the kindness of the reader.

St Mary's, Maynooth

1 December 1874

1

How the potato came to Europe

The Great Irish Famine, which reached its height in 1847, was, in many of its features, the most striking and most deplorable known to history. The deaths resulting from it, and the emigration which it caused, were so vast that, at one time, it seemed as if America and the grave were about to absorb the whole population of this country between them.

The cause of the calamity was almost as wonderful as the result. It arose from the failure of a root which, by degrees, had become the staple food of the whole working population: a root which, on its first introduction, was received by philanthropists and economists with joy, as a certain protection against that scarcity which sometimes resulted from short harvests. In 1662 Mr Buckland, a Somersetshire gentleman, sent a letter to the Royal Society, recommending the planting of potatoes in all parts of the kingdom, to *prevent famine,* for which he received the thanks of that learned body; and Evelyn, the well-known author of 'The Sylva', was requested to mention the proposal at the end of that work.

The potato was first brought into this country about three centuries ago. Tradition and, to some extent, history attribute its introduction to Sir Walter Raleigh. Whether this was actually the case or not, there seems to be no doubt about his having cultivated it on that estate in Munster which was bestowed upon him by his royal mistress after the overthrow of the Desmonds.[1]

Some confusion has arisen about the period at which the potato of Virginia, as I shall for the present call the potato, was brought to our shores, from the fact that another root, the *batatas* or sweet potato, came into these islands, and was used as a delicacy before the potato of Virginia was known; and what adds to the confusion is that the name potato, applied to the Virginian root, is derived

1

from *batatas*, it not bearing in Virginia any name in the least resembling the word potato. Up to 1640 it was called in England the potato of Virginia, to distinguish it from the sweet potato, which is another evidence that it derived the name potato from *batatas*.[2] The latter root was extensively cultivated for food in parts of America, but it never got into anything like general cultivation here, perhaps because our climate was too cold for it. It is now only found in our hot-houses, where it produces tubers from one to two pounds in weight.

It has been asserted that Sir John Hawkins brought the potato to Ireland in 1565, and his kinsman Sir Francis Drake to England in 1585. Although this is not improbable, writers generally assume that it was the sweet potato which was introduced by those navigators.

Whether or not Raleigh's third expedition, which sailed from England in 1584, was the *first* to bring into these countries the potato of Virginia, there can be no reasonable doubt of its having been brought home by that expedition. The story of Raleigh having stopped on some part of the Irish coast on his way from Virginia, when he distributed potatoes to the natives, is quite groundless. Raleigh was never in Virginia; for although by his money and influence, and perhaps yet more by his untiring energy, he organised nine exploring expeditions, he did not sail with any of them except the first, which was commanded by his half-brother, Sir Humphrey Gilbert. But this had to return disabled to England without touching land.[3]

Sir Joseph Banks, the well-known naturalist and President of the Royal Society from 1777 until his death in 1820, was at great pains to collect the history of the introduction of the potato into these countries. His account is that Raleigh's expedition, granted to him under patent 'to discover such remote heathen and barbarous lands not yet actually possessed by any Christian prince, nor inhabited by Christian people, as to him shall seem good', brought home the potato of Virginia. This character bears the date 25 March 1584 and was a new and more extensive one than the first granted to him, which was in June 1578.

With this expedition sailed one Thomas Heriot, called the Mathematician, who was probably sent out to examine and report upon the natural history of such countries as they might discover. He wrote an account of Virginia, and of the products of its soil, which was printed in the first volume of De Bry's collection of voyages. Under the article 'Roots', he described a plant which he called opanawk. 'These roots', he says, 'are round, some as large as a walnut, others much larger; they grow in damp soil, many hanging together as if fixed with ropes. They are good food

2

either boiled or roasted.' This must strike anyone as a very accurate description of the potato. Gerarde, in his *Herbal*, published in 1597, gives a figure of the potato under the name of the potato of Virginia. He asserts that he received the roots from that country, and that they were denominated naremberga.

Raleigh's expedition, which seems to have been already prepared, sailed in April and, having taken possession of that portion of America which was afterwards named Virginia in honour of Queen Elizabeth and by her own express desire, returned to England about the middle of September of the same year.

Although, as already stated, in all likelihood the potato of Virginia was introduced into England and Ireland by that expedition, Sir Joseph Banks was of the opinion that the root had come to Europe earlier. His reasons for thinking so are:

1. Clusius, otherwise L'Ecluse, the great botanist, when residing in Vienna in 1598, received the potato from the Governor of Mons, in Hainault, who had obtained it the year before from one of the attendants of the Pope's Legate under the name of taratouflè,[4] and learned from him that in Italy, where it was then in use, no one knew whether it came from Spain or America. From this we may conclude that the root was in Italy before it was brought to England, for this conversation happened only three years after the sailing of the expedition of 1584.

   It is further very probable that the root found its way from Spain into Italy, as those parts of America where the potato was indigenous were then subject to Spain.

2. Peter Cicca, in his *Chronicle* of 1553, said the inhabitants of Quito and its vicinity had, besides mays (maize), a tuberous root which they ate and called *papas*; which Clusius with much probability guessed to be the same sort of plant that he received from the Governor of Mons.

There is one obvious difficulty in this reasoning; we are not at all sure that it was the potato of Virginia that Clusius obtained from the Governor of Mons; it may have been the sweet potato. However, the conclusion which Sir Joseph Banks draws from these details is that potatoes were brought from the mountainous parts of South America in the neighbourhood of Quito and that, as the Spaniards were the sole possessors of that country, there can be little doubt of their having been first carried into Spain. Further, that as it would take a considerable time to introduce them into Italy, and make the Italians acquainted with them to the extent of giving them a name, there is good reason to believe that they had been several years in Europe before they had been sent to Clusius.

About 600,000 acres of land in Munster were declared forfeit to the Crown on the fall of the Desmonds. This was parcelled out to 'gentlemen undertakers' on certain conditions; one being that they were bound, within a limited time, to people their estates with 'well-affected Englishmen'. Raleigh became an undertaker and, by a legal instrument bearing the Queen's name, dated from Greenwich, last day of February 1586, he was given 42,000 acres of this land and, by a further grant the year after, the monastery of Molanassa and the Priory of Black Friars, near Youghal.[5]

Famine followed close upon the war with the Desmonds. 'At length,' said Hooker, 'the curse of God was so great, and the land so barren both of man and beast, that whatsoever did travel from one end to the other of all Munster, even from Waterford to Smerwick, about six score miles, he should not meet man, woman or child, saving in cities or towns, nor yet see any beast, save foxes, wolves, or other ravening beasts'.[6] Such was Munster when the great coloniser planted the potato there, in the hope, perhaps, of averting future famines!

It is generally assumed by writers on Ireland that soon after the introduction of the potato, it became a general favourite and was cultivated in most parts of the country as an important crop. This seems to be far from correct. Supposing the potato which we now grow, the *solanum tuberosum* of botanists, to have come to Ireland in 1586, the usually accepted date, it does not seem to have been in anything like general favour or cultivation 140 years later, at least in the richer and more important districts of the country.

In a pamphlet printed in 1723, 137 years after the introduction of the potato, speaking of the fluctuation of the markets, the writer said: 'We have always either a glut or a dearth; very often there are not ten days distance between the extremity of the one and the other; such a want of policy is there (in Dublin especially) on the most important affair of bread, without a plenty of which *the poor must starve'*.

If potatoes were at this time looked upon as an important food crop, the author would scarcely omit noticing the fact, especially in speaking of the food of the poor. At page 25 of the same pamphlet, after exposing and denouncing the corruptions of those who farmed tithes, the writer adds: 'Therefore an Act of Parliament to ascertain the tithe of hops, now in the infancy of their great growing improvement, flax, hemp, turnip fields, grass seeds, and dying roots or herbs, of all mines, coals, minerals, commons to be taken in, &c., seems necessary towards the encouragement of them'.[7] No mention of the potato.

In the next year, 1724, this pamphleteer was answered by an anonymous MP who mentions potatoes twice. Arguing against what he calls 'extravagant stocks', he says: 'Formerly (even since Popery) it was thought no ill policy to be well with the parson, but now the case is quite altered, for if he gives him *(sic)* the least provocation, I'll immediately stock one part of my land with bullocks and the other with potatoes .... so farewell tithes'.[8]

The fact of potatoes not being titheable at this period seems to have encouraged their cultivation. The next passage goes to show that they were becoming the food of those who could afford no better. Speaking of high rents, and what he calls 'canting of land' by landlords, he says: 'Again, I saw the same farm, at the expiration of the lease, canted over the improving tenant's head, and set to another at a rack-rent, who, though coming in to the fine improvements of his predecessor (and himself no bad improver), yet can scarce afford his family butter to their potatoes, and is daily sinking into arrears besides.'[9] From the tone of this passage, and from the context, the writer seems to regard the potato as food to be used only by the very poorest; for he adduces its use to show to what a state rack-renting can bring even an industrious farmer.

The burden of all the pamphlets of this period dealing with the land question was an attack on landowners for their excessive desire to throw land into grass. One published in 1727 has this passage: 'By running into the fancy of grazing after the manner of the Scythians, they (the landowners) are every day depopulating the country'.[10] In another, printed in the same type, and apparently by the same hand, we read: 'To bestow the whole kingdom on beef and mutton, and thereby drive out half the people who should eat their share, and force the rest to send sometimes as far as Egypt for bread to eat with it, is a most peculiar and distinguished piece of public economy of which I have no comprehension'.[11]

At this time there was extreme want in the country, on account, it was thought, of the great quantity of land which, within a short period, had been put out of tillage; graziers (whom the writer calls 'that abominable race of graziers') being mad after land then as they are now. But there were other causes. William III, at the bidding of the English Parliament, annihilated Ireland's flourishing woollen manufacture; her trade with the colonies was not only cramped, but ruined, by the navigation laws in force; which, amongst other things, enacted that no colonial produce would come to Ireland until it had first entered an English port, *and had been landed there.* Thus, whilst the fact that vast tracts of the soil had been put out of cultivation compelled the country

5

to buy food abroad, the unjust and selfish destruction of her trade and commerce by England left her without the money to do so.

The people being in a state of great destitution, the author of the *Memorial* quoted above said there should be taxes on a few commodities, such as tea, coffee, etc., in order to raise £110,000 — £100,000 to buy 100,000 barrels of wheat, and a £10,000 premium to those who would import it. To this the author of the *Answer* replied: 'By talking so familiarly of £110,000 by a tax upon a few commodities, it is plain you are either naturally or affectedly ignorant of our present condition, or else you would know and allow that such a sum is not to be raised here without a general excise; since, in proportion to our wealth, we pay already in taxes more than England ever did in the height of the war. And when you have brought over your corn, who will be the buyers? Most certainly not the poor, who will not be able to purchase the twentieth part of it.

'... If you will propose a general contribution in supporting the poor on potatoes and buttermilk till the new corn comes in, perhaps you may succeed better, because the thing at least is possible.'

Potato culture was clearly on the increase; the corn crop, however, was still looked to as the food of the nation. But if the growing of potatoes was on the increase, it seems to have partly arisen from the very necessity of the case. There was not land enough under tillage to give food to the people; it was laid down for grazing. Mountains, poor lands and bogs were unsuitable to graziers, nor would they yield wheat nor, in many instances, oats or any white crop whatever; but the potato was found to succeed very well in such places and to give a larger quantity of sustenance than such land would otherwise yield.

Its cultivation was therefore spreading but spreading, it would seem, chiefly amongst the poor Celtic natives, who had to take themselves to the despised wastes and barren mountains. In the rich lowlands, and therefore amongst the English colony (for whom alone all the publications of those times were intended), the potato was still a despised article of food. And to this the latter part of the above-cited passage points. The proposal to sustain the people on potatoes and buttermilk until the new corn should come in is evidently an ironical one, really meant to convey the degradation to which grazing had brought the country. Seventy or eighty years later the irony became a sad and terrible reality.

Meanwhile increased attention was given to the improvement of agriculture, arising, in a great measure, from the widespread panic which the passion for grazing had caused. Good and patriotic men saw but one result from it, a dangerous and unwise depopulation, and they called aloud for remedies against so terrible a calamity. The author of the *Answer to the Memorial* quoted above, said, with bitter sarcasm: 'You are concerned how strange and surprising it would be in foreign parts to hear that the poor were starving in a rich country.... But why all this concern of the poor? We want them not as the country is now managed; they may follow thousands of their leaders, and seek their bread abroad. Where the plough has no work, one family can do the business of fifty, and you may send away the other forty-nine. An admirable piece of husbandry never known or practised by the wisest nations, who erroneously thought people to be the riches of a country'.[12]

This anxious desire to prevent the country from 'running into grazing' called forth many treatises and pamphlets on the improvement of agriculture. Some writers undertook to show that agriculture was more profitable than grazing; others turned their attention to improve the implements of husbandry and to lay down better rules for the rotation of crops. Potatoes must have been pretty extensively grown at this time and yet they do not get a place in any of the rotations given. We have fallow, wheat, oats, rye, turnips, saintfoin, lucerne, barley, peas, beans, clover, rye-grass and even buckwheat, tares and lentils rotated in various ways, but the potato is never mentioned. The growth of turnips is treated with special importance. Hops, too, receive much consideration, and in 1733 the Royal Dublin Society published careful and elaborate instructions for their growth and management.

The reason the growing of potatoes gets no place in any of the rotations of this period seems to be that their culture was chiefly confined to the poor Celtic population in the mountainous and neglected districts; or, as the author whose pamphlet has a short introduction from Swift,[13] says, 'to the Popish parts of the kingdom'. Those who wrote in favour of tillage instead of grazing set great importance on the increase of population and bewailed emigration as the effect of bad harvests and want of tillage. All such observations made at this period must be taken as referring to the English colony, or Protestant population, exclusively, for there was no desire to keep the Catholics from emigrating — quite the contrary — but they were utterly ignored in the periodical literature of the time, except when some zealot called for a more strict enforcing of the laws 'to prevent the growth of Popery'. And this view is supported by the writer quoted above, who says it would be for the 'Protestant interest' to encourage tillage.

Primate Boulter, bewailing the emigration which resulted from the famine of 1728, 'the result of three bad harvests together', adds 'the worst is that it affects only the Protestants, and reigns chiefly in the north'.[14] He, in his tender anxiety for the Protestant colony, purchased corn in the south to sell it cheaply in the north, which caused serious food riots in Cork, Limerick, Waterford, Clonmel and other places. These riots were, of course, quelled and the rioters severely punished. The broad rich acres of the lowlands were in the hands of the Protestants; and these being specially suited to grazing were accordingly thrown into grass, whilst the Catholic Celts planted the potato in the despised half-barren wilds, and were increasing far more rapidly than those who were possessed of the choicest lands of the kingdom.

But a terrible visitation was at the threshold of Celt and Saxon in Ireland — the famine of 1740 and '41. There were several years of dearth, more or less severe, between 1720 and 1740. 'The years 1725, 1726, 1727 and 1728 presented scenes of wretchedness unparalleled in the annals of any civilised nation', says a writer in the *Gentleman's Magazine*.[15] A pamphlet published in 1740 deplores the emigration which was going forward as the joint effect of bad harvests and want of tillage: 'We have had', says the author, 'twelve bad harvests with slight intermission.'

To find a parallel for the dreadful famine which commenced in 1740, we must go back to the close of the war with the Desmonds.[16] Before 1740 the custom of placing potatoes in pits dug in the earth was unknown in Ireland. When the stems were withered, the farmer put additional earth on the potatoes in the beds where they grew, in which condition they remained till towards Christmas, when they were dug out and stored.[17]

An intensely severe frost set in about the middle of December 1739, whilst the potatoes were yet in this condition, or probably before they had got additional covering. There is a tradition in some parts of the south that this frost penetrated nine inches into the earth the first night it made its appearance. It was preceded by very severe weather. 'In the beginning of November 1739, the weather', says O'Halloran, 'was very cold, the wind blowing from the north east, and this was succeeded by the severest frost known in the memory of man, which entirely destroyed the potatoes, the chief support of the poor'.[18] It is known to tradition as the 'great frost', the 'hard frost', the 'black frost', &c. Besides the destruction of the potato crop it produced other surprising effects; all the great rivers of the country were so frozen over that they became so many highways for traffic; tents were erected upon the ice and large assemblies congregated upon it for various purposes. The turnips were destroyed in most places, but the parsnips survived. The destruction of shrubs and trees was immense, the frost making havoc equally of the hardy furze and the lordly oak; it killed birds of almost every kind; it even killed the shrimps of Irishtown Strand, near Dublin, so that there was no supply of them at market from that famous shrimp ground for many years.[19] Towards the end of the frost the wool fell off the sheep and they died in great numbers.[20]

On Saturday, 29 December, there was a violent storm in Dublin which did much damage to the shipping in the river; and the cruiser 'Man of War', which was at the North Bull, being in great danger, 'cut her cables and ran up between the walls as far as Sir John's Key,[21] where', adds the chronicler, 'she now lies frozen up'.[22] Another curious incident is recorded which proves the intensity of the frost at this time: the press-gang was very busy on the river catching sailors to man the navy for the war with Spain, and under the above date we are informed that more than 100 pressed men walked on shore on the ice with several of the crews; but it is added 'They gave their honour they would return'.[23]

The frost continued about eight or nine weeks, during which all employment ceased; the potato crop was destroyed and the mills being frozen up no corn could be ground. The effect on the population was general and immediate. In the middle of January the destitution was so great that subscriptions to relieve the people were set on foot in Dublin, Cork, Limerick, Waterford, Clonmel, Wexford and other places. Some landlords distributed money and food to their starving tenants; but I am sorry to have to say that the number of such cases on record is very limited.[24] There was no general combined effort to meet the calamity, the Government taking no action whatever, except that the Lord Lieutenant (the Duke of Devonshire) gave to the starving citizens of Dublin £150 in two donations and forbade, by proclamation, the exportation of grain, meal, bread *except to England*, 'apprehending', says his Excellency, 'that the exportation of corn will be bad for the kingdom during this extreme season.'

Later on in the famine, and when about 200,000 of the people had died of hunger and pestilence, there was another proclamation ordering a *general fast* for the success of His Majesty's army against the King of Spain! But the fasting does not seem to have had much effect; Admiral Vernon, commander of the fleet at the seat of war in the West Indies, took Portobello but had to give it up again; he attacked Carthagena with all his forces, was repulsed, and so the war ended.

To add to the miseries of the people, there was a great drought all the winter and spring.[25] A person writing from the west on 15 April, says: 'There has not been one day's rain in Connaught these two months.' The price of provisions continued to rise.

Wheat, quoted towards the end of January in the Dublin market at £2 1s 6d the quarter, reached £2 15s 6d in April, £3 14s in June, and £3 16s 6d in August.

Some days after a bread riot the Lord Mayor issued a proclamation giving permission to 'foreign bakers and others' to bake bread in Dublin; he also sent to all the churchwardens of the city to furnish him with information of any persons who had concealed corn on their premises; he denounced 'forestallers', who went to the suburbs to meet the people coming in with provisions, in order to buy them up before they reached the market; thus in a great measure justifying the rioters who were whipped and transported. The bakers began to bake household bread, which for some time they had ceased to do, and prices fell.[26]

Throughout the country there were numerous gangs of robbers, most of them undoubtedly having sprung into existence through sheer starvation; some, probably taking advantage of the famine, pursued with more profit and boldness a course of life to which they had been previously addicted. The most noted of these was the 'Kellymount gang'. Their headquarters seems to have been Coolcullen Wood, about seven miles from Kilkenny, but they extended their operations into the King's and Queen's Counties, and even to Galway. They were so formidable that a strong military force had to be sent against them. This gang committed no murders, disdained to take anything but money, horses and sheep; sometimes divided their plunder with the starving people and had at the outset pledged their honour not to rob any of the gentlemen of the County Kilkenny. They were dispersed, after giving much trouble to the military; many were taken prisoners, tried by a Special Commission and of course hanged; for, while the Government did nothing to alleviate the horrors of the famine, it enforced the law with a bloody severity.

The number of persons condemned to death at the Spring Assizes of 1741 was really appalling. There was a sort of small food riot at Carrick-on-Suir, where a boat laden with oats was about sailing for Waterford when the starving people assembled to prevent the food they so much needed from being taken away. Their conduct was clearly illegal, but they were at death's door with hunger, and ought to have been treated with some consideration and patience. A justice of the peace, with eighteen foot soldiers and a troop of horse, came out and ordered them to disperse; they would not, or at least they did not do so with sufficient alacrity. One account, published a fortnight or so after the occurrence, asserts with a feeble timidity akin to falsehood that stones were thrown by the people. Be that as it may, they were fired upon; five starving wretches were shot dead on the spot, and eleven badly wounded. To give the finishing touch to this wicked slaughter, the Lords Justices, Primate Boulter and Lord Chancellor Jocelyn, in the absence of the Lord Lieutenant, came out with a proclamation offering a handsome reward for the apprehension of any of those who had escaped the well-directed fire of the soldiery.

The famine continued throughout 1741, and even deepened in severity, provisions still keeping at starvation prices. The Duke of Devonshire met the Parliament in October, and in the course of his address said: 'The sickness which hath proved so mortal in several parts of the kingdom, and is thought to have been principally owing to the scarcity of wholesome food, must very sensibly affect His Majesty, who hath a most tender concern for all his subjects, and cannot but engage your serious attention to consider of proper measures to prevent the like calamity for the future, and to this desirable end the increase of tillage, which would at the same time usefully employ the industrious poor, may greatly contribute.' In answer to this portion of the speech, they promise to 'prepare such laws as, by encouraging tillage, and employing the industrious poor, may be the means for the future to prevent the like calamity.'

A committee was appointed to inquire into 'the late great scarcity', and some matters connected with tillage. They met many times; now and then reported to the House that they had made some progress, and at last the heads of a bill were presented by Mr Le Hunte, the chairman, which were ordered to be sent to England. Nothing, as far as I can discover, resulted from this proceeding, unless indeed it was a bill passed in 1743 'to prevent the pernicious practice of burning land', which is probable enough, as the heads of this bill were presented to the House by the same Mr Le Hunte. During the time this committee was sitting and reporting, and sitting again, Mr Thomas Cuffe, seconded by Mr George M'Cartney, presented the heads of a bill 'for the more effectual securing the payment of rents and preventing the frauds of tenants' which was received and read and committed by a committee of the whole House on presentation, and was hurried through its other stages, apparently without discussion, but certainly without opposition; and this in the second year of a famine, now combined with pestilence, which slaughtered one-eighth of the whole population.[27] The Act was a temporary one, but was never afterwards allowed to die out. It was renewed in various reigns, and is the foundation of the Acts which were in force up to 1870 'for the more effectual securing the payment of rents'.

The land had been thrown into grazing to an alarming extent for years, so that the acreage for producing grain and other such food was very limited; the people fell into listless despair from what they had endured in 1740 and did not cultivate the ground that was still left for tillage. The Catholics were paralysed and rendered unfit for industrious pursuits by an active renewal of the worst penal statutes. The prospect of a war with Spain, which was actually declared in October 1739, was made the pretext for this new persecution and all the severities recommended by Primate Boulter were put into rigid execution. These measures plunged the people into the deepest distress: horror and despair pervaded every mind.

Such was the state of Ireland in 1741, when bloody flux and malignant fever came to finish what the famine had left undone. These scourges, unlike the famine, fell upon the castle as well as on the hovel, many persons in the higher ranks of life having died of them during the year; amongst whom we find several physicians; the son of Alderman Tew; Mr John Smith, High Sheriff of Meath; the Rev. Mr Heartlib, Castle Chaplain; Mr Kavanagh of Borris House, and his brother; the son of the Lord Mayor-Elect; two judges, namely, Baron Wainright and the Right Honourable John Rogerson, Chief Justice of the King's Bench.

The prisoners died in thousands in the jails, especially poor debtors who had been incarcerated. In November 1741 the prisoners in Cork jail sent a petition to Parliament, in which they say that 'above seven hundred persons died there during the late severe seasons, and that the jail is now so full that there is scarce room for their lying on the floors.' The fever was so general in Limerick that there was hardly one family in the whole city who had not some member ill of it. Galway was cruelly scourged by the famine, to meet which little or nothing seems to have been done by those whose bounden duty it was to come to the relief of their starving brethren. When fever appeared on the terrible scene, the town became one great lazaretto. The following intelligence came from that unhappy place, dated 8 July: 'The fever so rages here that the physicians say it is more like a plague than a fever, and refuse to visit patients for any fee whatever.'[28]

The 'gentlemen of the county' met, in a way peculiar to themselves, this twofold calamity which threatened utter annihilation to their historic capital. To counteract the inevitable results of famine they announced that they would give the reward of £30 for the first, and £10 for every other robber that would be prosecuted to conviction, and this in addition to whatever the Government would allow. What excessive liberality! They must have had plenty of money. The plague, which no physician would attend, they dealt with by a proclamation also, of which they seemed proud, for they published it repeatedly in the journals of the time. Here is an extract: 'The town of Galway being at this time very sickly, the gentlemen of the county *think proper* to remove the races that were to be *run for* at Park, near the said town of Galway, to Terlogh Gurranes, near the town of Tuam, in the said county.' What humane, *proper thinking* 'gentlemen' they were, to be sure; and such precise legal phraseology![29] But their enticing bill of fare contained more than the 'races that were to be run for'; it announced balls and plays every night for the entertainment of the ladies.

The learned and kind hearted Dr Berkeley, Protestant Bishop of Cloyne, wrote to a friend in Dublin on 21 May 1741: 'The distresses of the sick and poor are endless. The havoc of mankind in the counties of Cork, Limerick and some adjacent places, hath been incredible. The nation probably will not recover this loss in a century. The other day I heard one from the county of Limerick say that whole villages are entirely dispeopled. About two months since I heard Sir Richard Cox say that five hundred were dead in the parish, though in a county I believe not very populous. It were to be wished people of condition were at their seats in the country during these calamitous times, which might provide relief and employment for the poor. Certainly if these perish the rich must be sufferers in the end.'

The author of a letter entitled *The Groans of Ireland*, addressed to an Irish Member of Parliament, thus opens his subject: 'I have been absent from this country for some years, and on my return to it last summer, found it the most miserable scene of universal distress that I have ever read of in history: want and misery in every face; the rich unable almost as they were willing to relieve the poor; the roads spread with dead and dying bodies; mankind of the colour of the docks and nettles they fed on; two or three, sometimes more, going on a car to the grave for want of bearers to carry them, and many buried only in the fields and ditches where they perished. This universal scarcity was ensued by fluxes and malignant fevers, which swept off multitudes of all sorts: whole villages were left waste by want, and sickness, and death in various shapes; and scarcely a house in the whole island escaped from tears and mourning. The loss must be upwards of 400,000, but supposing it 200,000, (it was certainly more) it was too great for this ill-peopled country, and the more grievous as they were mostly of the grown-up part of the working people.' 'Whence can this proceed?' he asks; and he answers, 'From the want of proper tillage laws to guide and to protect the husbandman in the pursuit of his business'.[30]

13

This writer further says the terrible visitation of 1740 and 1741 was the third famine within twenty years; so that in view of these and other famines, since and before, Ireland might be not inaptly described as the land of famines. Almost the first object one sees on sailing into Dublin Bay is a monument to famine. The Obelisk, as it is called, stands on Killiney Hill. The tourist reads: 'Last year being hard with the Poor, the walls about these Hills, and This, &c., erected by John Mapas, Esq., June, 1742'. The story of Ireland is before him; it is told in the landscape and the inscription; it may be expressed in two words — beauty and starvation.

The famine of 1741 did not deter farmers from the culture of the potato; on the contrary, it increased rapidly after that period and we now find it, for the first time, recognised as a rotation crop. They preferred to turn their attention to improve its quality and productiveness and to take measures for its protection from frost, rather than to abandon its culture. And, indeed, it was as much a matter of necessity as choice that they did so. The potato, on a given area, supplied about four times as much food as any other crop; and, from the limited breadth of land then available for tillage, the population would be in continual danger of falling short of food unless the potato were cultivated to a large extent.

The agricultural literature of the country from 1741 until the arrival of the celebrated traveller, Arthur Young, in Ireland, consisted chiefly of fierce attacks upon graziers — of a continual demand for the breaking up of grass lands into tillage, of plans for the establishment of public granaries to sustain the people in years of bad harvests, and of the results of experiments undertaken to improve the culture of the potato.

The writers on these subjects also frequently denounced the rich for the wretchedness and misery to which they allowed the labouring poor to be reduced. The author of a pamphlet, which went through several editions, thus attacks them in the edition of 1755: 'The want of trade and industry causes such inequality in the distribution of their (the people's) property, that while a few of the richer sort can wantonly pamper appetites of every kind, and indulge with the affluence of so many monarchs, the poor, alas! who make at least ninety-nine of every hundred among them, are under the necessity of going clad after the fashion of the old Irish, whose manners and customs they retain to this day, and of feeding on potatoes, the most generally embraced advantage of the inhabitants, which the great Sir Walter Raleigh left behind him.'[31] This writer's remarks apply chiefly to Cork, Waterford, Kerry and Limerick. He proceeds: 'The feeding of cattle on large dairies of several hundred acres together, may be managed by the inhabitants of one or two cabins, whose wretched subsistence, for the most part, depends upon an acre or two of potatoes and a little skimmed milk.'[32]

Many think that the yield per acre of potatoes has greatly increased with time in Ireland. This opinion, although true, is not true to the extent generally supposed; for, when Arthur Young travelled in this country, and even before it, the yield, as far as recorded, seems nearly equal to the quantity produced at present, except in some peculiar cases. A well-known agriculturist, John Wynne Baker, writing in 1765, says, in a note to his *Agriculture Epitomised* that he had in the past year (1764) of apple potatoes (not a prolific kind) in the proportion of more than 109 barrels an acre.

Arthur Young came to Ireland in 1776 and he brings his account of the country down to 1779. Thirty-six years had elapsed since the great famine, only one generation, and he found the famous root of Virginia a greater favourite than ever. From Slane, in Meath, he writes that potatoes were a great article of culture at Kilcock, where he found them grown for cattle; store bullocks were fed upon them, and they were even deemed good food for horses when mixed with bran. In Slane itself, the old custom, which was the chief cause of the famine of 1740, still prevailed; for, he says, the people there were not done taking up their potatoes until Christmas.

The potato culture, he elsewhere remarks, has increased twenty-fold within the last twenty years, all the hogs in the country being fattened on them. They were usually given to them half-boiled. Wherever he went he almost invariably found the food of the people, at least for nine months of the year, to be potatoes and milk, excepting parts of Ulster, where they had oatbread, and sometimes fresh meat. In the south, for the labourers of Sir Lucius O'Brien and their families, consisting of 276 souls, the quantity of potatoes planted, as appears from a paper given to him, was five acres and a quarter, ranging from a quarter of an acre to four acres for each family.

As to yield, the lowest he gives is forty barrels per acre, Irish of course; and the highest reported to him was at Castle Oliver, near Bruff, namely 150 barrels (Bristol).[33] The average produce of the entire country he gives at 328 bushels per acre — about sixty-six barrels. 'Yet, to gain this miserable produce', he says, 'much old hay, and nineteen-twentieths of all the dung in the kingdom is employed.' Potatoes grown on the coast were frequently sent to Dublin by sea; and Lord Tyrone told Arthur Young at Curraghmore that much of the potatoes grown about Dungarvan were sent thither, together with birch-brooms. The boats were said to be freighted with *fruit* and *timber*!

Amongst the endless varieties of the potato which appeared from time to time, that known as the 'apple' was the best in quality, and stood its ground the longest, having been a favourite for at least seventy or eighty years. The produce recorded above as raised by Mr Wynne Baker was as we have seen from this species; what kind gave the still greater yield at Castle Oliver is not recorded.

Thus it is perfectly clear that in 1780, and even before that time, the staple food of the Irish nation was once again the potato. In fact, it was cultivated to a far greater extent than before 1740, which caused the population to increase with wonderful rapidity.[34]

The prolific but uncertain root on which the Irish people became, year after year, more dependent for existence once again dashed their hopes in 1821 and threw a great part of the south and west into a state of decided famine. The spring of that year was wet and stormy, retarding the necessary work, especially the planting of potatoes. The summer was also unfavourable; May was cold and ungenial; in June there was frost, with a north wind, and sometimes a scorching sun. The autumn, like the spring, was wet and severe, rain falling to a very unusual extent.

The consequent floods did extensive injury; not merely were crops of hay floated off the lowland meadows, but in various places fields of potatoes were completely washed out of the ground and carried away. The crops were deficient, especially the potato crop, much of which was left undug until the ensuing spring, partly on account of the inclement weather, partly because it was not worth the labour. The low grounds were, in many instances, inundated to such a depth that even the potatoes in pits could not be reached. About the middle of December the 'Shannon at Athlone,' says an eye-witness, 'looked like a boundless ocean', covering for weeks the potato fields, souring the crop and preventing all access to the pits.

The loss of the potato in this year, and its cause, are thus epitomised in the following extract from the report of the London Tavern Committee: 'From the most authentic communications, it appeared that the bad quality and partial failure of the potato crop of the preceding year (1821) — the consequence of the excessive and protracted humidity of the season — had been a principal cause of the distress, and that it had been greatly aggravated by the rotting of the potatoes in the pits in which they were stored. This discovery was made at so late a period that the peasantry were not able to provide against the consequences of that evil.'[35] From the letters published in their own report, the committee would have been abundantly justified in adding that the distress was greatly increased by the almost total want of employment for the labouring classes, arising from the fact that very many of the landlords in the districts that suffered most were absentees.

A writer on this famine who, in general, is inclined to be severe in his strictures upon the people, thus opens the subject: 'The distress which has almost universally prevailed in Ireland has not been occasioned so much by an excessive population as by a culpable remissness on the part of persons possessing property, and neglecting to take advantage of those great resources, and of those ample means of providing for an increasing population, which nature has so liberally bestowed on this country.'[36]

The winter and spring of 1822 continued very wet and it was extremely difficult to perform any agricultural work. Seed potatoes were excessively scarce and the first relief that reached the country was a prudent and timely one; it consisted of 1,400 tons of seed potatoes, bought by the Government in England and Scotland. Charitable persons at home also gave seed potatoes, cut into sets, to prevent their being used for food; yet, in many instances, those sets were taken out of the ground by the starving people and eaten. Cork, Limerick, Kerry, Clare, Mayo and Galway were the counties most severely visited. These, according to the accounts given in the public journals of the time, were in a state of actual famine. Potatoes were eight pence a stone in districts where they usually sold from one penny to two pence.

But although the potato had failed, food from the cereal crops was abundant and cheap enough if the people had money to buy it. 'There was no want of food of another description for the support of human life; on the contrary, the crops of grain had been far from deficient, and the prices of corn and oatmeal were very moderate. The calamities of 1822 may, therefore, be said to have proceeded less from the want of food itself, than from the want of adequate means of purchasing it; or, in other words, from the want of profitable employment.'[37]

Poor Skibbereen, that got such a melancholy notoriety in the later and far more terrible Famine of 1847, was reported in May 1822 to be in a state of distress 'horrible beyond description'. Potatoes were not merely dear, they were inferior, not having ripened for want of sufficient heat; and, furthermore, they soured in the pits. The use of such unwholesome food soon brought typhus fever and dysentery upon the scene, which slaughtered thousands. In parts of the west the living were unable to bury the dead, more especially in Achill where, in many cases, the famine-stricken people were found dead on the roadside. A committee appointed by the House of Commons to investigate this calamity reported, amongst other things, that the famine was spread over districts representing half the superficies of the country and containing a population of 2,907,000 souls.

There are no statistics to give an accurate knowledge of the numbers that died of want in this famine and of the dysentery and fever which followed. If the census of 1821 can be relied on, which I much doubt, the famine and pestilence of the succeeding year did not in the least check the growth of the population, as it increased fifteen per cent in the ten years from 1821 to 1831; an increase above the average, even in absence of any disturbing cause.

This famine was met by Government grants; by the contributions from the London Tavern Committee; the Dublin Mansion House Committee and, to a limited extent, by private charity.[38] In June 1822 Parliament voted £100,000 'for the employment of the poor in Ireland, and other purposes relating thereto, as the exigency of affairs may require.' And in July £200,000, 'to enable His Majesty to take such measures as the exigency of affairs may require.' The London Tavern Committee, with the aid of a King's letter, received subscriptions amounting to £304,180 17s 6d, of which £44,177 9s was raised in Ireland. The Dublin Mansion House Committee collected £30,406 11s 4d. Thus, the whole sum from charitable collections was £334,587 8s 10d, of which £74,584, 0s 4d was raised in Ireland. This, with the grant of £300,000 from Government, makes a grand total of £634,587 8s 10d. The sum appears to have been quite sufficient, as the London Tavern Committee closed its labours whilst it had yet in hands £60,000, which sum was partly distributed and partly invested in ways considered beneficial to this country.[39]

Every two or three years from 1821 to the great blight of 1845 and 1846, a failure of some kind, more or less extensive, occurred to the potato crop, not merely in Ireland, but in almost every country in which it was cultivated to any considerable extent. Reviewing, then, the history of this famous root for over a period of 100 years, we find that, although it produces from a given acreage more human food than any other crop, it is yet a most treacherous and perishable one; and it may, perhaps, surprise future generations that the statesmen and landed proprietors of that lengthened period did nothing whatever to regulate the husbandry of the country in such a way as to prevent the lives of a whole people from being dependant on a crop liable to so many casualties. Perhaps the social and political condition of Ireland during these times will be found to have had something to do with this culpable apathy.

It is commonly assumed that the subjugation of Ireland was effected by Elizabeth, but the submission to English rule was only a forced one; the spirit of the nation was one of determined opposition, which was abundantly shown at Aughrim and Limerick, and on many a foreign field besides. Great Britain, knowing this and being determined to hold the country at all risks, was continually in fear that some war or complication with foreign powers would afford the Irish people an opportunity of putting an end to English rule in Ireland and of declaring the country an independent nation. As progress in wealth and prosperity would add to the probabilities of success in such an event, it was the all but avowed — nay, truth compels me to say, the *frequently avowed* policy of England to keep Ireland poor, and therefore feeble, that she might be held the more securely. For that reason she was not treated as a portion of a united kingdom but as an enemy who had become England's slave by conquest, who was her rival in manufactures of various kinds, who might undersell her in foreign markets and, in fact, who might grow rich and powerful enough to assert her independence.

The descendants of the Norman adventurers who got a footing here in the twelfth century; English and Scotch planters; officials and undertakers who, from time to time, had been induced to settle in Ireland by grants of land and sinecures were, by a legal fiction, styled the nation, although they were never more than a small fraction of it. For a great number of years every writer, every public man, every Act of Parliament, assumed that the English colony in Ireland was the Irish nation. Denunciations of Papists, the 'common enemy', gross falsehoods about their principles and acts, fears real or pretended of their wicked, bloodthirsty plots, thickly strewn in our path as we journey through this dismal period of our history, reveal to us, as it were by accident, that there was another people in this island besides those whom the law regarded as the nation; but they had no rights, they were outlaws — 'the Irish enemy'. One hundred and fifty years ago Primate Boulter expressed his belief that those outlaws made four-fifths of the population and the English colony only one-fifth; but the colonists held the rich lands; the bulk of the people, who formed the real nation, were in the bogs, the lonely glens and on the sterile mountains, where agriculture was all but impossible, except to the great capitalist. Capital they had none, and they were forced to subsist, as best they could, on little patches of tillage among the rocks, whose debris made the land around them in some sort susceptible of cultivation. By degrees those outlaws discovered that the potato, coming from the high moist soil of Quito, found in the half-barren wilds of Ireland, if not a climate, a soil at least congenial to its nature. It was palatable food, as it became acclimatised; it grew where no other plant fit for human food would grow; it was a great fertiliser; it was prolific: no wonder the poor Celt of our bogs and mountains, in time, made the potato more associated with the name of Ireland than it ever was with its native country, Virginia.

Before 1729 we have no record of the potato having suffered from blight or frost or anything else. But this is not to be wondered at; even though such things occurred, the outlaws, who were its chief cultivators, excited neither interest nor pity in the hearts of the ruling minority. They were watched and feared; they were known to be numerous; and many were the plans set on foot to reduce their numbers, and cause them to become extinct, like the red deer of their native hills. Surely then, a potato blight, followed by a famine, would not be regarded as a calamity, unless it affected the English colony. The Celtic nation in Ireland could have no record of such a visitation, unless in the fugitive ballad of some hedge schoolmaster.[40]

Anyhow, the Celt, forced to live for the most part in barren wilds, where it was all but impossible to raise sufficient food, found the potato his best friend and his race increased and multiplied upon it, in spite of that bloody code which ignored his existence, and with regard to which Lord Clare, no friend to Ireland, thus expressed his views in his speech on the Union: 'The Parliament of England seem to have considered the permanent debility of Ireland as the best security of the British crown, and the Irish Parliament to have rested the security of the colony upon maintaining a perpetual and impossible barrier against the ancient inhabitants of the country'.[41]

Another cause for the increased cultivation of the potato may be found in the poverty of the English colony itself. Whilst the people of whom that colony was composed, through the Parliament that represented them, pursued the Catholic natives with unmitigated persecution, they were themselves the object of jealous surveillance, both by the Parliament and the commercial classes of England. Long before the times of which I am writing, the English always showed uneasiness at the least appearance of amalgamation between the descendants of the Norman invaders and the natives, although their fears on this head were to a great extent set at rest by the change of religion in England, which change extended in a very considerable degree to the English colony in Ireland. After the Reformation there was not much danger of a union between the Catholic Celt and the Protestant Norman.

Still another jealousy remained — a commercial jealousy. The colonisation of Ireland meant, in the English mind, the complete extirpation of the natives and the peopling of this island by the adventurers and their descendants; but it is a strange fact that, even had this actually happened, we can, from what we know of the history of the period, assert with truth that still their commercial prosperity and progress would be watched and checked and legislated against, whenever they would seem to clash, or when there was a possibility of their clashing, with the commercial supremacy of Great Britain.

Not to go into all the commercial restraints imposed on Irish manufactures by the English Parliament, let us take what, perhaps, was the most important one — that imposed on the woollen manufacture. For a long period this branch of industry had flourished in Ireland. We not only manufactured what we required for ourselves, but our exports of woollens were very considerable. This manufacture existed in England also and the Englishmen engaged in it were determined to have the foreign markets to themselves. After many previous efforts, they at length induced both Houses of the English Parliament to address William III on what they were pleased to consider a grievance — the grievance of having foreign markets open to Irish woollens equally with their own.

To those addresses the King replied that he would do all in his power to 'discourage' the woollen trade in Ireland, to encourage the linen trade, and to promote *the trade of England.*[42]

Accordingly, a duty equal to a prohibition was imposed upon the exportation of Irish woollens, except, indeed, to England and Wales, where they were not required — England at the time manufacturing more woollens than were necessary for her home consumption. About 40,000 people in Ireland were thrown out of bread by this law, nearly every one of whom were Protestants; for that trade was almost entirely in their hands, so that neither Palesman nor Protestant was spared when their interests seemed opposed to those of England.

William's declaration on this occasion about encouraging the linen manufacture in Ireland was regarded as a compact, yet it was violated at a later period by the imposition of duties.[43] The jealousy and unkindness of the prohibitory duty on the export of woollens is exposed by the able author of *Groans of Ireland*, who says: 'It is certain that on the coasts of Spain and Portugal and the Mediterranean, in the stuffs &c., which we send them, we, under all the difficulties of a clandestine trade, undersell the French eight per cent, and it is as certain that the French undersell the English as much — it has been said — *eleven per cent.*'[44] So that although the English manufacturer was unable to compete with the Frenchman abroad, his narrow selfishness would not permit Ireland to do so, although she was in a position to do it with advantage to herself. Impoverished by such legislation, the English colony itself, Protestant and all as it was, had to lower its dietary standard and cultivate the potato or, at least, promote its cultivation by use of it.

Another of the alleged causes for the poverty of the country, and the consequent increase of potato culture, was absenteeism. In 1729 a list of absentees was published by Mr Thomas Prior, which ran through several editions. The list includes the Viceroy himself, then an absentee, which he well might be, at that time and for long afterwards, as Primate Boulter was the ruler of Ireland. Mr Prior sets down in his pamphlet the incomes of the absentees and the total amounts to the enormous annual sum of £627,769 sterling, a sum in excess of the entire revenue of the country which, though increasing year after year, even twenty-nine years afterwards was only £650,763.

Besides the exhausting drain by absentee proprietors, there was another kind of absenteeism, namely that of Englishmen who, through Court or other influence, obtained places in Ireland but discharged the duties of them, such as they were, by deputy. Mr Prior cites the following instance as an example: 'One of those Englishmen who got an appointment in Ireland landed in Dublin on a Saturday evening, went next day to a parish church, received the Sacrament there, went to the Courts on Monday, took the necessary oaths and sailed for England that very evening! This was certainly expedition, but still coming over at all was troublesome: so those who had obtained appointments in Ireland got an Act quietly passed in the English Parliament dispensing them from visiting Ireland at all, even to take possession of those offices to which they were promoted.'[45]

That a large proportion of the owners of the soil of a country should reside out of it has been always regarded as a great evil, as well as a real loss to that country. When taxes are to be levied and battles to be fought, we are always an integral part of the United Kingdom; but when there is a question of encouraging or extending manufacturers, we are treated as the rival and the enemy of England.

The avarice and tyranny of landlords is usually set down as a principal cause of the great poverty and misery of the Irish people, during a long period. If we examine the rents paid 150, or even 100 years ago, they will appear trifling when compared with the rents of the present day; so that, at first, one is inclined to question the accuracy of those writers who denounce the avarice and rack-renting propensities of the landlords of their time. But when we examine the question more closely we find so many circumstances to modify and even to change our first views that by degrees we arrive at the belief that the complaints made were substantially true.

If the rents of those times seem to us very low, we must remember that the land, for the most part, was in a wretched condition; that the majority of farms had much waste upon them and that the portions tilled were not half tilled; so that whilst the acreage was large, the productive portion of the lands was only a percentage of it. Then, agricultural skill was wanting; good implements were wanting; capital was wanting; everything that could improve the soil and make it productive was wanting. These and many other causes made rents that seem trifling to us, rack-rents to the farmers who paid them.

Swift had no doubt at all upon the matter, for he says: 'Another great calamity is the exorbitant raising of the rents of lands. Upon the determination of all leases made before the year 1690, a gentleman thinks that he has but indifferently improved his estate if he has only doubled his rent-roll. Farms are screwed up to a rack-rent; leases granted but for a small term of years; tenants tied down to hard conditions, and discouraged from cultivating the lands they occupy to the best advantage by the certainty they have of the rent being raised on the expiration of their lease proportionably to the improvements they shall make.'[46] As to the unlimited power of the landlords and its tyrannical use, Arthur Young, writing in 1779, less than 100 years ago, says: 'The age has improved so much in humanity, that even the poor Irish have experienced its influence and are every day treated better and better, but still the remnant of the old manners, the abominable distinction of religion, united with the oppressive conduct of the little country gentlemen, or rather vermin, of the kingdom, who were never out of it, altogether bear still very heavy on the poor people, and subject them to situations more mortifying than we ever behold in England. The landlord of an Irish estate inhabited by Roman Catholics, is a sort of despot who yields obedience in whatever concerns the poor to no law but that of his will .... A long series of oppressions, aided by very many ill-judged laws, have brought landlords into a habit of exerting a very lofty superiority, and their vassals into that of an almost unlimited submission. Speaking a language that is despised, professing a religion that is abhorred, and being disarmed, the poor find themselves in many cases slaves even in the bosom of *written* liberty.' And again, this enlightened Protestant English gentleman says of the Irish landlord that 'nothing satisfied him but an unlimited submission.'[47]

Forty years later, some of their more obvious, not to say essential duties, were brought under the notice of Irish landlords, but in vain. The writer quoted above on the famine of 1822 says: 'It is therefore a duty incumbent on all those who possess property, and consequently have an interest in the prosperity of this country, to prevent a recurrence of this awful calamity [the famine], and to provide for those persons over whom fortune has placed them, and whom they should consider as entrusted to their care, and entitled to their protection; and this can only be successfully carried into execution by their procuring and substituting other articles of food, so as to leave the poor only partially dependant on the potato crop for their support.'[48]

Some Acts of Parliament, without perhaps intending it, gave a further impulse to potato cultivation in Ireland. As if the violation of the treaty of Limerick by William III; the exterminating code of Anne; its continuance and intensification under the first and second Georges were not a sufficient persecution of the native race, statutes continued to be enacted against them, during the first twenty-five years of George III's reign — that is, up to 1785. But although this was the case, the necessity of making some concessions to them began to be felt by their rulers, from the time the revolt of the American colonies assumed a dangerous aspect. So that, whilst, on the one hand, the enactment of persecuting laws was not wholly abandoned, on the other, there sprang up a spirit, if not of kindness, at least of recognition, and perhaps of fear.

'It was in the year 1744', says Sir Henry Parnell, 'that the Irish legislature passed the first Act towards conciliating the Catholics.'[49] And a very curious concession it was. It was entitled 'An Act to enable His Majesty's subjects, of whatever persuasion, to testify their allegiance to him'.[50] Previously the Catholics dared not to approach the foot of the throne even to swear that they were ready to die in defence of it. But two years before this an Act was passed of no apparent political significance, which was of much more practical value to the Catholics. It was 'An Act to encourate the reclaiming of unprofitable bogs'.[51] This Act made it lawful 'for every Papist, or person professing the Popish religion', to lease fifty acres, planting measure, of such bog, and one half acre of arable land thereunto adjoining, 'as a site for a house, or for the purpose of delving for gravel or limestone for manure.' Certain immunities were granted and certain restrictions imposed. The immunities were that, for the first seven years after the bog was reclaimed, the tenant should be free from all tithes, cesses or applotment. The restrictions were: (1) that no bog should be deemed unprofitable unless it were at least four feet from the surface to the bottom of it, when reclaimed — the Act having been especially passed for the reclaiming of *unprofitable* bogs; (2) that no person should be entitled to the benefit of the Act unless he reclaimed ten plantation acres; (3) that half whatever quantity was leased should be reclaimed in twenty-one years; (4) that such bog should be at least one mile from any city or market-town.

Alas, how utterly prostrate the Catholics must have been when this was regarded as a concession to them! Yet it was, and one of such importance that 'in times of less liberality it had been repeatedly thrown out of Parliament, as tending to encourage Popery, to the detriment of the Protestant religion'; and to counter-balance it, the pension allotted to apostate priests in Anne's reign was, in the very same Session of Parliament, raised from £30 to £40 per annum by the Viceroy, Lord Townsend.[52] The wretched serfs were, of course, glad to get any hold upon the soil, even though it was unprofitable bog, and largely availed themselves of the provisions of the Act. Ten or twelve years later, we find Arthur Young speaking with much approval of the many efforts that were being made, in various parts of Ireland, to reclaim the bogs — efforts resulting, no doubt, in a great measure, from this Bill. In the process of reclaiming the bogs, the potato was an essential auxiliary.

But of all the means of increasing the growth of that renowned esculent in Ireland, the Catholic Relief Act of 1793 must, at least in more recent times, be accorded the first place. That Act, it is said, was the result of the fears excited in England by the French Revolution. Whether this was so or not, the concessions it made were large for the time; and its effect upon potato culture in Ireland is unquestionable. Dr Beaufort, in his Ecclesiastical Map, gives our whole population in 1789 as 4,088,226. Sir Henry Parnell says the Catholics were, at this time, at least three-fourths of the population.[53] And this agrees with the estimate which the Catholics themselves made of their numbers at the period; for, in a long and remarkable petition presented to the House of Commons in January 1792, they say: 'Behold us then before you, 3,000,000 of the people of Ireland.' These 3,000,000 became, by the Bill of '93, entitled to the elective franchise; or, as the Bill itself more correctly expressed it, 'such parts of all existing oaths', as put it out of their power to exercise the elective franchise, were repealed.

The Catholics were not slow in availing themselves of this important privilege, which they had not enjoyed since the first year of George II's reign — a period of sixty-six years.[54] They soon began to influence the elections in at least three out of the four provinces; but they influenced them only through their landlords, not daring, for a full generation after, to give independent votes. A landlord had political influence in proportion to the number of voters he brought, or rather drove, to the poll. To secure and extend this influence, the manufacture of forty-shilling freeholders went on rapidly and to an enormous extent. The Catholics were poor, numerous, subservient and doubtless grateful for recent concessions; so bits of land, merely sufficient to qualify them for voting, were freely leased to them, which they as freely accepted.[55] On these they built cabins, relying on the potato for food and on a little patch of oats or wheat to pay their rent and taxes.

By the influence of O'Connell and the Catholic Association, the forty-shilling freeholders broke away from landlord influence in the great General Election of 1826, and supported the candidates who promised to vote for Catholic Emancipation, in spite of every threat. From that day their doom was sealed; the landlords began to call loudly for their disfranchisement and accordingly they were disfranchised by the Relief Bill of 1829, but of course they still retained their little holdings.

Immediately the landlords began to utter bitter complaints of surplus population; they began to ventilate their grievances through the English and Irish press, saying that their land was overrun by cottiers and squatters — the main cause of all this being kept in the background, namely, the immense and continuous increase of forty-shilling freeholders, by themselves, and for their own purposes. But the moment those poor men presumed to vote according to the letter and the spirit of the Constitution they were sacrificed to landlord indignation; they were declared to be an encumbrance on the soil that ought to be removed.

Landlords began to act upon this view: they began to evict, to exterminate, to consolidate; and in this fearful work the awful Famine of 1847 became a powerful, and I fear in many cases even a welcome, auxiliary to the Crowbar Brigade.[56]

Thus was the cultivation of the potato extended in various ways until it had become the principal food of nineteen-twentieths of the population long before the Famine of 1847.

2

The blight arrives

The disease which cut off at least one-half of the potato crop of Ireland in 1845, and completely destroyed that of 1846, had made its appearance several years before in other countries. It is said to have existed for a long time in the western parts of America before it appeared in Europe; but, as it was at first confounded with dry rot and wet rot, the American may have been a different disease from ours. What seems certain is that the potato disease, as known to us, made its first appearance in Germany; and in the year 1842, travelling thence into Belgium, it manifested itself in a very destructive form in the neighbourhood of Liège. It visited Canada in 1844, and in 1845 it appeared in almost every part of the United Kingdom, being observed first of all in the Isle of Wight, where it was most virulent on wheat lands which had been manured with guano.

In the first week of September the potatoes in the London market were, to a very considerable extent, found to be unfit for human food. To the eye they did not show any sign of disease but, when boiled and cut, its presence was but too evident by the black, or rather brownish-black, mass they presented. The potato fields began to be examined and the provincial journals soon teemed with accounts of the destructive visitation, with speculations concerning its cause and suggestions as to probable remedies.

The descriptions of the disease given by the English newspapers do not quite agree with the symptoms observed somewhat later in Ireland. 'Whatever may have been the cause', says one account, 'it is certain that, externally, the disease indicates itself by a fungus or moss producing decomposition of the farinaceous interior.'[1] 'The disease is very general in this locality', says another, 'beginning with a damp spot on some part of the potato.'[2] A third observer writes: 'The commencement of the attack is generally dated here from Tuesday, 19 ultimo. A day

Woman begging at Clonakilty.

of the heaviest rain almost ever known. It first appears a bluish speck on the potato, and then spreads rapidly.'[3]

Whether it was that, in England, in their anxiety about the tuber, people paid little or no attention to the stems or leaves of the potato; or that the earlier symptoms differed from the later, matters but little — the disease was certainly the same throughout the United Kingdom. In Ireland it was first observed on the leaves of the plant as brown spots of various shapes and sizes, pretty much as if a dilution of acid had fallen upon them like drops of rain. Sometimes the blight made its appearance near high hedges or under trees; sometimes portions of a field would be greatly affected with it before other parts were touched at all; and I have sometimes observed the very first symptoms of the disease opposite an open gateway, as if a blighting wind had rushed in, making for some distance a sort of avenue of discoloured leaves and stalks, about the width of the gateway at first but becoming wider onwards.

When the decomposition produced by the blight was in a somewhat advanced stage, the odour from the potato field, which was very offensive, was perceptible at a considerable distance. There may have been cases in this country in which the disease was first observed in the tubers but they must have been rare. It appeared in Scotland with the same symptoms as in Ireland. A contemporary account says: 'In various parts of Scotland the potatoes have suffered fearfully from the blight. The leaves of the plant have, generally speaking, first been affected, and then the root.'

From this mode of manifesting itself, the potato disease was commonly called in Ireland, as in Scotland, the potato blight. It had other names given to it; potato murrain, cholera in the potato and so on; but potato blight, in Ireland at least, was and is its all but universal name. The whole stem soon became affected after the blight had appeared on the leaves, more especially if the weather was damp; and for some time before the period for digging out the crop had arrived, the potato fields showed nothing but rank weeds, with here and there the remains of withered-up stems — bleached skeletons of the green healthy plants of some weeks before.

I have a vivid recollection of the blight as it appeared in the southern portion of Kildare in 1850. In that year St Swithin's day — 15 July — was a day of clouds and lightning, of thunder and terrific rain. It was one of those days that strike the timid with alarm and terror: sometimes it was dark as twilight; sometimes a sudden ghastly brightness was produced by the lightning. That the air was charged with electricity to a most unusual extent was felt by everybody. Those who had an intimate knowledge of the various potato blights from 1845 said, 'This is the beginning of the blight.' So it was.

It is well known that after the blight of 1845 the potatoes in Ireland had scarcely shown any blossom for some years, even those unaffected by the blight, or affected by it only to a small extent; and the few exceptional blossoms which appeared produced no seed. This feebleness of the plant was gradually disappearing, and in 1850 it was remarked as a very hopeful sign that the potatoes blossomed almost as of old. The crop having been sown much earlier than was customary before 1845, most of the fields, on this memorable 15 July, were rich with that beautiful and striking sheet of blossom, which they show when the plant is in vigorous health.

Next day — a still, oppressive, sultry, electric sort of day — I, in company with some others, visited various potato fields. There was but one symptom that the blight had come; all the blossoms were closed, even at midday: this was enough to the experienced eye — the blight had come. Heat, noontide sun, nothing ever opened them again. In some days they began to fall off the stems; in eight or ten days other symptoms appeared, and so began the Potato Blight of 1850, a mild one, but still the true blight. How like this 15 July must have been to 19 August 1845, described above by the *Cambridge Chronicle*.

The blight of 1845 was noticed in Ireland about the middle of September. Like the passage birds, it first appeared on the coast and, it would seem, first of all on the coast of Wexford. It soon travelled inland and accounts of its alarming progress began to be published in almost every part of the country. Letters in the daily press from Cork, Tyrone, Meath, Roscommon and various other places gave despairing accounts of its extent and rapidity. A Meath peasant wrote: 'Awful is our story; I do be striving to blindfold them (the potatoes) in the boiling. I trust in God's mercy no harm will come from them.' The Very Rev. Dr McEvoy, PP, writing from Kells, 24 October, says: 'On my most minute personal inspection of the state of the potato crop in this most fertile potato-growing *locale*, is founded my inexpressibly painful conviction, that one family in twenty of the people will not have a single potato left on Christmas Day next.... With starvation at our doors, grimly staring us, vessels laden with our whole hopes of existence, our provisions, are hourly wafted from our every port. From one milling establishment I have last night seen no less than fifty dray-loads of meal moving on to Drogheda, thence to go to feed the foreigner, leaving starvation and death the soon and certain fate of the toil and sweat that raised this food.'

From other places the accounts were more favourable. 'I have found no field without the disease,' wrote Mr Horace Townsend to the *Southern Reporter*, 'but in great variety of degree; in some at least one-third of the crop is tainted, in others to a tenth, and all the remainder seems sound as ever.' From Athy, Kilkenny, Mayo, Carlow and Newry, the accounts were that the disease was partial and seemed in some cases arrested. But these hopeful accounts had, almost in every instance, to be contradicted later on. The blight did not appear in all places at once; it travelled mysteriously but steadily, and from districts where the crop was safe a few days before, the gloomiest accounts were unexpectedly received. The special correspondent of a Dublin newspaper, writing from the west, explained this when he said: 'The disease appeared suddenly, and the tubers are sometimes rotten in twenty-four hours afterwards.' But the disease was not so rapid as this in all cases.

On 18 October, The Royal Agricultural Improvement Society of Ireland held a special meeting relative to the disease in the potatoes. They had, some short time before, appointed a sub-committee on the subject, Professor (now Sir Robert) Kane being its Chairman. He stated to the meeting that the sub-committee had sat the two previous days but were not as yet prepared with anything definite on the subject. They, however, communicated some advice to farmers, under eight heads, founded on experiments. This advice, whether useful or not, was, for the most part, not within the power of small farmers to put in practice; but the sub-committee made one observation that should have aroused all the energies of those who had the lives of the people in their hands. They said that 'on mature consideration of the evidence now before them, it was advisable that the Council should direct the attention of the Irish Government to the now undoubted fact that a great portion of the potato crop in this country was seriously affected by the disease in question'. A cautious, well-weighed sentence which, coming from such a responsible quarter, was full of portentous meaning for the future.

The Dublin Corporation took up the question of the Potato Blight with much and praiseworthy earnestness. They appointed a committee to enquire and report on the subject. A meeting of this committee was held in the City Assembly House on 28 October; the Lord Mayor, John L. Arabin, presided, who, from the accounts which had reached him, gave a gloomy picture of the progress of the disease. The late Mr William Forde, then Town Clerk, in a letter to the committee, said he had recently inspected the produce of eight or ten acres dug and housed in an apparently sound state three weeks before, and that now it was difficult to find a sound potato amongst them. That all might not, however, be gloom, he added that he never saw so much corn safe and thatched in the haggards as he had seen this year.

It was at this meeting that O'Connell first brought forward his plan for dealing with the impending famine, a plan which met with no favour from those in power, there not having been a single suggestion put forward in it which was taken up by them. The crisis, he said, was one of terrible importance; the lives of the people were at stake; the calamity was all but universal; something must be done, and done immediately, to meet it. Private subscriptions would not be sufficient; they might meet a local but not a national calamity like the present. By a merciful dispensation of Providence there was one of the best oat crops that they ever had in the country, but that crop was passing out of Ireland day by day. Then, quoting from the *Mark Lane Express*, he said 16,000 quarters of oats were imported from Ireland to London alone in one week.

His proposal was that a deputation should be appointed to wait on the Lord Lieutenant (Lord Heytesbury) to urge certain measures on the Government in order to mitigate the calamitous state of the country.

1. The first measure he proposed was the immediate stoppage of distillation and brewing.

2. Next, that the export of provisions of every kind to foreign countries should be immediately prohibited and our own ports open to receive provisions from all countries. From this prohibition he, strangely enough, excepted England, although he had just shown that it was England which was carrying away our provisions with the most alarming rapidity. He probably made this exception to induce the Government to lend a more willing ear to his other propositions. He adduced the example of Belgium, Holland and even of Russia and Turkey, in support of this view; all these countries having closed their ports against the exportation of provisions, under analogous circumstances.

3. But all this, he said, was not enough; the Government must be called on to assist the country in buying provisions, called on, not in a spirit of begging or alms-seeking but called on to supply from the resources of Ireland itself money for this purpose. Let our own money be applied to it. The proceeds of the woods and forests in this country were, he said, £74,000

a year; money, which instead of being applied to Irish purposes, had gone to improve Windsor and Trafalgar Square — two millions of Irish money having been already expended in this manner. This is no time to be bungling at trivial remedies; let a loan of a million and a half be raised on this £74,000 a year, which, at four per cent, would leave a portion of it for a sinking fund; let absentees be taxed fifty per cent, and every resident ten per cent. By these means abundant funds would be found to keep the people alive. Let there be got up in each county machinery for carrying out the relief: let the projected railways be commenced and let the people be put to work from one end of the country to the other, and let them be paid in food. He concluded, amidst the applause of the gentlemen present, by moving that a deputation do wait on His Excellency to lay this plan before him, and to explain to him the pressing necessity which existed for its adoption.

To the Tory Government of the day, especially to a politician like Lord Heytesbury, the scheme, in all likelihood, appeared very extravagant, and yet at this distance of time and with the history of that terrible period before us, it was, on the whole, sound, statesmanlike and practical.

In accordance with O'Connell's suggestion, a deputation was appointed to wait on the Lord Lieutenant. He received them at the Phoenix Park, on Wednesday, 3 November. They were coldly received. This may be in part accounted for by the fact that the two or three previous years were remarkable for the great Repeal agitation; O'Connell himself having baptised the year 1843 the Repeal year. Then the State trials came, in which the Repeal leaders fought the Government, inch by inch, putting it to enormous cost, trouble and anxiety. To be sure it succeeded, at last, in securing a verdict and in sending O'Connell and some four or five others to Richmond prison; but their imprisonment there, like their journey to it, was a continuous triumph. Besides, the Government were in the end defeated by an appeal to the House of Lords and the State prisoners set free in the fall of 1844.

O'Connell, it was known through the press, had propounded a scheme to meet the impending famine, which was, in substance, the one laid before the Viceroy. It is not much to be wondered at that a small politician and narrow partyman, as Lord Heytesbury was, should think it a victory to make the deputation feel his high displeasure at the manner in which agitators had been, for so long a period, bearding the Government to which he belonged.

The deputation was highly respectable and ought to have been influential, consisting, as it did, of the Duke of Leinster, Lord Cloncurry, the Lord Mayor, O'Connell, Henry Grattan, Sir James Murray, John Augustus O'Neill, and some twenty other gentlemen of position. The journals of the next morning informed the public that the deputation was 'most formally' received. The Lord Mayor read to His Excellency the resolutions drawn up by the committee by which the deputation was appointed. They stated:

1. That famine and pestilence were immediately imminent, unless the Government took prompt measures against them;

2. That this could be best done by employing the people in works of national utility;

3. That the ports ought to be closed against the exportation of corn;

4. That public granaries ought to be established in various parts of the country, the corn to be sold to the people at moderate prices;

5. That the use of grain for distillation ought to be stopped.

The Lord Lieutenant read the following reply:

'My Lord Mayor and Gentlemen,
   It can scarcely be necessary for me to assure you that the state of the potato crop has for some time occupied, and still occupies, the most anxious attention of the Government.
   Scientific men have been sent over from England to co-operate with those of this country, in endeavouring to investigate the nature of the disease and, if possible, to devise means to arrest its progress. They have not yet terminated their enquiries; but two reports have already been received from them, which have been communicated to the public.
   The Government is also furnished with constant reports from the stipendiary magistrates and inspectors of constabulary, who are charged to watch the state of the potato disease and the progress of the harvest. These vary from day to day, and are often contradictory; it will, therefore, be impossible to form an accurate opinion on the whole extent of the evil till the digging of the potatoes shall be further advanced. To decide, under such circumstances, upon the most proper measures to be adopted, would be premature; particularly as there is reason to hope that,

though the evil exists to a very great extent in some localities, in others it had but partially manifested itself.
There is no immediate pressure in the market. I will, however, lose no time in submitting your suggestions to the consideration of the Cabinet. The greater part of them can only be enforced by legislative enactment and all require to be maturely weighed before they can be adopted. It must be clear to you that, in a case of such great national importance, no decision can be taken without a previous reference to the responsible advisers of the Crown.'

When the Lord Lieutenant had concluded reading the above answer, he immediately commenced bowing the deputation out. As they were about to withdraw, O'Connell made an observation about distilleries. Lord Heytesbury, not condescending to mention him by name, said that the observation *of the gentleman who had spoken* was one deserving of much consideration and one which had not been overlooked by the Government, 'when it had the matter under discussion'; and again began bowing them out, 'which', writes one of those present, 'was *distinctly* understood, and the deputation forthwith retired.'

Although there is clear evidence in Sir Robert Peel's memoirs of himself that Lord Heytesbury immediately submitted the views of the deputation to the Cabinet, His Excellency's letter, which no doubt accompanied them, is not given, neither is the address itself; nor does the Premier or Home Secretary discuss these views or in any way allude to them in subsequent communications. The evidence we have, that they were in the hands of the Cabinet without delay, is contained in a letter of Lord Heytesbury himself, dated 8 November, given in the Peel Memoirs, the name of its recipient, contrary to his usual practice, being suppressed by Sir Robert Peel.

The Lord Lieutenant's address to the deputation was evidently found fault with, at least in one particular, at headquarters and he is on his defence in this letter. 'It is perfectly true', writes His Excellency, 'that I did, in my answer to the Lord Mayor, say there was no immediate pressure on the market; but you must not give too wide a meaning to that observation, which had reference merely to his demand that the exportation of grain should be prohibited and the ports immediately thrown open. My meaning was that there was nothing so pressing as to require us to act without waiting for the decision of the responsible advisers of the Crown. But the danger may be upon us before we are aware of its being near; for, as I said in a former letter, the sudden decay of potatoes dug up in an apparently sound state sets all calculation at defiance. Some precautionary measures must be adopted, and adopted promptly, for there is danger in delay.'

It is worthy of remark that the only part of the Viceroy's answer to the deputation that could weaken the arguments in favour of Free Trade, was his saying, 'there was no immediate pressure on the market'; and this was the only part found fault with by the unnamed minister to whom the above defence was addressed.

The reception accorded to the deputation was soon known through the city, and the chief liberal daily journal opened its leader on the subject next morning in this indignant fashion: 'They may starve! Such in spirit, if not in words, was the reply given yesterday by the English Viceroy, to the memorial of the deputation, which, in the name of the Lords and Commons of Ireland, prayed that the food of this kingdom be preserved, lest the people thereof perish.'[4]

Meanwhile the newspapers were filled with accounts of the progress of the disease, with remedies to arrest it and with suggestions of various kinds for warding off the impending famine. Mr Campbell Foster, then travelling in Ireland as *Times'* Commissioner, made some very sensible suggestions which, he says, he had obtained during his journeys through the country. He said it was generally agreed that the potato crop of 1845 was about one-fifth more than the average of other years. This arose partly from the greater breadth of land that had been placed under potato culture and partly from the unusually abundant produce of the crop. Although he admits the general opinion that, at the time[5] about one-third of the crop was lost, still, if even then the disease could be arrested, his opinion was that there would be food enough in the country for the wants of the people.

'Various plans,' he wrote, 'such as quick lime, layers of ashes, kiln drying, exposure to the air and ventilation have been suggested, to obtain dryness. Most of these are utterly futile, as beyond the general means and comprehension of the people.' He then gives a simple plan of ventilation which was within the reach of every peasant. It was to make an air passage under the whole length of the potato pit and to have one or two vent holes, or chimneys, on the surface of it. The next thing to guard against was frost, which always descends perpendicularly. This being the fact, the only thing required was simply a sod to place over the chimney, or vent hole, every night, or when it might be raining hard, to keep the potatoes dry and free from frosting.

His second important suggestion was to save seed for the coming year, a point, strange to say, that was never sufficiently attended to throughout the whole of this calamitous time, though occasionally spoken of. He said truly, that the vitality of the potato being at the top, where the eyes cluster, in preparing to boil the meal of potatoes each day, the tops ought to be cut off and preserved for seed. In doing this, carefully and sufficiently, the quantity of the edible portion of the potato lost would be the merest trifle. He might have added that the top is usually the least nutritious, or 'mealy' part of the potato, which would make the loss still less.

His third suggestion, he said, he received from a Sligo miller. It was a plan to prevent extortion and high prices, should a famine really come. It consisted in this, that a 'nominal subscription' should be entered into by each county and that a committee of the leading men of each county should be formed, having at their disposal this subscription, should it be found necessary to call it in: that these committees should each purchase, as they might deem it expedient, say 1,000 tons of oatmeal at the lowest present price, holding this oatmeal over in stores till the next spring or summer and that then it should be retailed, under proper superintendence by a storekeeper *for cash*, at a moderate profit, merely sufficient to cover the storage and salary of the storekeeper: that the committee should raise money for the purchase of the oatmeal by their *joint notes,* which the banks would at once discount; all sales of the meal to be lodged each day in the bank to the account of the promissory notes outstanding. On winding up the transaction the oatmeal would be at least worth its present value; and if sold at a small profit, enough to cover the expenses, there would be no necessity for calling in any portion of the subscriptions; but should there be a loss on the sale, the proportion to each subscriber, according to the amount of his subscription, would be trifling. One good effect of this plan would be that these stores would regulate the prices of oatmeal in the market and would prevent the ruin of the farmers by extortioners and meal-mongers, and insure to them, if they must unfortunately buy food, *that* food at a reasonable rate.

Mr Foster added: 'These three plans will, if carried out, I feel assured by all that I have seen and heard, insure, first, *the arrest of the disease in the potatoes,* and the preservation of food for the *people;* secondly, *seed for next* year; and lastly, if there should occur the calamity of a famine, *there will be a substituted food secured for the people at a reasonable price'*.

All these suggestions were well worthy of serious and immediate attention when they were written and although every mode of saving the tuber was, to a great extent, a failure, the mode suggested above was at least as good as any other and far simpler than most of them. But the third suggestion, about a county organisation to keep the food in the country was admirable, practicable, effective; but as the poorer classes, from various causes, could not and, in some instances, would not carry out any organised plan, the *Times'* Commissioner warned the Government to look to it. He said: 'I am as firmly convinced as that I am now writing to you, such is the general apathy, want of exertion and feeling of fatality among the people, such their general distrust of everybody, and suspicion of every project, such the disunion among the higher classes, with similar apathetic indifference, that unless the Government steps forward to carry out, to order, to enforce these or similar plans for the national welfare, *not any of them will be generally adopted, and nothing will be done.* Christmas is approaching, when the potato pits, most of them, will be opened; the poor people will clasp their hands in helpless despair, on seeing their six months' provisions a mass of rottenness; there will be no potatoes for seed next season; a general panic will seize all and oatmeal for food will be scarcely purchasable by the people at *any price.* The Government, however, have been *warned* — let them act promptly, decisively, and *at once,* and not depend on the people helping themselves; for such is the character of the people that *they will do nothing till starvation faces them.'*[6]

Mr Foster collected his letters on Ireland into a volume in March 1846 and said, with justice, in a note to the above passage, 'the truth of this prediction, in every particular, is now unhappily being verified'.

Although Mr Foster is here, as in several other places throughout his letters on Ireland, unjustly severe upon the people — poor, helpless, unaided, uncared for as they were by those whose sacred duty it was to come to their assistance — still many of his views, as in the present instance, were full of practical good sense. He gave many valuable hints for the amelioration of Irish grievances, and several of his recommendations have since been embodied in Acts of Parliament; but when he says the people will do nothing, are apathetic and so on, he ought to remember that in such a fearful crisis, combined effort alone is of value. This must come from the leaders of the people. The best army cannot fight without generals, and in this battle against famine the Irish people had no leaders: their natural leaders, the proprietors of the soil, did next to nothing — the Government of the country did next to nothing. The Government alone had the power to combine, to direct, to command; it was called upon from all parts of the country to do so — the Viceroy was waited on — Mr Foster himself, in the passage quoted above, warned the Government to act, and to act at once, and yet what had it done up to the

Family viewing rotten potatoes, August 1846.

time he closed his Irish tour? Where was the real, the culpable, the unpardonable apathy?

Mr Gregory, writing from Coole Park on 12 November, said he could not get the people to take precautions against the disease. By putting drains under his own pits and holes in them for ventilation and throwing turf mould and lime upon them, he said they were still safe. His opinion was that half the potatoes in his neighbourhood were tainted. The police- sergeant of the Kinvara district made a return, the result of an examination of fifty-two acres of potatoes in eighteen fields of from one-and-a-half to seven acres. The least diseased field, one of four acres, had twelve tubers in the 100 diseased. In a field of seven acres, ninety-six in every 100 were diseased and the average loss in all the fields was seventy per cent.

Charles K. O'Hara, Chairman of the Sligo Board of Guardians, wrote to the Mansion House Committee: 'In many instances the conacre tenants have refused to dig the crops and are already suffering from want of food.' Mr Crichton of Somerton, Ballymote, said the disease in his locality was not so bad as it was elsewhere, but still it was his opinion that many families about him could not count on having a potato left in January.

Mr Christopher Hamilton, Land Agent, of Leeson Street, Dublin, writing to the Marquis of Lansdowne, said he 'ascertained by personal inspection that a great proportion of the ordinary food of the people had become useless, and that from the nature of the blight it is impossible to depend on any adequate proportion being saved'. Mr Hamilton praised the submission of the people under the trial.

On 24 November Sir James Murray, MD, published a remarkable letter, headed 'Surgery *versus* Medicine', in which, I believe, he came as near the immediate cause of the disease as any writer who had dealt with the subject. He attributed it to electrical agency. 'During the last season,' he wrote, 'the clouds were charged with excessive electricity, and yet there was little or no thunder to draw off that excess from the atmosphere. In the damp and variable autumn this surcharge of electrical matter was attracted by the moist, succulent, and pointed leaves of the potato.' As medicine is found to be useless for the disease, he recommended the use of the knife to cut away the diseased parts and to keep the sound portions on shelves.

The clergy of every denomination came forward with a zeal and charity worthy of their sacred calling. Out of hundreds of letters written by them, I cannot deny myself the pleasure of making a few extracts. The Rev. Mr Killen, Rector of Tyrrilla, Co. Down, wrote: 'This is the famous potato-growing district. One-third of the crop is already affected, both in the pits and those in the ground.' The Rev. Mr McKeon, of Drumlish, in his letter to the Mansion House Committee, said: 'The people must starve in summer, *having paid their rents by selling their oats*; their rents being rigorously exacted on the Granard and Lorton estates.' The Rev. James McHall, of Hollymount, Mayo, mentioned the startling fact that a poor man in his neighbourhood having opened a pit, where he had stored six barrels of potatoes, of sixty-four stone each, found he had not one stone of sound potatoes! The Rev. John Stuart, Presbyterian minister in Antrim, declared that fully one half of the crop was lost in his district. He added: 'Some have tried lime dust, and pits aired with tiles, and in a few days have found a mass of rottenness'. The Rev. Mr Waldron, Parish Priest of Cong, wrote that he had examined the crop in every village in his parish, and reported that more than one-half of it was lost on sound lands, above three-fourths on others. 'The panic', he continued, 'which at first took the people has lately subsided into silent despair and hopelessness.' A Protestant clergyman in Mayo, who had thirty men digging his potatoes, of the species called Peelers, 'thinks they did not dig as much sound potatoes as two men would do in a sound year'. The Rev. Mr Cantwell, of Kilfeacle, made the suggestive announcement that 'parents are already counting the potatoes they give their children'. The good Rector of Schull, Dr Robert Traill Hall, wrote to Lord Bernard with prophetic grief. 'Am I to cry peace, peace, where there is no peace? But what did I find in the islands? *The pits, without one single exception in a state of serious decay, and many of the islanders apprehending famine in consequence.* Oh, my heart trembles when I think of all that may be before us.'

Meanwhile the accounts of the progress of the disease were every day more disheartening; the Government appeared to do nothing except publish a few reports from those 'scientific men sent over from England', alluded to by the Viceroy in his reply to the deputation of November. The Mansion House Committee met on the nineteenth of that month and unanimously passed the following resolutions, Lord Cloncurry being in the chair:

1. 'That we feel it an imperative duty to discharge our consciences of all responsibility regarding the undoubtedly approaching calamities, famine and pestilence, throughout Ireland, an approach which is imminent, and almost immediate, and can be obviated only by the most prompt, universal and efficacious measures for procuring food and employment for the people.

2. That we have ascertained beyond the shadow of doubt, that considerably more than one-third of the entire of the potato crop in Ireland has been already destroyed by the potato disease; and

that such disease has not, by any means, ceased its ravages, but, on the contrary, it is daily extending more and more; and that no reasonable conjecture can be formed with respect to the limits of its effects, short of the destruction of the entire remaining potato crop.

3. That our information upon the subject is positive and precise and is derived from persons living in all the counties of Ireland. From persons also of all political opinions and from clergymen of all religious persuasions.

4. We are thus unfortunately able to proclaim to all the inhabitants of the British Empire, and in the presence of an all-seeing Providence, that in Ireland famine of a most hideous description must be immediate and pressing, and that pestilence of the most frightful kind is certain, and not remote, unless immediately prevented.

5. That we arraign in the strongest terms, consistent with personal respect to ourselves, the culpable conduct of the present administration, as well in refusing to take any efficacious measure for alleviating the existing calamity with all its approaching hideous and necessary consequences; as also for the positive and unequivocal crime of keeping the ports closed against the importation of foreign provisions, thus either abdicating their duty to the people or their sovereign, whose servants they are, or involving themselves in the enormous guilt of aggravating starvation and famine, by unnaturally keeping up the price of provisions, and doing this for the benefit of a selfish class who derive at the present awful crisis pecuniary advantages to themselves by the maintenance of the oppressive Corn Laws.

6. That the people of Ireland, in their bitter hours of misfortune, have the strongest right to impeach the criminality of the ministers of the Crown, inasmuch as it has pleased a merciful Providence to favour Ireland in the present season with a most abundant crop of oats. Yet, whilst the Irish harbours are closed against the importation of foreign food, they are left open for the exportation of Irish grain, an exportation which has already amounted in the present season to a quantity nearly adequate to feed the entire people of Ireland, and to avert the now certain famine; thus inflicting upon the Irish people the abject misery of having their own provisions carried away to feed others, whilst they themselves are left contemptuously to starve.

7. That the people of Ireland should particularly arraign the conduct of the ministry in shrinking from their duty, to open the ports for the introduction of provisions by royal proclamation, whilst they have had the inhumanity to postpone the meeting of Parliament to next year.

8. That we behold in the conduct of the ministry the contemptuous disregard of the lives of the people of Ireland, and that we, therefore, do prepare an address to her Majesty, most humbly praying her Majesty to direct her ministers to adopt without any kind of delay the most extensive and efficacious measures to arrest the progress of famine and pestilence in Ireland.

Signed,
John L. Arabin,
Lord Mayor of Dublin.'

It does not appear that the address to the Queen agreed to by the last resolution was ever presented, which omission is sufficiently accounted for by the resignation of the Peel Cabinet, which occurred a few days afterwards, on 8 December.

Not to prolong those extracts, I will here quote an analysis of 500 letters received by the Mansion House Committee, which was given by the Earl of Mountcashel at a meeting of farmers held in Fermoy, Co. Cork. 'I have seen', said his Lordship, 'an analysis of 500 letters received by the Mansion House Committee, made by Mr Sinnott, the Secretary. Of those, 197 have come from clergymen of the Established Church; 143 from Roman Catholic clergymen; thirty from Presbyterian clergymen; 107 from deputy-lieutenants and magistrates; and the remainder from poor-law guardians and so forth. Taking all these communications together, 158 calculated upon a loss of less than one-third of the potato crop; 135 upon the loss of a full third; 134 that one-half of the crop was destroyed, and forty apprehended a destruction of more than one-half. With respect to the residue of the crops, there are 216 letters in which no opinion is given, whilst the writers of 101 think that the remainder of the crop may be saved, and 118 are of a contrary opinion. Thus, we have all classes and parties in the country — Protestant and Presbyterian clergymen more numerous than Roman Catholic clergymen — peers, deputy-lieutenants, magistrates, poor-law guardians all concurring in the main fact, that a vast portion of the food of millions of the people has been destroyed whilst all is uncertainty as to the remainder'.

With this information before them and a vast deal more besides, it is not to be wondered at that the Mansion House Committee passed the resolutions given above. A strong protest, indeed, but it came from a body of men who had laboured with energy and diligence from the very first day the Committee was formed. One of the earliest acts of that Committee was to prepare a set of queries that, through them, they might put themselves in communication with persons of position and intelligence throughout the entire country. The result was that they felt themselves compelled to pass a deliberate censure upon the apathy of the Government; and it will be found, in the course of this narrative, that the want of prompt vigorous action on the part of the Government, more especially at this early stage of the Famine, had quite as much to do with the Famine as the failure of the potato crop itself.

In November a cessation of the rot was observed in some districts, but in that month the assertion made in the first resolution of the Mansion House Committee, that more than one-third of the potato crop was lost, was not only vouched for by hundreds of most respectable and most trustworthy witnesses, as we have seen, but it was accepted as a truth by every party. Moreover, the Government, whose culpable apathy and delay was denounced on all sides, except by its partisans, was in possession of information on the subject, which made the loss of the potato crop at least one-half instead of one-third. Professors Lindley and Playfair made a report to Sir Robert Peel, bearing the date 15 November, from which he quoted the following startling passage in his speech on the address, on 22 January 1846: 'We can come to no other conclusion, they write, than that one-half of the actual potato crop of Ireland is either destroyed, or remains in a state unfit for the food of man. We, moreover, feel it our duty to apprise you that we fear this to be a low estimate'.[7]

Estimating the value of the potato crop of 1845 in Ireland at £18,000,000, not a high estimate, it was now certain that food to the value of £9,000,000 was already lost, yet no answer could be had from the Viceroy or the Premier but the stereotyped one, that the matter was receiving the most serious consideration of the Government. And on they went enquiring when they should have been acting. With the information given by Professors Lindley and Playfair in their hands, they appointed another Commission about this time, which sat in Dublin Castle and was presided over by Mr Lucas, then Under-Secretary. Its Secretary, Captain Kennedy, applied to the Mansion House Committee for information. That body at once placed its whole correspondence at the disposal of the Commissioners; the Lord Mayor had an interview with Sir Thomas Freemantle, one of them, by whom he was assured that the Government was fully prepared to take such steps as might be found necessary for the protection of the people, when the emergency should arise.

Most people thought it had arisen already.

On 8 December, a full fortnight after this interview, a set of queries, similar to those issued months before by the Mansion House Committee, were printed and circulated by the new Commissioners, asking for information that had already come in from every part of the country even to superabundance.

On 10 December the Corporation of Dublin agreed to an address to the Queen, calling her Majesty's attention to the potato blight and the impending famine consequent upon it. In their address they respectfully brought before her two facts then lately elicited, or rather confirmed, by the Devon Commission — namely, that 4,000,000 of the labouring population of Ireland 'are more wretched than any people in Europe, their only food the potato, their only drink water'. They added that even these facts did not convey to her Majesty an adequate idea of the destitution by which the Irish people were threatened, or of the numbers who would suffer by the failure of the potato crop; facts related of the inhabitants of a country which, of late years, might be justly styled the granary of England, exporting annually from the midst of a starving people food of the best kind in sufficient abundance for treble its own inhabitants. They assured her Majesty that fully one-third of their only support for one year was destroyed by the potato blight, which involved a state of destitution for four months of a great majority of her Majesty's Irish subjects. They said, with a respectful dignity, that they asked no alms; they only asked for public works of utility; they asked that the national treasury should be 'poured out to give employment to the people at remunerative wages'. Finally they prayed her Majesty to summon Parliament for an early day.

The Corporation did not get an opportunity of presenting their address to the Queen until 3 January following — four-and-twenty days after it was agreed to. This delay, no doubt, chiefly arose from the resignation of the Peel ministry on 5 December; the failure of Lord John Russell to form a Government and the consequent return of Sir Robert Peel to office on the twentieth of the month, after a fortnight's interregnum.

In the Queen's reply to the Dublin address she deplored the poverty of a portion of her Irish subjects, their welfare and prosperity being objects of her constant care; she had, she said, ordered precautions to be taken; she had summoned Parliament for an early day, and looked with confidence to the advice she would receive from the united council of the realm.

The Corporation of London addressed her Majesty on the same occasion, deploring the sufferings and privations of a large portion of her subjects in England, Ireland and Scotland, which they attributed to 'erroneous legislation, which, by excluding the

Mother and child search for potatoes.

importation of food, and restricting commerce, shuts out from the nation the bounty of Providence'. They, therefore, prayed that the ports of the kingdom might be opened for the free importation of food. While the Corporation of London did not, we may presume, exclude the peculiar distress of Ireland from their sympathies, their real object in going to Windsor was to make an anti-Corn Law demonstration. So much was this the case that the deputation consisted of the enormous number of 200 gentlemen. The Queen's reply to them was hopeful. She said she would 'gladly sanction any measure which the legislature might suggest as conducive to the alleviation of this temporary distress, and to the permanent welfare of all classes of her people'.

It is a noticeable fact, and one to be deplored, that even the potato blight was made a party question in Ireland. If we except the Protestant and dissenting clergy and a few philanthropic laymen, the upper classes, especially the Conservatives, remained aloof from the public meetings held to call attention to it and its threatened consequences. The Mansion House Committee, which did so much good, was composed almost exclusively of Catholics and Liberals; and the same is substantially true of the meetings held throughout the country — in short, the Conservatives regarded, or pretended to regard, those meetings as a new phase of the Repeal agitation. Then, as the distress must chiefly occur amongst the poor Catholics, who were repealers, it was, they assumed, the business of repealers and agitators to look to them and relieve them.

The Premier himself was not free from these feelings. In the memorandum which he read to the Cabinet on 1 November, amongst many other things, he said: 'There will be no hope of contributions from England for the mitigation of this calamity. Monster meetings, the ungrateful return for past kindness, the subscriptions in Ireland to Repeal rent and O'Connell tribute, will have disinclined the charitable here to make any great exertions for Irish relief'.[8] There was even, I fear, something behind all this — the old feeling of the English colony in Ireland that it was no business of theirs to sustain the native race, whose numerical strength they regarded, now as ever, to be a standing threat and danger to themselves.

The sentiments of the leading journals of the Tory party quite coincided with this view. They kept constantly asserting that the ravages of the potato blight were greatly exaggerated; and they eagerly seized on any accidental circumstance that could give them a pretext for supporting this assertion. The chief Dublin conservative journal, the *Evening Mail*, on 3 November, writing about the murder of Mr Clarke, 'inclines to believe that the

47

agrarian outrage had its origin in a design to intimidate landlords from demanding their rents, at a season when corn of all kinds is superabundant, and the partial failure of the potato crop gives a pretence for not selling it. And if we recollect', it continued, 'that the potato crop of this year far exceeded an average one, and that corn of all kinds is so far abundant, it will be seen that the apprehensions of a famine in that quarter are unfounded, and are merely made the pretence for withholding the payment of rent.' Such was the language of a newspaper supposed largely to express landlord feeling in Ireland and supposed, too, to be the chief organ of the existing Governments, represented by Lord Heytesbury.

Later on in the month, a Protestant dignitary, Dean Hoare of Achonry, wrote a letter to the Mansion House Committee, in which, whilst he gave substantially the same views of the potato failure as hundreds of others, he complained in a mild spirit of the people in his locality as being 'very slow' to adopt the methods recommended for preserving the potatoes from decay. Another Tory journal of the time, since amalgamated with the former, made this letter the pretence of an attack on the Mansion House Committee, accusing it of withholding Dean Hoare's letter, because it gave a favourable account of the state of the potato crop, and an unfavourable one of the peasantry — charging it with 'fraud, trickery and misrepresention', and its members with 'associating for factious purposes alone'. In reply, it was clearly shown that the Committee did not withhold the Dean's letter, even for an hour, and was clearly shown that the *Evening Packet*, the journal in question, antedated his letter by a day, in order to sustain its charge of suppression.

The *Packet* also omitted those portions of the letter which represented the loss of the potato crop as extensive, and which called on the Government to employ the people.[9]

The *Freeman's Journal* of 24 November, in commenting on the way in which its Tory contemporary dealt with Dean Hoare's letter, said: 'The *Packet*, in its last issue, has returned to its appointed task of denying that the failure of the potato crop is so extensive as to demand extraordinary measures on the part of the Government.' Although, at the time, this could be nothing more than a bold guess, it is highly probable that the writer of it hit the mark for, in his memoirs, published by his literary executors, Earl Stanhope and Lord Cardwell, we find the Premier, in the middle of October, giving this caution to the Lord Lieutenant: 'I need not recommend to you the utmost reserve as to the future, I mean as to the possibility of Government interference'.[10]

A few days after the *Packet* had published the above sentiment, the *Evening Mail* said 'there was a sufficiency, an abundance, of sound potatoes in the country for the wants of the people'. And it went on to stimulate farmers to sell their corn, by threats of being forestalled by Dutch and Hanoverian merchants. In the beginning of December, a Tory provincial print, not probably so high as its metropolitan brethren in the confidence of its party, wrote: 'It may be fairly presumed the losses have been enormous.... We repeat it, *and we care not whom it displeases,* that there are not now half as many sound potatoes in the country as there were last December.' The editor seemed to feel he was doing a perilous thing in stating a fact which he knew would be displeasing to many of his readers.

3

Government reaction

As stated in the last chapter, the deputation that waited on the Lord Lieutenant was superciliously bowed out the moment his Excellency had finished the reading of his reply; so that the usual courtesy extended to such bodies, of having some conversation and friendly discussion on the subject of the address, was denied to the noblemen and gentlemen who presented themselves at the Viceregal Lodge on 3 November. Yet, more than a fortnight previously, Lord Heytesbury had written to the Premier, expressing great concern at the accounts daily received of the blight. 'The reports', he wrote, 'continue to be of a very alarming nature, and leave no doubt upon the mind but that the potato crops have failed almost everywhere'.[1] This admission he took care not to make to the deputation, although its truth had not only been verified but strengthened by the accounts which he continued to receive between the date of the letter and 3 November.

In the Premier's communication, to which Lord Heytesbury was replying, were, amongst others, the following queries: 'At what period would the pressure be felt? Would it be immediate, if the reports of the full extent of the evil are confirmed, or, *is there a stock of old potatoes* sufficient to last for a certain time?' The Viceroy replied that he was assured '*there is no stock* whatever of *last year's* potatoes in the country'. That is, in the middle of October 1845 no stock of the potatoes grown in 1844 had remained! Such was the knowledge which the Premier of England (once an Irish Secretary) and the Lord Lieutenant of Ireland possessed of the nature and constitution of the potato!

One of Sir Robert Peel's biographers, evidently a great admirer of his, says of him that he was a freetrader in principle long before 1845;[2] whilst his enemies assert that, having been placed by the Tory party at the head of a Protectionist Government, he betrayed that party and suddenly threw himself into the arms of the Corn

Law League. Neither of these views appears to be quite correct. The common and, it would seem, the more accurate opinion about him is that he was a politician by profession — a man of expediency — and that on the question of the Corn Laws he did no more than he had previously done with regard to Catholic emancipation — followed the current of public opinion, which he always watched with the most anxious care — and turning round, carried through Parliament a measure which he had long and strenuously opposed. There was, to be sure, this difference in his conduct with regard to those two great measures, that, whilst up to the time he undertook, in conjunction with the Duke of Wellington, to free the Catholics, he never advocated their claims; on the other hand he had been twice a party to modifications of the Corn Laws, first in 1828 and secondly in 1842. In the latter year he, cautiously indeed, but not unsubstantially, legislated in the direction of free trade.

He became First Lord of the Treasury in August 1841 and soon afterwards brought before the Cabinet the question of the duties on the importation of food, more especially of corn. He recommended his colleagues to make the revision of those duties a Cabinet question; and he further submitted 'a proposal in respect of the extent to which such revision should be carried, and to the details of the new law'.[3] A bill founded on his views was passed in the Parliament of 1842 'providing for a material diminution in the amount of the import duties on the several kinds of foreign grain'.

But these changes did not satisfy the Corn Law Leaguers, who sought complete repeal; but they had the effect of alarming the Premier's Tory supporters and led to the resignation of one Cabinet Minister, the Duke of Buckingham. His partisans endeavoured to obtain from him a guarantee that this Corn Law of 1842 should, as far as he was concerned, be a final measure; but, although he tells us that he did not then contemplate the necessity for further change, he uniformly refused to fetter either the Government or himself by such an assurance.

Yet, in proposing the introduction of the tariff in 1842, he seems to have foreshadowed future and still more liberal legislation on the subject. 'I know that many gentlemen,' he said, 'who are strong advocates for free trade may consider that I have not gone far enough. I know that, I believe that on the general principle of free trade there is *now no great difference of opinion; and that all agree* in the general rule, that we should purchase in the cheapest market, and sell in the dearest.'

The opposition, more especially the freetraders, received this sentiment with rapturous applause, so the adroit statesman added: 'I know the meaning of those cheers. I do not now wish to raise a discussion on the Corn Laws or the sugar duties, which (I contend) are exceptions from the general rule.[4] His exceptions were futile, because they were illogical, which of course he must have known; they were therefore only meant to reassure, to some extent, the affrighted Protectionist gentlemen behind him.

The anti-Corn Law League, not accepting the concessions made in 1842 as final, continued to agitate and insist upon total repeal. They held meetings, made able speeches, published pamphlets, delivered lectures and continued to keep before the English public the iniquity, as they said, of those laws which compelled the English artisan to eat dear bread.

Sir Robert, as a politician and statesman, watched the progress of this agitation, as also the effect of the changes made in 1842; and he tells us he was gradually weakened in his views as to the protection of British-grown corn. 'The progress of discussion', he says, 'had made a material change in the opinions of many persons with regard to the policy of protection to domestic agriculture, and the extent to which that policy should be carried.[5] The success of the changes made in 1842, falsifying, as they did, all the prophecies of the Protectionists, tended further to shake his confidence in the necessity of maintaining those laws.

Since its formation in August 1841 Sir Robert Peel's Government had continued to carry its measures through Parliament with overwhelming majorities; still the question of free trade was making rapid progress throughout the country, especially in the great towns, the anti-Corn Law League had become a power, and thoughtful men began to see that the principle it embodied could not be long resisted in a commercial nation like England.

The Parliamentary Session of 1845 opened with an attempt, on the part of Lord John Russell, the leader of the Opposition, to compel the Government to declare its policy on free trade. Sir Robert Peel was silent, probably because at the moment he had no fixed policy about it; or, if he had, he was not the man to declare it at an inconvenient time. Great agricultural distress prevailed, a fact admitted by both sides of the House: the Protectionist members maintained that it was caused by the concessions already made to free trade; the free traders, on the contrary, held it to be the result of the continuance of absurd protective duties.

On 9 August the Parliamentary Session of 1845 closed, leaving Sir Robert Peel still at the head of that imposing majority which had sustained him since 1841. Not long after commenced those gloomy reports of potato blight which continued to increase, until the fact was placed beyond the possibility of doubt.

It was not originally Sir Robert Peel's desire to propose a repeal of the Corn Laws in the session of 1846; he would have much preferred the postponement of the question for a year or so in order to prepare the public mind for his altered opinions; besides, he not unreasonably hoped that the success of the changes of 1842 would have so enlightened his party as to induce them to accept further and greater changes in the commercial tariff. Meanwhile, he could be feeling his way with them by the aid of trusted friends and be making them, in various ways, familiar with the new sacrifices he was about to require at their hands. Hence, the potato blight was, in more senses than one, an untoward event for himself and his Cabinet, since it hurried him into the doing of that which he hoped to have done without giving any very violent shock to the opinions or prejudices of his Tory supporters.

Sir Robert, if not a man of great forecast or intuition, was certainly one to make the most of circumstances as they arose, provided he had time for reflection. When the news of the potato failure in Ireland became an alarming fact, he recast his plan and put that failure foremost amongst his reasons for repealing the Corn Laws; in fact, in his own adroit way he left it to be understood that this was the immediate and urgent cause for dealing with the question — nay more, that the real, the *only* question he was dealing with was the potato blight and the threatened famine in Ireland; and that, in anxiously seeking for an adequate remedy for such terrible evils, he could find but one — the total repeal of the Corn Laws.

Some in his own Cabinet, and numbers of thoughtful people throughout the country, saw a variety of plans for meeting the failure distinct from such repeal; very many even, far from regarding it as a remedy against Irish famine, considered it would be a positive injury to this country, under existing circumstances; but Sir Robert Peel, with that charming frankness and simplicity, the assumption of which had become a second nature to him, could see but one remedy for poor Ireland — a repeal of the Corn Laws. Others, which were hinted to him by some of his colleagues, he dexterously avoids discussing and only repeats his own great conviction — repeal the Corn Laws and save poor, famine-threatened Ireland.

From the end of August to the beginning of October several communications passed between the Premier and Sir James Graham, relative to the failure of the potato. During that period the accounts were very varied, partly from the disease not having made very much progress and partly because there was not as yet sufficient time to examine the crop with care; but a perusal of the correspondence which reached the Government, so far as it is given in Sir Robert Peel's memoirs and his speeches in Parliament, prove that the accounts in newspapers and, above all, in letters received and published by the Mansion House Committee, did not overstate the failure, but rather the reverse — this fact is more especially evident from the joint letter of Professors Lindley and Playfair already quoted.

Of all the ministers, Sir James Graham seems to have had the greatest share of the Premier's confidence; Sir Robert thus wrote to him from Whitehall on 13 October: 'The accounts of the state of the potato crop in Ireland are becoming very alarming. I enclose letters which have very recently reached me. Lord Heytesbury says that the reports which reach the Irish Government are very unsatisfactory. I presume that if the worst should happen which is predicted, the pressure would not be *immediate*. There is such a tendency to exaggeration and inaccuracy in Irish reports that delay in acting upon them is always desirable; but I foresee the necessity that may be imposed upon us at an early period of considering whether there is not that well grounded apprehension of actual scarcity that justifies and compels the adoption of every means of relief which the exercise of the prerogative of legislation might afford. *I have no confidence in such remedies as the prohibition of exports or the stoppage of distilleries. The removal of the impediments to import is the only effectual remedy.'*

Sir James Graham wrote to the Premier from Netherby on the same day enclosing a communication from the Lord Lieutenant of Ireland *which is not given* in the Peel memoirs, but which Sir James says 'conveys information of the most serious kind, which requires immediate attention'. He goes on to give it as his opinion that the time had come when speculation was reduced to certainty, as the potatoes were being taken out of the ground; it was therefore the duty of the Government to apply their attention without delay to measures for the mitigation of this national calamity.

He referred to Belgium and Holland and said it was desirable to know, without loss of time, what had been done by our Continental neighbours in similar circumstances. Indian corn might, of course, he said, be obtained on cheap terms, *'if the people would eat it'*, but unfortunately it was an acquired taste. He thought the summoning of Parliament in November a better course than the opening of the ports by an Order in Council.[6]

On receipt of the above Sir Robert again wrote to the Home Secretary: 'My letter on the awful question of the potato crop will have crossed yours to me. Interference with the due course of the law respecting the supply of food is so momentous, and so lasting in its consequences, that we must not act without the most accurate information. I fear the worst. I have written to the Duke also.'

It was about this time that the Premier appointed Drs Lindley and Playfair to come to Ireland for the purpose of investigating the causes of the blight and, if possible, to apply remedies. He summoned the latter to Drayton Manor before leaving and both were struck by the very short time in which the blight rendered the potato worthless for food.

Sir Robert said to Sir James Graham on 18 October: 'We have examined here various potatoes that have been affected; and witnessing the rapidity of decay, and the necessity of immediate action, I have not hesitated to interrupt Playfair's present occupation, and to direct his attention to this still more pressing matter'.[7] Two days later Sir James sent his chief a desponding letter in reply and, with much good sense, said he was not sanguine about any chemical process, *within the reach of the peasantry*, arresting the decay in tubers already affected; besides the rainfall continued so great that, independently of disease, he felt the potatoes must rot in the ground from the wet, unless on very dry lands. He then mentioned a matter of the utmost consequence which had not been alluded to before. 'There are many points', he said, 'on which a scientific inquiry may be most useful, particularly the vital one with respect to the seed for next year'.[8]

In his letter of 13 October, given above, the Premier opened his mind to his friend, the Home Secretary, that he was a convert to the repeal of the Corn Laws, but even to him he put forward the potato blight in Ireland as the cause. Some days afterwards, in a very carefully worded letter to Lord Heytesbury, he introduced the same business. 'The accounts from Ireland of the potato crop, confirmed as they are by your high authority,' said Sir Robert, 'are very alarming, and it is the duty of the Government to seek a remedy for the "great evil".'

Of course it was, and he had made up his mind to apply one which he knew was distasteful to most of his colleagues; but time was pressing and he must bring it forward; so making a clean breast of it, he stated his remedy in a bold clear sentence to the Protectionist Lord Lieutenant of Ireland. 'The remedy', he wrote, 'is the removal *of all impediments* to the import of all kinds of human food; that is the total and absolute repeal for ever of all duties on all articles of subsistence'.[9] Sir Robert Peel seldom penned so clear a sentence, but its very clearness had an object, for he seemed to desire to shut out discussion on any of the other remedies which were put forward in Ireland. He then went on to join the *temporary* relief of Irish distress with the *permanent* arrangement of the Corn Law question. 'You might', he said, 'remit nominally for one year; but who will re-establish the Corn Laws once abrogated, though from a casual and temporary pressure? I have good ground therefore for stating that the application of a temporary remedy to a temporary evil does in this particular case involve considerations of the utmost and most lasting importance.'

These passages were written by a minister who, coolly and without any sufficient authority whatever, assumed that there was no other remedy for the failure of the potato crop in Ireland but a repeal of the Corn Laws and that it was the remedy the Irish public were calling for, to meet the threatened danger. And yet so far from this being the case, it was never propounded by anyone as a principal remedy at all.

What the Irish public thought about the impending famine and what they said about it was that the oat crop was unusually fine and more than sufficient to feed the whole population and that it should be kept in the country for that purpose. A most obvious remedy; but the Premier had other plans in his head and could not see this one, because he would not. Like Nelson on a memorable occasion, he persisted in keeping his telescope to the eye that suited his own purpose. He did not condescend to give a reason for his views, he only expressed them.

He had no confidence in the old-fashioned remedy of keeping the food in the country but he did put his trust in the remedy of sending 3,000 miles for Indian corn — a food which, he elsewhere admitted, he feared the Irish could not be induced to use. He thought it quite right and in accordance with political science to allow, or rather to compel Ireland, threatened with famine, to sell her last loaf and then go to America to buy maize, the preparation of which she did not understand. Political economists will hardly deny that people ought not to sell what they require for themselves — that they should only part with *surplus* food. But to sell wheat and oats and oatmeal and flour with one hand and buy Indian corn with the other to avoid starvation could be hardly regarded as the act of a sane man.

'There had been — it was hinted, and we believe truly, in Lord John Russell's letter from Edinburgh — some talk in the Cabinet, and there was some discussion in the press, about opening the Irish ports by proclamation. *Opening the Irish ports!* Why, the real remedy, had any interference with the law been necessary, would have been to *close* them — the torrent of food was running *outwards*'.[10] So did the leading Tory periodical put this obvious truth some months later.

The Viceroy, replying to the Premier's letter on 17 October, said he was deeply impressed with the extent and alarming nature of the failure of the potato crop and had no doubt in his mind that it was general. The Premier had, sometime before, suggested Special Commissioners to collect information but the Lord Lieutenant did not think they would be able to collect more accurate information than that *already* furnished by the county inspectors. He suggested that when the potato digging was more advanced it would be well to move the Lieutenants of counties to call meetings of the resident landholders, with a view to ascertaining the amount of the evil and their opinion of the measures most proper to be adopted. He saw no objection to such a course, though he dutifully added that the Premier might.

There could be no objection whatever to such a course. It was, so far as it went, the right course, because it would have called upon the proprietors of the soil to discharge the duties of their position and to take counsel as to the best mode of doing it. In his later correspondence with Lord Heytesbury the Premier *never alluded to this suggestion in any way!* Of course it fell to the ground.

On 19 October, Mr Buller, Secretary to the Royal Agricultural Society of Ireland, wrote to Sir Robert Peel that he had made the tour of several of the counties of the Province of Connaught and the result was that he found the potato crop affected in localities where people thought the blight had not reached. Mr Buller's was a private letter to the Premier in anticipation of a more formal report from the Society, because, as he said, he 'did not wish a moment to elapse' before informing him of the extent of the fearful malady, in order that no time should be lost in adopting the necessary measures of precaution and relief for Ireland. He concluded by announcing that a panic had seized all parties to a greater extent than he ever remembered since the cholera; which panic, he thought, would go on increasing as the extent of the failure became better known.

Subordinates like Lord Heytesbury and Sir James Graham, writing to their chief, could only hint their views. Both did so more than once with regard to the immediate action to be taken in securing food for the Irish people, to replace the potatoes destroyed by the blight. In one of the Viceroy's letters to the Premier, he quoted some precedents of what had been done in former years by proclamation in Ireland, especially referring to proclamations issued by Lord Cornwallis in 1800-1. He also referred to some Acts of Parliament, no longer, however, in force. Sir James Graham, writing some days later to the Premier, said: 'The precedents for proceeding by proclamation from the Lord Lieutenant of Ireland, and not by Order in Council, *are directly in point*; adding, of course, that such proclamations should be followed by an Act of Indemnity'. Surely anybody can see that for a Government to meet an extraordinary evil by an extraordinary remedy would not only be sanctioned by an Act of Indemnity but would be certain to receive the warm approval of Parliament.'

Sir Robert Peel wanted neither county meetings nor proclamations; so, writing to Sir James Graham on 22 October, he said — all but misstating Lord Heytesbury's views on proclamations: 'Lord Heytesbury, from his occasional remarks on proclamations, seems to labour under an impression that there is a constitutional right to issue them. Now there is absolutely none. There is no more abstract right to prohibit the export of a potato than to command any other violation of law. Governments have assumed, and will assume in extreme cases, unconstitutional power and will trust to the good sense of the people, convinced by the necessity to obey the proclamation, and to Parliament to indemnify the issuers. The proclamations to which Lord Heytesbury refers may be useful as precedents but they leave the matter where they found it in point of law; they give no sort of authority. I have a strong impression that we shall do more harm than good by controlling the free action of the people in respect to the legal *export* of these commodities, or the legal use of them'.[11]

The above passage naturally drew from Sir James Graham the following remarks: 'I enclose another letter from the Lord Lieutenant, giving a worse account of the potato crop as the digging advances but stating that we are as yet unacquainted with the full extent of the mischief. *I think* that Lord Heytesbury is aware that the issue of proclamations is the exercise of a power beyond the law, which requires subsequent indemnity, and has not the force of law. *The precedents which he cites illustrate this known truth;* yet proclamations remitting duties, backed by an order of the Custom-house not to levy, are very effective measures, though the responsibility which attaches to their adoption is most onerous, especially when Parliament may be readily called together'.[12]

Some days later the Lord Lieutenant announced to the Premier that Professors Lindley and Playfair had arrived in Dublin, and also gave a set of queries which he had placed in their hands — all very useful, but one of special importance: 'What means can be adopted for securing seed potatoes for next year?'

This communication contained the following passage: 'There is a great cry for the prohibition of exportation, particularly of oats. With regard to potatoes, it seems to be pretty generally admitted that to prohibit the exportation of so perishable a produce would be a very doubtful advantage. Towards the end of next week we shall know, I presume, the result of the deliberations of her Majesty's Government; and as by that time the digging will be sufficiently advanced to enable us to guess at the probable result of the harvest, I shall then intimate to the several Lieutenants the propriety of calling county meetings, unless I should hear from you that you disapprove of such proceedings. The danger of such meetings is in the remedies they may suggest, and the various subjects they may embrace in their discussions, wholly foreign to the question before them'.[13]

Three days later, on 27 October, he again wrote to the Premier: 'Everything is rising rapidly in price, and the people begin to show symptoms of discontent which may ripen into something worse. Should I be authorised in issuing a proclamation prohibiting distillation from grain? This is demanded on all sides.'

There is no reply to this letter given by Sir Robert Peel in his memoirs, and yet he must have written one. He certainly wrote to the Lord Lieutenant between 3 and 8 November; for the Mansion House deputation was received at the Viceregal Lodge on the third and we find the Viceroy in a letter to the Premier on the eighth explaining what he had said to the deputation on the third; so that the Premier must, in the meantime, have put him on his defence; 'it is perfectly true,' wrote Lord Heytesbury, 'that I did, in my answer to the Lord Mayor, say there was no immediate pressure in the market; but you must not give too wide a meaning to that observation, which had reference merely to his demand that the exportation of grain should be prohibited and the ports immediately thrown open.' But neither this passage, nor anything in the subsequent part of the letter, sufficiently explains what he had written eleven days before, namely that everything was rising rapidly in price.

During the last days of October two very desponding reports were made to the Premier by Dr Playfair, in the latter of which he says that Dr Lindley was after making a tour of the potato shops of the city; that he had examined the potatoes, 'carefully picked as good', and warranted to be sound, and that he had found 'nineteen bad for fourteen good'.

The first Cabinet Council assembled at the Premier's house on 31 October, on which occasion he read for his colleagues all the information received either by himself or the Home Secretary, after which the sitting was adjourned until next day, 1 November, when he put his views before them in the shape of an elaborate memorandum.

He began by calling their attention to the great probability of a famine in Ireland consequent upon the potato blight. The evil, he thought, might be much greater than the reports would lead them to anticipate, but whether it was or was not, the Cabinet could not exclude from its consideration 'the contingency of a great calamity'. He told them that he had sent eminent men of science to Ireland to examine and report on the question; that they were proceeding cautiously, but would suggest at the earliest period the simplest and most practical remedies which their inquiries and scientific knowledge might enable them to offer. Inquiries had also been addressed to the consular agents in different parts of Europe as to the available supply of potatoes for the purpose of seed.

The noticeable fact in this, the first portion of the memorandum, is that the Premier kept his Cabinet in ignorance of the private reports made to himself by the 'scientific men', assuring him that half the potato crop in Ireland had ceased to be fit for the food of man.

Sir Robert next proceeded to discuss measures of relief to meet the danger. His first suggestion was a commission to be appointed by the Lord Lieutenant to inquire into the mode of giving relief, the head of the Board of Works to be a member of the Commission. The Commissioners were to see how money could be advanced and employment given and also how remote outlying districts could be relieved, where no employment existed; the power of calling this Commission into existence to be immediately given to the Lord Lieutenant, who could nominate its members after consulting with others, or immediately if he thought it necessary.

In the third and last part of his memorandum the Premier came to the really delicate and dangerous question — the repeal of the Corn Laws. He thought the potato blight and the measures he proposed to meet its probable consequences would necessitate the calling of Parliament before Christmas — a very important step, as 'it compels', he said, 'an immediate decision on these questions — 'Shall we maintain unaltered — shall we modify — shall we suspend — the operation of the Corn Laws?'

The first vote the Cabinet proposed, say a vote of £100,000 to be placed at the disposal of the Lord Lieutenant for the supply of food, opened the whole question. Could the Government, then, vote public money for the sustenance of the people and maintain existing restrictions on the free importation of grain? He thought not, and he went on to give the example of other countries threatened with scarcity, which were opening their ports for foreign grain and prohibiting their own to be exported, thereby closing some of our ordinary sources of supply. If, he asked, the Corn Laws were suspended, was it to be done by an act of prerogative or by legislation at the instance of the Government?

Such were the leading points placed before his Cabinet by Sir Robert Peel in his memorandum of 1 November. 'In the course of the conversation which followed the reading of the above memorandum, it became evident', he said, 'that very serious differences of opinion existed as to the necessity of adopting any extraordinary measures, and as to the character of the measures which it might be advisable to adopt.'

The Cabinet broke up to meet again on 6 November, on which day the Premier submitted to his colleagues the following memorandum: 'To issue forth an Order in Council remitting the duty on grain in bond to one shilling, and opening the ports for the admission of all species of grain at a smaller rate of duty until a day named in the Order. To call Parliament together on the 27th instant, to ask for indemnity and a sanction of the Order by law. To propose to Parliament no other measure than that during the sitting before Christmas. To declare an intention of submitting to Parliament immediately after the recess, a modification of the existing law, but to decline entering into any details in Parliament with regard to such modification. Such modification to include the admission at a nominal duty of Indian corn and of British Colonial corn to proceed with regard to other descriptions of grain upon the principle working of the present machinery for taking the averages'.[14]

These proposals were rejected by a very decided majority of the Cabinet, only three ministers, Lord Aberdeen, Sir James Graham and Mr Sidney Herbert, supporting them. Sir Robert tells us that he would, at this juncture, have felt himself justified in resigning office, but that on weighing all the circumstances of his position, he resolved to retain it until the end of November, when the Cabinet would meet again, as he thought by that time new information would be forthcoming and in all likelihood new phases of the crisis would have arisen, to induce his colleagues to change or modify their views. He also thought his immediate resignation, if not a cowardly, would be an undignified course, as it would be sure to create excitement and even panic in the country. The most decided opponent of the Premier's views was Lord Stanley. After the Cabinet Council of 1 November, he wrote a memorandum detailing his objections to those views, and sent it to his chief, who said 'it contained a very detailed, clear, and able exposition of the grounds on which Lord Stanley dissented from the proposals he had submitted to the Cabinet'.[15]

The Cabinet re-assembled on 25 November and agreed to the

instructions which were to be issued to the Lord Lieutenant and by him given to the Commission which had been appointed, to consider and adopt such measures as they deemed useful to mitigate the apprehended scarcity.

In these instructions the opinion of Drs Lindley and Playfair, that half the potato crop was destroyed, was not only given but emphatically put forward. Apprehension was expressed at the difficulty of substituting a dearer for a cheaper food, the probability of fever closely succeeding famine and the formidable danger of not having a sufficiency of sound seed for the ensuing crop.

'The proportion', said the instructions, 'which seed bears to an average crop of potatoes is very large; it has been estimated at not less than one-eighth; and when we remember that a considerable portion of this year's crop in Ireland is already destroyed, and that the remaining portion, if it be saved, must supply food for nine months as well as seed for next year, it is obvious that no ordinary care is required to husband a sufficient quantity of sound potatoes for planting in the spring. Unless this be done, the calamity of the present year is but the commencement of a more fatal series'.[16] No prophecy was ever more accurately and terribly verified.

The Cabinet met again next day and the Premier read to them a memorandum, which opened thus: 'I cannot consent to the issue of these instructions, and undertake at the same time to maintain the existing Corn Law.' And again he said, towards the close, 'I am prepared, for one, to take the responsibility of suspending the law by an Order in Council, or of calling Parliament at a very early period, and advising in the Speech from the Throne the suspension of the law.'

On 29 November, the Premier sent to each of his colleagues a more detailed and elaborate exposition of his views, in order that they might be prepared to discuss them at the next Cabinet Council.

According to the course he had evidently laid down for himself, he made the whole question of the repeal of the Corn Laws turn on the impending Irish famine. He began with the question he intended to discuss in this manner: 'What is the course most consistent with the public interests under the present circumstances, in reference to the future supply of food?' His answer to his own question was 'that the proper precaution, though it may turn out to be a superfluous one, is the permission, for a limited time, to import foreign grain free of duty.'

He repeated that several of the countries of Europe had taken precautions to secure a sufficiency of food for their people. He went into a history of what the English Government had done on former occasions, when a scarcity of food was imminent, admitting that, while in 1793 it opened the ports for food supplies, it also prohibited their exportation. He went on to show the advantages to be derived from the opening of the ports.

He touched the repeal of the Corn Laws but slightly, knowing full well that the other points treated in the memorandum must raise a discussion on that question in the Cabinet. However he did say enough to show it must be treated. He asked: 'Is the Corn Law in all its provisions adapted to this unforeseen and very special case?' He summed up his views in these words: 'Time presses, and on some definite course we must decide. Shall we undertake without suspension to modify the existing Corn Law? Shall we resolve to maintain the existing Corn Law? Shall we advise the suspension of that law for a limited period? My opinion is for the last course, admitting as I do that it involves the necessity for the immediate consideration of the alterations to be made in the existing Corn Law, such alterations to take effect after the period of suspensions. I should rather say it involves the question of the principle and degree of protection to agriculture'.[17]

Several of the Cabinet Ministers sent replies to the Premier's memorandum before the day for their next meeting, which replies he thought might lead to long discussions without any practical result, so on 2 December he brought before them, in another memorandum, what he called a specific measure — the announcement, in fact, that if the ports were once opened the corn duties could not be re-imposed; and, whether the ports were or were not opened, he said the state of those laws must be re-considered — nay more, that they must gradually, but, 'at no distant day', be repealed. He finally stated in this paper the principles on which he was ready to undertake that repeal.

When this last memorandum was prepared, the Cabinet was in a sort of permanent session: Sir Robert Peel tells us its discussions continued from 25 November to 5 December. With the exception of the Duke of Buccleugh and Lord Stanley, his colleagues gave their consent to his proposal; in some instances, however, he felt it was a reluctant consent. Under such circumstances, he considered he could not succeed in a complete and final adjustment of the Corn Law; so, on 5 December, he repaired to Osborne and placed his resignation in the hands of the Queen.

Lord John Russell was summoned by the Queen on 8 December; he was still at Edinburgh and was unable to present himself before her Majesty until the eleventh. He was in the unfortunate position of being in a minority in the House of

Commons. However, being empowered to form an administration, he asked for time to consult his political friends; besides which he also opened a communication with the late First Lord, to see how far he could reckon on his support, at least with respect to the question of the Corn Laws.

He received from Sir Robert Peel what seemed a kind and reassuring answer; but although Sir Robert, in his letter to the Queen of 8 December, told her Majesty he would support the new Government in carrying out the principles, to carry out which a majority of the members of his own Cabinet refused to aid him, still he did not, when interrogated on the subject, pledge himself to support Lord John who then saw the promised aid could not be relied on; for any change in the programme might be regarded as a change of principle, and no minister takes up the precise programme of his predecessor.

Still, on 18 December Lord John undertook to form a Government; on 20 December he wrote to the Queen to say he found it impossible to do so. It was no secret that Lord Grey's objection to *one* appointment was the immediate cause of this failure, nor was it a secret that the person objected to was Lord Palmerston.[18] Some, however, thought that this incident was cleverly laid hold of by Lord John, to free himself from an untenable position.

On the same day Sir Robert Peel found himself again in the Queen's presence. She at once announced to him that, instead of taking leave of him, she must request him to continue in her service. On his return to town he immediately summoned his late colleagues to meet him. All but two agreed to enter the Cabinet again. These were Lord Stanley and the Duke of Buccleugh; the former stood firm to his principles of protection, the latter asked time for consideration, which resulted in his re-accepting his former place; the rapid changes and events since 6 December giving, he said, such a new character to things that he was now of the opinion that a measure for the absolute repeal of the Corn Laws, at an early period, was the true policy.

Thus, after an interregnum of fifteen days, the old Government, Lord Stanley excepted, was back in power. Mr Gladstone replaced Lord Stanley at the Colonial Office, giving 'the new administration the weight of his high character and great abilities and acquirements'.[19]

4

More talk in the Commons

Sir Robert Peel, thus reinstated as Prime Minister of England for the third time, met Parliament on 22 January with a Queen's speech in which her Majesty's first allusion to Ireland was one of deep regret at the deliberate assassinations so frequent in that country.

The speech then went on to deplore the failure of the potato in the United Kingdom — the failure being greatest in Ireland — assuring Parliament that 'all precautions that could be adopted were adopted for the purpose of alleviating the calamity'. An eulogium was next passed on previous legislation in the direction of Free Trade, and upon the benefits conferred by it, with a recommendation that Parliament should take into early consideration the principles which guided that legislation, with a view of having them more extensively applied.

Her Majesty was finally made to say that she thought further reductions in the existing duties 'upon many articles, the produce of other countries, will tend to ensure the continuance of these great benefits'. The wily Premier did not allow the word 'corn' or 'Corn Laws' to have a place in the speech of his Royal Mistress.

Anxious to explain, at the very earliest moment, the causes which led to the dissolution of his Ministry and their return to office, he spoke upon the address, and went into the whole question. He put the potato blight in the foreground; for, with the instinct of the caddis worm, he felt that this was the piece of bulrush by which he could best float his Free Trade policy, his Government and himself. And, indeed, from the first night of the session until the resolutions on the Corn Laws were carried, the members of the Government showed the greatest anxiety to keep the terrible consequences of the potato failure before Parliament. They did not exaggerate the failure, nor its then probable effects; they gave to both that importance which they really demanded, but which, only the admission helped the repeal of the Corn Laws, they would hardly be so ready to concede.

The Protectionists, on the contrary, took up the cry of

'exaggeration', against the most undoubted evidence, supplied from every part of the country, by persons in every rank of life, and of every shade of political opinion. 'We have', said one of them, Mr Calhoun, 'famine in the newspapers, we have famine in the speeches of Cabinet Ministers, but we find abundance in the markets; the cry of famine is a pretext, but it is not the reason for the changes.'

There is some truth in the latter part of this sentence — famine was not all a pretext but it was certainly used by ministers as a cry to strengthen their Corn Law policy. 'It was', said Sir Robert Peel, 'that great and mysterious calamity, the potato failure, that was the immediate and proximate cause which led to the dissolution of the Government on 6 December 1845.' Two most important points, he said, they had now before them:

1. the measures to be immediately adopted in consequence of the potato blight and

2. the ultimate course to be pursued in relation to the importation of grain.

His opinions, he went on to say, on the subject of protection had undergone a change, and chiefly because the prophecies of the protectionists, when the tariff was altered in 1842, were falsified by experience. Now, if the free traders had a watchword which they used more frequently than any other, it was the cry of 'cheap bread'; and yet in the face of this the Premier said: 'I want, at the same time, to show that concurrently with the increase of importation there had been an increase in the prices of the articles'. He then quoted several of the Government contracts to prove this assertion, which was quite correct.

Once again, he put prominently forward the advice he gave his Government at the beginning of November 1845, which was, either to open the ports by an Order in Council, or to call Parliament together as soon as possible, to meet the 'great and pressing danger of the potato failure'; but what he did not put forward was that he grounded both these proposals on the condition that the Corn Laws should be repealed. To be sure he stated this condition mildly, when he told his colleagues that once the ports were opened, he would not undertake to close them — yet what was this but saying to a protectionist Cabinet that there was great danger of a famine in Ireland — we ought to open the ports or assemble Parliament, but I will not agree to one or the other unless you all become free traders — thus making the feeding or the starving of the Irish people depend on the condition that the members of his Government were to change their views, and preach free trade from those benches to which they had been triumphantly carried on the shoulders of protection.

In truth, Sir Robert, more than most politicians, was in the habit of suppressing those portions of a question which he found inconvenient; limiting his statement to such parts of it as suited his present purpose. In his communications with his colleagues he was very fond of such phrases as 'to lay aside all reserve', 'to speak in the most unreserved manner', etc., thus forcibly impressing one with his habitual love of reserve, even with his greatest intimates. And in his speech of 22 January, on the Address, he said, with suspicious indignation, that 'nothing could be more base or dishonest' than to use the potato blight as a means of repealing the Corn Laws.

The great twelve nights' debate on the repeal of these laws commenced five days after the speech referred to above was made. The Premier, at great length and very ably, repeated the arguments he had been putting forward since the previous November in favour of taking the duty off everything that could be called human food; he even proposed to repeal the duty on the importation of potatoes, by which, he said, he hoped to obtain sound seed from abroad.

Sir Robert, in this speech, may be said to have been in his best vein — full, explanatory, clear, assumptive, persuasive — often appealing to the kindness and forbearance of his hearers, always calculating a good deal on his power of bending people to his views by a plausible, diplomatic treatment of the whole question. Addressing Mr Greene, the chairman of the Committee, he said, with solemn gravity: 'Sir, I wish it were possible to take advantage of this calamity, for introducing among the people of Ireland the taste for a better and more certain provision for their support than that which they have heretofore cultivated.' Surely the Indian meal, which he so often boasted of having ordered on his own responsibility, was not a step in that direction. To have purchased and stored for their use the wheat and oats of their own soil would have been, one should suppose, the direct way of achieving this philanthropic desire.

On the fifth night of the debate, Sir Robert rose again, and in his speech applied himself almost exclusively to the famine part of the question. He read many letters from persons in high position in Ireland, to prove to the House what was unfortunately but too well known in that country for many months, that the greater portion of the only food of four millions of the people was destroyed. Reading from an official report, substantially embracing the whole kingdom, he said: 'In four electoral divisions, nearly nine-tenths of the potato crop are gone; in ninety-three, between seven-tenths and eight-tenths; and in 125 the loss approaches to seven-tenths of the whole crop; in sixteen divisions, to six-tenths; in 596, nearly one-half; and in 582, nearly four-tenths are destroyed.'

Appealing to the House, he said it had but two courses, 'to maintain the existing law, or make some proposal for increasing the facilities of procuring foreign articles of food'. 'Will you not then', he concluded, in an elaborate peroration, 'will you not then cherish with delight the reflection that, in this, the present hour of *comparative prosperity*, yielding to no clamour, impelled by no fear except, indeed, that provident fear which is the mother of safety, you had anticipated the evil day and, long before its advent, had trampled on every impediment to the free circulation of the Creator's bounty.'

The old Tory party had, in the beginning, admitted, to a great extent, the failure of the potato crop in Ireland; but seeing the use the Peel Government were making of it they seem to have agreed to maintain that the reports — Government as well as others — were greatly exaggerated, and for a purpose. Lord George Bentinck, the coming leader of the Protectionists, said that 'in his opinion, which every day's experience confirmed, the potato famine in Ireland was a gross delusion — a more gross delusion had never been practised upon the country by any Government'. Mr Shaw, the member for the University of Dublin, maintained that 'great exaggeration existed'. 'The case', he said, 'was not extraordinary — *fever, dysentery* and *death* being a kind of normal state' in Ireland!

Members on both sides of the House soon began to see that there was no necessary connection between the potato failure in Ireland and the repeal of the Corn Laws, although, in all his speeches on the subject, Sir Robert Peel assumed it as a matter of course. The only member of the Government who attempted to prove this connection was Sir James Graham.

Mr Stafford O'Brien, the member for North Northamptonshire, but connected by marriage with the County Clare and one of the ablest men in the Tory ranks, said he had just returned from Ireland, that there was no exaggeration about the failure of the potato crop there, but that it had nothing to do with the question of the Corn Laws. He accused the Government of introducing a new principle for a disaster which he hoped would be casual, and of announcing that new principle without, in the least, tracing out how the Corn Laws had contributed to the famine in Ireland or how the total abrogation of those laws was likely to alleviate that country's distress. The Irish members, he said, all asked for employment; they wished the railways to be made; they expressed their fears about the want of seed for the ground; but they said, 'if you wish to complete our ruin destroy our agriculture'. Whilst he expressed the opinion that there never was a country which called for more urgent attention on the part of the Government than Ireland did at the moment, he did not believe, he said, that if they passed the Government Bill tomorrow, one more quarter of corn or one more hundredweight of meal would be placed within the reach of the poor of Ireland, unless it was accompanied by other measures.

Sir James Graham replied that it did appear to him that this matter of the coming scarcity, if not of famine, in Ireland, had an immediate and indissoluble connection with the question of the Corn Laws; and that he, for one, would not propose to the people of Great Britain to take out of the taxes of Great Britain public money, to aid in the sustenance of their fellow-countrymen in Ireland while, artificially, by the laws, the price of the food of the people of Great Britain is enhanced.

With regard to this logic of Sir James, it may be remarked 1. that the immediate effect produced, *and sought to be produced,* by a repeal of the Corn Laws, was to cheapen in the market the only thing Ireland had to sell — corn; 2. that the Irish members did not ask any portion of the taxes of Great Britain to feed their countrymen — they proclaimed and proved that the resources of their own country were sufficient for this purpose; and this view was frequently put forward by O'Connell and other leading Irish representatives.

William Smith O'Brien, the member for Limerick county, spoke but little during the session. He and that advanced party in the Repeal Association which acknowledged him as leader had made up their minds that Irish parliamentary business should be transacted in Ireland and that St Stephen's was not the place where patriotic Irish members could best serve their country. Agreeably to this view, he remained in Ireland for nearly two months after the meeting of Parliament, in regular attendance at the Repeal Association, throwing out suggestions for the formation of an Irish party on a basis wide enough to admit Liberals, Conservatives and all others with national aspirations.

He also paid much attention to the measures brought forward by the Government for the relief of his famishing countrymen; he prepared and brought up reports in the Association on those measures and reviewed and criticised them in his speeches. At length, he entered an appearance in the House of Commons on 13 March. There was a motion before the House, brought forward by the Home Secretary, Sir James Graham, that provision should be made to meet the impending fever and famine in Ireland.

Sir James, in his speech, boasted of the sums of money already advanced, with such liberality, for the relief of Ireland. Smith O'Brien made a brief reply, in which he said that the moneys advanced were badly expended, having found their way into other channels than those intended. 'He would', he further observed, 'tell them frankly — and it was a feeling participated in by the majority of Irishmen — that he was not disposed to appeal to their generosity. There was no generosity in the matter. They had taken and they had tied the purse-strings of the Irish purse. They should compel the landlords', he again urged, 'to do their duty to the people, and if they did, there would be neither disturbance nor starvation.'

In making these observations he must have spoken with unaccustomed energy, and with a boldness unusual in Parliament, as he apologised for his tone and manner which, he said, he knew could not be acceptable to the House.

When he sat down, Lord Claud Hamilton rose and replied to him by one of those fierce invectives which, after the lapse of a quarter of a century he still, on occasion, could summon up vigour enough to deliver. He taunted the honourable member for Limerick with having then, for the first time during the session, made his appearance in the House. He told him that, having neglected his own duties both as a representative and a landlord, an attack upon the landlords of Ireland came from him with a bad grace. He further accused him with lending himself to a baneful system of agitation, by which Ireland was convulsed and prosperity rendered unattainable in that country.

Lord Claud having resumed his seat, Smith O'Brien again rose and said he would not take up their time in replying to him, but he wished to tell the House that the tone, not so much of the House as of the English press, 'about those miserable grants' had exasperated him, and a large number of his fellow-countrymen. 'If Parliament met in November', he continued, 'to enact good laws, instead of now coming forward with a Coercion Bill, they would not be under the necessity of making those painful appeals to Parliament.'

On 18 March he spoke again, calling for a tax of ten per cent on absentees which would at once, he said, produce £400,000. But it was on 17 April he made his longest and most effective speech. On that occasion he began by reading extracts from the provincial press of Ireland, giving accounts of 'fearful destitution', 'deaths from famine', and so forth.

He then said 'the circumstance which appeared most aggravating was that the people were starving in the midst of plenty and that every tide carried from the Irish ports corn sufficient for the maintenance of thousands of the Irish people'. He put forward the sound, but then unpopular view of the repeal of the Corn Laws, which was that its immediate effect would be injurious to Ireland. He could not, he told the House, refrain from expressing his regret that Government should think it necessary to couple the question of Ireland with the question of the Corn Laws. These laws did not affect the description of food available for the people of Ireland... he was one of those who differed from the great majority of the honourable members at his side of the House — he meant with respect to measures to alter the Corn Law, which he had no doubt would be of service to this country, but would for some time be injurious to Ireland. He closed his speech by the declaration that he felt it his duty to throw the responsibility upon Government; and in his conscience he believed that, for whatever loss of life might arise from want of food, or from outbreaks, the result of want, ministers would be answerable.[1]

Meanwhile, the Irish liberal members grew sick of the endless debate upon the Corn Laws, out of which they expected nothing would come to relieve their starving countrymen. During its progress, O'Connell made a motion that the House would resolve itself into a committee, to take into consideration the state of Ireland, with a view to devise means to relieve the distress of the Irish people. He called attention to the vast exports of food from Ireland; showed that, while Poor Laws might mitigate distress in ordinary seasons, they were not capable of meeting a famine; and, speaking from the depths of his conviction, he declared that in his conscience he believed the result of neglect on the part of the House, in the present instance, would be deaths to an enormous amount.

'It may be said', the Liberator continued, with a dignity worthy of him, 'that I am here to ask money to succour Ireland in her distress: *No such thing, I scorn the thought;* I am here to say Ireland has resources of her own.'

The Home Secretary replied, admitted O'Connell's facts but begged of him 'to leave the matter in the hands of the responsible advisers of the Crown'. Lord John Russell counselled the withdrawal of the motion, as he considered the measures of the Government judicious. It was accordingly withdrawn and so the matter ended for that time.

But again, on 9 March, O'Connell asked the First Lord of the Treasury if he were prepared to lay before the House a statement of the measures taken by the Government to obviate the impending famine and disease in Ireland. Delay, he said, would be fatal, and the sums of money already voted would not be of the least avail. He repeated that the Irish people were not suing *in forma pauperis*; there were resources in the country and some further measures should be adopted to meet the exigencies of their case.

Sir Robert Peel replied that 'the statement did not fall much short of the impression *first formed in his mind* in October and November last', and concluded thus: 'I again assure the honourable and learned member that *every precaution that can be taken by Government had been taken, not within the last week, or fortnight, but long ago.*'

In the Speech from the throne, her Majesty was made to say that she observed with deep regret the very frequent instances in which the crime of deliberate assassination had been, of late, committed in Ireland; and that it would be the duty of Parliament to consider whether any measure could be devised to give increased protection to life in that country.

In accordance with this striking passage in the Royal Message, Lord St Germans, Chief Secretary for Ireland, introduced in the House of Lords, on 23 February, a bill for the protection of life in Ireland, better known by the title of Coercion Bill, given to it by the liberal Irish members and by the Irish people. Of course it passed without difficulty, Lord Bingham, as became one of his name and blood, making a furious speech in its favour.

Strong as the Peel Cabinet had been for years, the Premier's newly announced policy on the Corn Law question led to such a disruption of party ties that the progress of the Coercion Bill through the Commons could not be regarded by the Government without apprehension. When it went down from the Lords, the unusual though not unprecedented proceeding of opposing its first reading was had recourse to by O'Connell and his supporters. O'Connell led the opposition in a speech of two hours, which Mr Disraeli called his last speech in the House of Commons; but this is a mistake. He spoke on 8 February 1847 nearly a year after, on the famine. It is quite possible that Mr Disraeli confounded the two occasions, for the account he gives of O'Connell on 3 April 1846 was far more applicable to him in February 1847.

Of the speech delivered on the former occasion, against the first reading of the Coercion Bill, Mr Disraeli said: 'It was understood that the House would adjourn for the Easter recess on the eighth instant. There were, therefore, only two nights remaining for Government business, before the holidays. On the first of these (Friday, 3 April), Mr O'Connell had announced that he should state his views at length on the condition of Ireland and the causes of these agrarian outrages. Accordingly, when the order of the day for resuming the adjourned debate was read, he rose at once to propose an amendment to the motion. He sat in an unusual place, in that generally occupied by the leader of the Opposition, and spoke from the red box, convenient to him, from the number of documents to which he had to refer. His appearance was of great debility and the tones of his voice were very still. His words, indeed, only reached those who were immediately around him and the ministers sitting on the other side of the green table, and listening with that interest and respectful attention which became the occasion. It was a strange and touching spectacle to those who remembered the form of colossal energy and the clear and thrilling tones that had once startled, disturbed and controlled senates. Mr O'Connell was on his legs for nearly two hours, assisted occasionally, in the management of his documents, by some devoted aide-de-camp. To the house generally it was a performance of dumb show, a feeble old man muttering before a table; but respect for the great parliamentary personage kept all as orderly as if the fortunes of a party hung upon his rhetoric; and though not an accent reached the gallery, means were taken that next morning the country should not lose the last, and not the least interesting of the speeches of one who had so long occupied and agitated the minds of nations. This remarkable address was an abnegation of the whole policy of Mr O'Connell's career. It proved, by a mass of authentic evidence, ranging over a long term of years, that Irish outrage was the consequence of physical misery and that the social evils of that country could not be successfully encountered by political remedies. To complete the picture, it concluded with a panegyric of Ulster and a patriotic quotation from Lord Clare'.[2]

That the rich and splendid voice which had so often sounded in the ears of his countrymen, like the varied and touching music of their native land, and led them where he would, had lost its finest tones was true enough; but it had not so utterly failed as Mr Disraeli asserts. I heard O'Connell speak in public after this time, and although the marks of age and feebleness were in his whole manner, he managed his voice so as to be heard and understood at a considerable distance. 'Respect for the great parliamentary personage kept all as orderly as if the fortunes of a party hung upon his rhetoric', Mr Disraeli said. He ought to have recollected that the fortunes of a party did really hang upon his rhetoric on this very occasion; for, to the uncompromising opposition of O'Connell and his friends may be fairly attributed the ultimate defeat of this Coercion Bill, which defeat drove Sir Robert Peel from power and brought in Lord John Russell.

As to some means or other having been taken to publish a

speech that had not been heard, there can be little doubt but the reporters took it down substantially, with the exception of the documents read. It was not O'Connell's habit to write his speeches; where then could the means of publishing this one come from, except from the reporters? He made several short speeches during the progress of the bill, which were printed in the newspapers in the usual way; surely they must have been reported in the usual way.

But this is a trifle: the most unkind and groundless assertion the author of the letters of Runnymede made with regard to the man who called him the lineal descendant of the impenitent thief, was when he said that 'this remarkable address was an abnegation of the whole policy of Mr O'Connell's career'. This is strangely inexact: nay more, if Mr Disraeli heard the speech, as is to be inferred, or if he read it, it is disingenuous. The speech was a bold denunciation of the system of evictions, carried out by Irish landlords, to which O'Connell attributed the murders the Government relied on to justify them in bringing forward the Coercion Bill.

Speaking of the murder of Mr Carrick, he said: 'Here again let me solemnly protest — I am sure I need not — that I do not consider any of these acts as an excuse, or a reason or even as the slightest palliation of his murder [hear, hear]; no, they are not; it was a horrible murder; it was an atrocious murder; it was a crime that was deserving of the severest punishment which man can inflict, and which causes the red arm of God's vengeance to be suspended over the murderer [hear, hear].'

But he added: 'I want the House to prevent the recurrence of such murders. You are going to enact a Coercion Bill against the peasantry and the tenantry, and my object is that you should turn to the landlords and enact a Coercion Bill against them.' Who but Mr Disraeli can perceive any abnegation of O'Connell's principles in these sentiments? He quoted Parliamentary reports to prove what tyrannical use had been made of the powers conferred by Coercion Acts and he enumerated those passed since 1801, under some of which trial by jury was abolished. He cited Blue Books to show the misery and destitution to which ejected tenants were sometimes reduced, closing his proofs with the sentence: 'Such is the effect of the ejectment of tenantry in Ireland.'

He next dwelt on the physical wretchedness of the people in general, relying chiefly for his facts on the Devon Commission. He reminded Sir James Graham of a statement of his that the murders in Ireland were a blot upon Christianity. 'Is not', said O'Connell, 'the state of things I have described a blot upon

Christianity? [hear, hear]. This, be it recollected', he continued, 'is forty-five years after the Union, during which time Ireland has been under the government of this country, which has reduced the population of that country to a worse condition than that of any other country in Europe' [hear, hear].

His great object was to prove that the state of the Land Laws was the cause of agrarian murders and that Coercion Acts were not a remedy. In the County Tipperary, where there were most ejectments, there were also most murders, and he called the particular attention of the House to this fact. He referred to the Land Commission report with regard to ejectments and showed from it that in the year 1843 there were issued from the Civil Bill Courts 5,244 ejectments, comprising 14,816 defendants, and from the Superior Courts 1,784 ejectments, comprising 16,503 defendants, making a total of 7,028 ejectments and 31,319 defendants; or within the period of five years 1839 to 1843 comprised in the return, upwards of 150,000 persons had been subjected to ejectment proceedings in Ireland.

He complained of the administration of justice in that country. The government had, he said, appointed partisan judges (he named several of them) and partisan magistrates, in whom the people had no confidence, whilst they took away the commission of the peace from seventy-four gentlemen, simply because they advocated a repeal of the Legislative Union.

He came to remedies. His opinion was that the great cause of the existing state of Ireland was the land question. The fact was, he said, the House had done too much for the landlord and too little for the tenant. He enumerated the principal laws conferring power on the landlords, adding that he did not believe there was a more fertile source of murder and outrage than those powers. *'Thus'*, said he, *'the source of crime is directly traceable to the legislation of this House.'* The repeal of those Land Laws was one of the remedies which he called for, but not the only one. He wanted the House to determine at once to do justice to Ireland politically as well as in relation to the laws of landlord and tenant. In the first place, he said, Ireland had not an adequate number of members to represent her in the House, next she wanted an extension of the franchise, thirdly, corporate reform and, lastly, a satisfactory arrangement of the temporalities of the Church. These four general remedies he demanded from the House, as a mode of coercing the people of Ireland, by their affections and their interests, into a desire to continue the Union with England. 'I want', he said, 'the House to determine at once to do justice to Ireland politically as well as in relation to the law of landlord and tenant.'

He maintained that the Land Laws passed since the Union should be repealed and, above all, he called for full compensation for every improvement made by the tenant. 'Labour', he said, 'is the property of the tenant, and if the tenant by his labour and skill improved the land, and made it more valuable, let him have the benefit of those improvements, before the landlord turns him out of possession.' In Lord Devon's report he found the superior tranquillity of Ulster was traced to the security given to the tenant by tenant right, in proof of which he quoted the evidence of Mr Handcock, Lord Lurgan's agent, and other Northern witnesses who were examined before the Devon Commission.

'This then', he continued, 'is the evidence of the North of Ireland as to the value of tenant right. How often have I heard all the boast of the superior tranquillity of the North? It was because they were better treated by their landlords and, generally speaking, there was a better feeling there towards the landlords, and because the tenants were allowed to sell their tenant right. In the County Tipperary there is an agrarian law, which is the law of ejectment; in the province of Ulster there is a general law giving the tenants valuable rights. He (Mr O'Connell) called upon the House to make their choice between the two. Now was the time for the choice. The country had arrived at a state when something must be done.' This is what Mr Disraeli calls "a panegyric of Ulster".

'Are you', he concluded, 'desirous of putting an end to these murders? Then it must be by removing the cause of the murder. You could not destroy the effect without taking away the cause. I repeat, the tranquillity of Ulster is owing to the enjoyment of tenant right; when that right was taken away, the people were trodden under foot and, in the words of Lord Clare, "ground to powder". This is what Mr Disraeli calls "a patriotic quotation from Lord Clare".'

It would seem to me that any impartial reader of the Liberator's speech on this occasion would regard it as an iteration of the whole policy of his career, rather than an abnegation of it; but smooth and kind as Mr Disraeli's words appear, it is manifest he did not forget their ancient feud and he therefore adroitly tries to give a parting stab, ungenerous as it was false, to the expiring lion.

That portion of the Tory party which remained faithful to Protection, being deserted by their leaders, rallied round Lord George Bentinck and in some sense forced him to become their champion against their late chief, the Premier, and his policy. Thus was formed the Protectionist party, strictly so called. This party being of opinion that there was sufficient necessity for the

Government Coercion Bill were in 'great difficulty to find a plausible pretext for opposing it'. Lord George himself hit upon one. The party held a meeting at the house of Mr Bankes, and after anxious discussion on the part of many members present, Lord George at last spoke. He said 'he was for giving the Government a hearty support, provided they proved they were in earnest in their determination to put down murder and outrage in Ireland, by giving priority in the conduct of public business to the measure in question', the Coercion Bill.[3]

This was ingenious. The party supported what was called public order in Ireland, but with a proviso that might eventually defeat free trade by postponement. After some finessing, the Government showed a determination to go on with both bills. Lord John Russell and the Whigs saw their opportunity and, to the dismay of the First Lord, he found the strange, incongruous, unprecedented combination of Irish Repealers, Tory Protectionists, Whigs and Manchester League-men prepared to vote against him on his Irish Coercion Act. The debate on it occupied six nights. It was closed on 25 June by Mr Cobden; the division was taken, and the Government was left in a minority of seventy-three.

It was a memorable night in the life of Sir Robert Peel. Although a night of defeat, it was also a night of triumph for him; for, two hours before the division, and whilst the debate was going on, commissioners from the House of Lords announced to the Commons that their lordships had finally passed the bill for the repeal of the Corn Laws. It was the law of the land!

Sir Robert expressed himself satisfied, but the coincidence which caused this satisfaction was not in the slightest degree influenced either by himself or any member of his Government. Neither was it the result of chance or good fortune; it was solely brought about by the nice calculation of the anti-Corn Law party, who had resolved to prolong the debate on the Coercion Act until the Corn Bill would be passed. And as soon as they heard the welcome announcement, they were satisfied and the division took place.

During the session, the Peel Government proposed and carried several measures for the employment of the people of Ireland, the principal of which were:

1. An Act for the further amendment of the 1st Victoria, cap. 21;

2. An Act empowering Grand Juries at the Assizes of 1846 to appoint extraordinary presentment sessions for county works;

Village scene at height of famine, possibly Meanus, Co. Kerry.

3. An Act to consolidate the powers hitherto exercised by the Commissioners of Public Works in Ireland; and,

4. An Act to facilitate the employment of the labouring poor for a limited period in the distressed districts. Up to 15 August 1846, there was expended for the relief of Irish distress the sum of £733,372; of which £368,000 was in loans and £365,372 in grants. The sum raised in voluntary subscriptions, through the Relief Committees, was £98,000. The largest number of persons employed at any one time in this first season of relief was 97,000; which was in August 1846.[4]

There was very considerable delay in affording relief to the people under the above acts. New Boards, new Commissioners, new forms, new everything had to be got up and all were commenced too late; it was, therefore, long, provokingly and unnecessarily long, before anything was done. The Rev. Mr Moore, Rector of Cong, in one of his letters, complained that he was superciliously treated at the relief office in Dublin Castle and finally told relief was only to be had in the workhouse. He then wrote to the Lord Lieutenant asking for a consignment of meal to be sold in his neighbourhood, undertaking to be responsible to the Government for the amount. A promise was given to him that this would be done, but I cannot discover that it was ever fulfilled.

Great numbers were in a starving condition in the southern and western counties, and in districts of Ulster also. A correspondent of the London *Morning Chronicle*, writing from Limerick under date of 16 April said: 'The whole of yesterday I spent in running from hut to hut on the right bank of the Shannon. The peasantry there were in an awful condition. In many cases they had not even a rotten potato left. They have consumed even the seed potatoes, unable any longer to resist the pangs of hunger.'

The Rev. Mr Doyle, of Graig, in the County Kilkenny, writing on 13 April, said he had made a visitation of his parish and found 583 distressed families, comprising 2,730 individuals; of this number fifty-one had constant employment, 270 none at all; the rest got occasional work; three-fourths of the whole had not three days' provisions.

Sir Lucius O'Brien (afterwards Lord Inchiquin), as Chairman of the Ennis Board of Guardians, took occasion to remark, 'on the heartlessness of some of the Dublin papers, when speaking of the famine.' 'Everyone acquainted with the country knew', he said, 'that at this moment the people are in many places starving'.[5]

The people assembled in considerable numbers in parts of the South calling for food or employment. A man died of starvation on the public works in Limerick. At a meeting in Newry for the purpose of taking measures against the scarcity, and whilst some were denying its existence in that locality, the Right Rev. Dr Black, the Catholic bishop, said that since he had entered the meeting, a letter had been handed to him stating that a person had just died of starvation in High Street. In April and May potatoes had risen to a famine price in the provinces. They were quoted in Galway and Tuam at 6d. a stone, but in reality, as the local journals remarked, the price was double that, as not more than one-half of those bought could be used for food.

The humane and philanthropic, who went about endeavouring to save the lives of the people, often asked, as they travelled through the country: 'Are the landlords making any efforts?' The common answer was, with very rare exceptions, 'None whatever'. The correspondent of a Dublin newspaper,[6] writing from Cashel, quoted a notice he had copied in Cahir, which was posted all about the town. It ran thus:

'The tenantry on the Earl of Glengall's estate, residing in the manor of Cahir, are requested to pay into my office on the 12th of May, all rent and arrears of rent due up to the 25th of March, otherwise the most summary steps will be taken to recover same.

John Chaytor

1st April, 1846.'

The same correspondent, in a letter from Templemore, informed his readers that a certain noble proprietor was just after paying a visit to his estate in that locality and he had no sooner taken his departure than notices were served on his tenantry to pay the November rent. The tenants asked time, saying they had only a few black potatoes left. The bailiff's reply was characteristic, and no doubt truthful: 'What the d_____ do we care about you or your black potatoes? — it was not *us* that made them black — you will get two days to pay the rent, and if you don't you know the consequence.'[7]

When the relief depots, the local committees and the public works got into gear, much was done during the summer months to alleviate the terrible distress; but as soon as the Government advances and subscriptions to the committees began to be exhausted, the cry for food was again heard from many parts of the country.[8]

At this time there were 123 workhouses open and, great as the people's aversion was to them, the inmates went on steadily increasing. In the month of December 1845 the total number in those workhouses was 41,118; in March 1846, 50,717; and on 13 June, the highest point attained during the year was arrived at, there being, on that day, 51,302 persons receiving indoor relief. On 29 August, owing, of course, to the harvest having come in, the number had fallen to 43,655.

In ordinary years, when there was neither blight nor fear of blight, it was deemed good husbandry to procure foreign seed potatoes, and if this could not be done, farmers at least tried to procure 'strange' seed, grown at a distance from their own farms. A larger and in every way a better crop was the usual result of this practice. After the potato blight of 1845, the procuring of sound and, if possible, foreign seed for planting in Ireland was of the utmost importance, and indeed Sir Robert Peel had included, in his new tariff, the admission of foreign potatoes free, in the hope of securing good seed for the planting of 1846; but as the Corn and Customs' Bill did not become law until the end of June, this provision could be of no avail for that year.

The Peel Government was defeated on the Irish Coercion Act on 25 June, and the Duke of Wellington and Sir Robert Peel announced their resignation on 29 June in the Upper and Lower House respectively. The Duke contented himself with the simple announcement but Sir Robert made a speech, reviewing and defending his conduct whilst minister. Of Ireland he said little, except that he had the full intention of serving her in every way, by dealing with the land and other questions, telling us patronisingly that she was entitled to a 'complete equality of municipal and political rights'. But this was only the old stereotyped liberality of a beaten minister — beaten on an Irish Coercion Act — speaking by anticipation from the opposition benches and endeavouring to plant thorns in the path of his successful rival. The sentiment, such as it was, was received with much cheers and *some murmurs*.

Strangely enough the *murmurs* are not to be found in Hansard, although reported in the newspapers of the day.

Although Sir Robert Peel lived four years after this defeat, he never returned to the treasury benches. In opposition, however, he was almost as powerful as when minister; giving to Lord John Russell's Government an independent and most valuable support, without which it could not have continued to exist. On 28 June 1850 he spoke in the House on the celebrated Don Pacifico's claims against the Greek Government, and refused his support to Mr Roebuck's motion approving of Lord Palmerston's foreign policy. He rode out next day, SS Peter and Paul's day, his horse shied and became restive whilst he was saluting a lady on Constitution Hill; he was thrown heavily; on being taken up, partly insensible, he was conveyed to his house, where, having suffered much pain, he died three days afterwards.

The manner in which Peel dealt with the potato blight, and consequent Famine, is indefensible. His policy from first to last was a policy of delay — delay in a case in which delay was ruin. He went on by slow and almost imperceptible degrees preparing his colleagues for his altered views on the corn duties; talking and writing all the time pathetically about the deep apprehensions he entertained of an impending famine in Ireland, while his whole heart was set on quite another object.

To aid this masked policy of his, there was Commission after Commission — the Scientific Commission, the Castle Commission, the Police Inquiry; and these went on analysing, printing and distributing hundredweights of query sheets and making reports, long after it was proved, beyond all doubt, that half the food of the Irish people had been irretrievably lost, the money value of which was estimated at from £8-10,000,000 sterling.

As early as the end of October 1845 Dr Playfair, his own scientific investigator, expressed to him his opinion that fully one half of the potatoes in Ireland were perfectly unfit for human food; he said he had made a careful tour of the potato shops of Dublin and had found that those potatoes picked as sound had nineteen bad for fourteen good! Sir Robert Peel knew this in October 1845; admitted its truth more than once during the session of Parliament that followed, and yet the bill which he persisted in regarding as the only panacea for such a national calamity did not become law until 25 June 1846, eight months afterwards; but of course four millions of foodless Irish must battle with starvation until the Premier had matured and carried his measure for securing cheap bread for the artisans of England; and further, those same famishing millions had, day after day, to submit to be insulted by his false and hollow assertion that all this was done for them.

Nor can it be urged in his favour that the delay in repealing the Corn Laws was the fault of his opponents, not his own; for no one knew better than he, a shrewd experienced party leader, that every available weapon of parliamentary warfare would be used, as they were used, against his bill for the repeal of the Corn Laws, in order to strike it down by sheer defeat if possible, but if not, at least to maim and lop it of its best provisions.

5

Irish ranks split

Sir Robert Peel's defeat on the Irish Coercion Bill made it a matter of course that Lord John Russell, the leader of the Opposition, should be called upon to form a Government. In fulfilling this task his first anxiety seems to have been to conciliate every section of the Liberals. Important offices were given to several Irish Catholics. This fact was accepted by some as a desire on his part to act justly towards Ireland; while others looked upon it with suspicion, regarding it as an attempt to buy up independent liberal representatives, corrupt the national leaders and thus crush the agitation for a repeal of the Legislative Union.

Ireland is generally regarded as one of the chief difficulties of English Cabinets, but at no period was it a greater difficulty than on the day Lord John Russell accepted the seals of office, as First Minister of the Crown. Nine million people were passing through the terrible ordeal of a famine year; a far more awful year of famine was before them; the Repeal of the Union was still regarded by them as the only true remedy for their grievances; the hopes awakened by the great public meetings of Clifden, Mullaghmast and Tara were still clung to and fostered; whilst the fierce indignation resulting from the sudden, and therefore treacherous suppression of the projected meeting at Clontarf, and above all the persecution and unjust imprisonment of O'Connell and his compatriots, caused the Irish people to turn a deaf ear to every promised concession short of complete legislative independence.

But, like the keen-eyed warrior of classic story, the English minister detected a flaw in the armour of this bold, defiant nation — it was the old and fatal one of disunion. The men whose influence, lofty patriotism and burning eloquence had marshalled the whole people into one mighty phalanx, began to differ among themselves.

The Liberator, who had been long proclaiming himself the apostle of a new doctrine, namely that 'no political amelioration was worth one drop of blood,' now began to insist upon it more frequently than ever; probably on account of the warlike tone assumed by some of the young fiery spirits who followed, but hardly obeyed him. Thomas Francis Meagher, as their mouthpiece, proclaimed his conviction that there were political ameliorations worth many drops of blood; and adhesion to one or the other of these principles cleft in two the great Irish Repeal party, namely, into Old and Young Ireland. Of the former O'Connell was of course the leader, and William Smith O'Brien allowed himself to be placed at the head of the latter.

No English Government could hope to win or seduce to its side the Young Ireland party — the soul of that party being its opposition to every Government that would not concede a Repeal of the Legislative Union; but to the Old Ireland section of Repealers Lord John Russell's Cabinet looked with hopefulness for support, both in the House of Commons and with the county. It was only through O'Connell this party could be reached; the Government, therefore, and the Government press, were not slow in making advances to him.

The *Times*, which can always see what is right and just and true, when it is useful to English interests to do so, commenced praising O'Connell; and that journal, which for years had heaped upon him every epithet of insolence and contempt, now condescended to call him 'Liberator', and warned the Government to coalesce with him: 'Assisted by him', it said, 'but not crouching to him — it [the Government] may enlist the sympathies of the majority on its side, and thus be able to do real good'.[1]

In its next issue it followed up the subject, saying: 'O'Connell is to be supported, if possible, by the Government, but at least by the feeling and sympathies of the English people, against agitation of the worst kind — convulsive civil war.' 'Hitherto', it continued, 'no Government had come into immediate contact with the sympathies of the people. *The power of the Executive has been felt in acts of harshness, seldom of beneficial or parental interference.*[2] A Government which should employ itself in improving the material and social condition of the Irish people would awaken sentiments of gratitude, affection and joy, such as no people hitherto had shown to their rulers. But a Government beginning to act thus would need an interpreter between itself and the people. Such an interpreter would O'Connell be, if he would consent to prefer the prosperity and happiness of his country to hopeless struggle for an ideal advantage.' There can be little doubt that the foregoing passages are from what are termed 'inspired' articles — inspired if not actually written by some member of the Government. They contain a bold bid for the support of O'Connell and his adherents.

Whether it was that he thought Repeal would not be granted, or that the concession of some measures of substantial benefit, besides being good in themselves, would strengthen his hands to carry Repeal; or that he feared the people might be driven into a hopeless rebellion, entailing disaster upon the country; or that his high spirit was subdued by his late imprisonment, or his intellect impaired by the incipient inroads of that malady of which he died within a year; or from all those causes combined, O'Connell did not by any means turn a deaf ear to the overtures of the Whigs.

The first time he appeared in the Repeal Association after they had entered into office, he made a speech which showed his inclination to support them, provided they would make certain concessions to Ireland. He, on that occasion, detailed eleven measures which he required them to pass during the current session. They consisted of three Acts for enlarging the franchise and simplifying the registration of voters; an Act for a full and effective municipal reform; an Act to secure the perfect freedom of education for all persuasions in Ireland; one for tenant right; one for giving compensation for all valuable improvements; one for taking away in certain cases the power to distrain for rent; one for the abolition of the fiscal powers of grand juries, substituting instead a County Board; and finally an Act to tax absentees twenty per cent.

The whole of these could not be even introduced during the remnant of the session which remained, it being now July. It is noteworthy that the abolition of the Established Church in Ireland was not called for by O'Connell on this occasion. Lord John Russell was known to be opposed to such a measure. As to Repeal, he said, even if he got those eleven measures, he would not give it up.

But the advanced Repealers took a different view and believed he was either about to relinquish Repeal, or at least to put it in abeyance to avoid embarrassing the new Government. His line of action with regard to the elections was calculated to increase the suspicion; he said he would not sanction any factious opposition to the re-election of the liberal Irish members who had accepted office: if he could find honest Repealers to put forward to contest the seats he would contest them, but he would be no party to opposition for the sake of opposition.

Smith O'Brien, the organ of the other section of Repealers, took the opposite view. Writing from Kilkee on 9 July he said Repeal candidates must be put in opposition to the Government candidates, no matter how good they might be.

For a considerable time the dissensions in the Repeal

Association were painfully evident to the whole country. O'Connell saw a rupture must be the result and he accordingly made preparations for it. On 13 July he, as chairman of a committee appointed for the purpose, brought up a Report reiterating the principles on which the Association had been founded, and in which were embodied the 'Peace Resolutions', as they were called.

'There are already upon record', said the Report, 'the following declarations and resolutions of the Repeal Association: The basis of the Repeal Association was laid on 15 April 1830. The following were the three first propositions constituting such basis:

1. Most dutiful and ever inviolate loyalty to our most gracious and ever-beloved Sovereign, Queen Victoria, and her heirs and successors for ever.

2. The total disclaimer of and the total absence from all physical force, violence or breach of the law; or, in short, any violation of the laws of man, or the ordinances of the eternal God, whose holy name be ever blessed.

3. The only means to be used are those of peaceable, legal and constitutional combinations of all classes, sects and persuasions of her Majesty's loyal subjects, and by the power of public opinion, concentrated upon most salutary and always legal means and objects'.

The Report gave rise to a stormy discussion, but in the end it was adopted all but unanimously, Thomas Francis Meagher alone saying 'no' to it.

A fortnight later, after a fierce debate of two days' duration, the complete and final separation between Old and Young Ireland occurred on 28 July. Monday, 27 July, was the usual day for the weekly meeting and on that day the business commenced by Mr Ray, the Secretary, reading a letter from O'Connell, who had gone to London to attend Parliament, in which he expressed his sorrow at the miserable dissensions which had arisen amongst them, at a period, too, when unanimity was most necessary and most likely to be useful.

He, in substance, repeated the principles contained in the Report adopted a few days before: 'Here we take our stand', he wrote, 'peaceable exertions and none others — no compromise, no equivocation — peaceable exertions and none others. Let it, however, be borne in mind that these peaceable doctrines leave untouched the right of defence against illegal attack or unconstitutional violence. It has become', he added, 'more essential than ever to assent to those peace principles, as the

Association was sought to be involved in proceedings of a most seditious nature, stated in the *Nation* newspaper to have been perpetrated in and by the writers for that publication.'

Smith O'Brien was the first to speak. Although he might, he said, be in error, he conceived that the present discussion had been raised with a view to call upon the Association to say that there were no circumstances, in this or any other country, to justify the use of physical force for the attainment of political amelioration — a doctrine to which he did not subscribe. He instanced various countries which had attained their liberty by means of physical force.

Then, referring to the period of 1782 in Ireland: 'I say', said Mr O'Brien, 'if the Parliament of England refused to accede to the national demand of the Volunteers to have a free constitution that the Volunteers would have been fully justified in taking up arms in defence of the country.' He, however, for his part, considered the question a merely speculative one as, so far as he knew, no one contemplated an appeal to physical force, under the present circumstances, which would be madness, folly and wickedness. He considered it very unwise to be putting those tests when there was no occasion for them. He declared against permitting those Liberals, who had taken places under the Whigs, to have a walk-over; they should, he maintained, be opposed by Repeal candidates, as nothing in the Whig programme called for the anticipative gratitude of Ireland.

Finally, he expressed the hope that no rash attempt would be made to expel certain members of the Association. 'Let nothing', he said, 'be done rashly; let nothing be done to destroy this glorious confederacy, the greatest and most powerful that ever existed for the preservation and achievement of the liberties of a people.'

Several other members addressed the meeting. At its close Mr O'Brien suggested that if both parties wished, everything which had transpired on that day regarding the questions in dispute should be laid aside, binding neither party to any course of action and reserving any measures to be adopted, so as to apply to what might occur at the meeting of next day.

At the adjourned meeting next day, the Secretary read a letter from Mr Charles Gavan Duffy, the proprietor of the *Nation* newspaper. That journal had been charged by several members of the Association with inciting the people to overthrow English rule in Ireland by armed force. Mr Duffy's letter was written to explain and defend the articles of the *Nation*, which were said to have such a tendency. It must be admitted that, in his earlier days of agitation, O'Connell did not seem to hold the single-drop-

87

of-blood theory; on the contrary, he often threatened England, at least indirectly, with the physical strength of the Irish millions.

The Young Ireland party, in defending themselves, referred to this but Mr John O'Connell explained in his speech of the previous day that all those allusions to physical force pointed but to a single case in which it could be used — 'the resistance of aggression, and defence of right.'

The Liberator himself, in the letter quoted above, also fully admitted this one case, when he said it was to be borne in mind that those peaceable doctrines left untouched the right of defence against illegal attack or unconstitutional violence.

Referring to this admission, Mr Duffy, in a postscript to his letter, wrote: 'Mr O'Connell says his threatening language pointed only to defensive measures. I have not said anything else. I am not aware of any great popular struggle for liberty that was not defensive.'

Mr John O'Connell spoke at great length on the second day; his speech mainly consisting in a bill of indictment against the *Nation*. He quoted many passages from it to show that its conductors wrote up physical force.

Mr John Mitchell, in an able speech, interrupted by cheers, hisses and confusion, undertook to show that O'Connell was, to all appearance, formerly for physical force. He was accustomed, he said, to remind his hearers that they were taller and stronger than Englishmen and had hinted, at successive meetings, that he had then and there at his disposal a force larger than the three armies at Waterloo.

'I cannot,' said Mr Mitchell, 'censure those who may have believed, in the simplicity of their hearts, that he did mean to create in the people a vague idea that they might, after all, have to fight for their liberties. It is not easy to blame a man who confesses that he, for his part, thought when Mr O'Connell spoke of being ready to die for his country, he meant to suggest the notion of war in some shape; that when he spoke of ''a battle line'', he meant a line of battle and nothing else.'[3]

Tom Steele having addressed the meeting for some time, Thomas Francis Meagher rose and delivered what was subsequently known as 'the sword speech', a name given to it on account of the following passage:

'I do not disclaim the use of arms as immoral, nor do I believe it is the truth to say that the God of Heaven withholds his sanction from the use of arms. From the day on which, in the valley of Bethulia, he nerved the arm of the Jewish girl to smite the drunken tyrant in his tent, down to the hour in which he blessed the insurgent chivalry of the Belgian priests, his almighty hand hath ever been stretched forth from his throne of light, to consecrate the flag of freedom, to bless the patriot's sword. Be it for the defence, or be it for the assertion of a nation's liberty, I look upon the sword as a sacred weapon. And if it has sometimes reddened the shroud of the oppressor; like the anointed rod of the High Priest it has, at other times, blossomed into flowers to deck the freeman's brow. Abhor the sword and stigmatise the sword? No; for in the cragged passes of the Tyrol it cut in pieces the banner of the Bavarian, and won an immortality for the peasant of Innsbruck. Abhor the sword and stigmatise the sword? No; for at its blow a giant nation sprung up from the waters of the far Atlantic, and by its redeeming magic the fettered colony became a daring free Republic. Abhor the sword and stigmatise the sword? No; for it scourged the Dutch marauders out of the fine old towns of Belgium back into their own phlegmatic swamps, and knocked their flag and laws and sceptre and bayonets into the sluggish waters of the Scheldt. I learned that it was the right of a nation to govern itself, not in this hall but upon the ramparts of Antwerp. I learned the first article of a nation's creed upon those ramparts, where freedom was justly estimated, and where the possession of the precious gift was purchased by the effusion of generous blood. I admire the Belgians, I honour the Belgians, for their courage and their daring; and I will not stigmatise the means by which they obtained a citizen king, a Chamber of Deputies.'

Here Mr John O'Connell rose to order. He said the language of Mr Meagher was so dangerous to the Association that it must cease to exist, or Mr Meagher must cease to be a member of it. Mr Meagher again essayed to speak, but failed to obtain a hearing. Mr John O'Connell continued: 'Unless', he said, 'those who acted with Mr Meagher stood by the Peace Resolutions, they must adopt other resolutions and another leader'; upon which Mr O'Brien and the Young Ireland party abruptly left the hall, amid much excitement and confusion. They never returned to it: the rupture was complete.

Thus, at a most critical moment, standing between two years of fearful, withering famine, did the leaders of the Irish people, by their miserable dissensions, lay that people in hopeless prostration at the mercy of the British Cabinet, from which, had they remained united, they might have obtained means of saving the lives of hundreds of thousands of their countrymen.[4]

It matters but little now which party was in the right and which in the wrong. Looking back, however, through the cool medium of a quarter of a century, it would seem that each side had something of right to support its views. In the earlier part of his career O'Connell did not disclaim the use of physical force, nor denounce the employment of it in the cause of liberty, as it became his habit to do towards the close of his life; and if ever he did so, it was usually after telling his audience, as Mr Mitchel said, that Ireland contained seven millions of people, as brave as any upon the face of the earth.

Subsequent professions of loyalty and assurances of his never intending to have recourse to the bravery of those millions were interpreted by the people as nothing more than a clever touch of legal ability, to keep himself out of the power of the Crown lawyers who were ever on the watch to catch him in his words. O'Connell himself may have never contemplated any effort beyond legal and constitutional agitation, but the fear that he might intend something more, founded on his bold allusions to the strength and courage of those whom he led, gave undoubted force to the demands he made upon the Government — in a strictly legal and constitional manner.

When the 'single-drop-of-blood' principle became the guiding star of his political life, his demands had public opinion and their own inherent justice only to support them; so that physical force no longer played a part in Irish politics, except from the fact that, inasmuch as it undoubtedly still existed, it might some day act without him, or in spite of him, or act when he should be dead and gone. It is hard to think that a people who had been resisting English oppression for twenty generations, with nothing else but physical force, ever believed him in earnest when he told them they should win their rights by legal and constitutional means alone. The more educated may have given some credence to his words, but I do not think the great bulk of the people ever did.[5]

At any rate, the principle was distasteful to them; and when the *Nation* newspaper began to publish what seemed to them the good old threatening physical force articles, and when a talented band of young gentlemen, in the Repeal Association, began to pronounce eulogiums on the physical force patriots of other countries in fervid eloquence, they soon became the prime favourites of the people; and it was not long until the *Nation* surpassed, in circulation, every other journal in the country.

Those enthusiastic young men saw that the oft-repeated maxim, that 'no political amelioration is worth one drop of human blood', took the strength and manhood out of the agitation; so they determined to return to the older doctrine of moral force — a doctrine which neither makes it independent of physical force, nor antagonistic to it, but rather its threatening shadow. A principle well expressed by the motto on the cannon of the Volunteers of 1782 — 'Free Trade, or else' — a motto often quoted by the Liberator himself, with a disclaimer, to be sure, in order to avoid the law, as the people believed.

Smith O'Brien was right, then, when he said he could not see the utility of continually assuring England that, under no circumstances whatever, would Ireland have recourse to any but peaceable means to right her wrongs, quoting at the same time Davis's happy definition of moral force:

> When Grattan rose, none dared oppose
> The claim he made for freedom;
> They knew our swords to back his words
> Were ready, did he need them.

Had Mr O'Brien and his friends stopped here, all would have been well; but they did not. The two parties in the Repeal Association, having the same object in view — the good of Ireland — chose different and diverging routes for arriving at it; and every day saw them further and further from each other. The Young Ireland party, to the sorrow of their best friends and exposing themselves to the sneers of their enemies, drifted rapidly into an armed outbreak, feeble and ill-planned, if planned at all, and ending in miserable disaster. The Old Ireland agitation went on; but the hand of death was upon the mighty spirit who alone could sustain it and it may be said to have expired with him.

Moral force, with physical force in the not too dim perspective behind it, was a giant power in the hands of O'Connell, and it won emancipation; physical force by itself, when brought to the test, resulted in ridiculous failure.

Lord John Russell met Parliament as Prime Minister on 16 July; on which occasion he gave a brief outline of the Government business for the remainder of the session. He said they would take up and endeavour to pass some of the measures of the late Administration. As to Irish bills, he postponed the most important one, the Tenants' Compensation Bill which, he said, was complicated and was therefore reserved for further consideration. Referring to the waste lands, the reclamation of which he had, a short time before, put so prominently forward, he said he would make preparation for the introduction of a general measure on the subject. Thus were disposed of in a very brief speech, and in a very cool manner, the eleven measures which O'Connell required to be passed before the rising of the Session, and on the passing of which he had grounded any support he intended to give the Whig Government.

Whilst people were absorbed with the change of Ministry, and the wretched conflict in Conciliation Hall, the fatal blight began to show itself in the potato fields of the country. Its earliest

Old Chapel Lane, Skibbereen, at the time of the famine.

recorded appearance was in Cork, on 3 June. Accounts of its rapid increase soon filled the public journals, and the gloomiest forebodings of the total loss of the crop of 1846 immediately took hold of the public mind.

Here are a few specimens of the manner in which the dreadful calamity was announced: 'Where no disease was apparent a few days ago all are now black.' 'Details are needless — the calamity is everywhere.' 'The failure this year is universal; for miles a person may proceed in any direction, without perceiving an exception to the awful destruction.'

The South and West suffered more in 1845 than the North; but this year the destroyer swept over Ulster the same as the other provinces. 'We have had an opportunity', said a writer, 'of observing the state of the potato crop from one end of the county Antrim to another, and saw only one uniform gloomy evidence of destruction. The potatoes everywhere exhibit the appearance of a lost crop.' The same account was given of Tyrone, Monaghan, Londonderry and, in fact, of the entire province. On 18 August the fearful announcement was made that there was not one sound potato to be found in the whole county of Meath! Again: 'The failure of the potato crop in Galway is universal; in Roscommon there is not a hundredweight of good potatoes within ten miles round the town.' 'In Cavan, Westmeath, Galway and Kerry, the fields emit intolerable effluvia.' 'The failure this year is universal in Skibbereen.'[6]

In a letter published amongst the Parliamentary papers, Father Mathew wrote: 'On the 27th of last month [July] I passed from Cork to Dublin, and this doomed plant bloomed in all the luxuriance of an abundant harvest. Returning on the 3rd instant [August] I beheld with sorrow one wide waste of putrefying vegetation. In many places the wretched people were seated on the fences of their decaying gardens, wringing their hands and wailing bitterly the destruction that had left them foodless.'[7]

Such were the words of terror and despair in which the destruction of the food of a whole people was chronicled; a people who had but just passed through a year of deadly famine; a people still surrounded with starvation — looking forward with earnest and longing expectancy to the new harvest — but alas! their share of it had melted away in a few short days before their eyes and there they were, in their helpless myriads before Europe and the world, before God and man, foodless and famine-stricken, in a land renowned for its fertility and this, before the terrible fact could be fully realised by many of their countrymen at home; whilst it was doubted, or only half believed by unsympathising absentees who, distant from the scene, are always inclined to think, with a grudging suspicion, that accounts of this kind are either false or vastly exaggerated, to furnish an excuse for withholding rent, or for appealing in some way to their pockets.

The failure of 1845 did not prevent the people from planting potatoes very largely in 1846, in which year, according to one account, the quantity of land under potatoes in Ireland was 1,237,447 acres; the produce being valued at £15,947,919 sterling,[8] but according to another account it was very much larger, being, as estimated by the Earl of Rosse, 2,000,000 acres valued at £33,600,000.[9] The great discrepancy between these two accounts arises from there being no authoritative official returns on the subject. The truth, no doubt, lies somewhere between them.

The crop looked most healthy in the earlier part of Summer. Towards the close of July, the potato fields were in full blossom, and in every way so promising, that the highest hopes of an abundant yield were entertained, and the people had so little fear on the subject of the blight that there was no appearance of that nervous anxiety which was so strongly manifested at the same period of the previous year.[10]

A strong opinion prevailed that imported potatoes, at least, would resist the blight, but there was no considerable importation of them into Ireland in 1846. There is no doubt that new or strange sets, if of a good quality, produce a healthier and a better crop than seed raised on the same or neighbouring land, but from the general prevalence of the potato blight, it is very doubtful if there would have been much advantage in importing seed. An admittedly surer way of producing sound tubers is to raise them from the actual seed as ripened and perfected on the stalk in the apples, as the notch berries are commonly called in Ireland, yet Mr Niven,[11] an excellent authority, being Curator of the Botanic Gardens belonging to the Royal Dublin Society, said: 'The seedlings I have had, both of 1845 and 1846, have been equally affected with the leaf disease, as have been the plants from the tubers; whereas the seedlings I raised on the experimental ground in the Royal Dublin Society's Botanic Gardens, in Glasnevin, in 1834, at the time I instituted my first experiments, were not at all infected with the root disease then prevalent, but were, without an exception, sound and perfect as could be desired.'

The blight of 1846 was identical with that of 1845, but more rapid and universal. The leaves of the potato plant were spotted in the same way; the stalk itself soon became discoloured — not completely but in rings or patches; it got cankered through at those places and would break short across at them like rotten wood. Moisture, it was observed, either brought on or increased the blight, yet the rainfall of 1846 rose very little above the average of other years; probably not more than from two to three inches; but the rain fell very irregularly, being most copious at those times when it was likely to do most injury to the crops.

The Spring was harsh and severe; snow, hail and sleet fell in March; at Belfast there was frost and snow even in the first week of April. In contrast with this, the greater part of June was exceedingly warm, which must have stimulated vegetation to an unnatural degree, thus exposing the growing crops all the surer to danger, whenever the temperature should fall. It fell suddenly and decidedly, and the month closed with thunderstorms and heavy rains. On 19 June it was reported that the weather at Limerick underwent a sudden change from tropical heat to copious rain, with thunder and lightning, followed by intense cold — there were hail showers on the 24th. St Swithin, true to his traditional love of moisture, ushered in his feast, 15 July, with a downpour of rain and next day a fearful thunderstorm broke over Dublin, followed by a deluge of rain. The same sort of weather prevailed in almost every part of the country throughout July and August.

On the evening of 3 August, Mr Cooper, of Markree Castle, observed a most singular cloud, which extended itself over the east of the range called the Ox Mountains, in County Sligo, accurately imitating in shape a higher range of mountains somewhat more distant; afterwards an extremely white vapour, resembling a snow-storm, appeared along the southern slopes of the range. Mr Cooper remarked to a friend at the time that he thought this vapour might be charged with the fluid causing the disease in the potato. The friend to whom this observation was made, being a resident near those mountains, Mr Cooper requested him to make enquiries on the subject. He afterwards informed him that on the same evening, or night, the blight fell upon the whole of that side of the mountain where they had witnessed the strange appearance.

It was noticed in various districts that some days before the disease appeared on the potatoes a dense cloud, resembling a thick fog, overspread the entire country, but differing from a common fog in being dry instead of moist and in having, in almost every instance, a disagreeable odour. It is worthy of remark that from observations made by Mr Cooper for a series of years, the average number of fogs for each year was a fraction under four — the night fogs for each year not being quite two. In the year 1846, the night fogs were ten, the day two, being a striking increase of night fogs, in the year of greatest potato blight in Ireland.[12]

On the last day of July, Lord Monteagle brought forward, in the House of Lords, a motion for the employment of the people of Ireland, of which he had given notice whilst the Peel Government were yet in office. He gave credit to that Government for good intentions in passing several Acts for the employment of the people, but these Acts were not, he said, so successful as was expected, or as the wants of Ireland required. Without any desire of being an alarmist, he told the Government that the prospects of the coming year were infinitely worse than those of the year then passing away and that precautionary measures were much more necessary than ever. The hopes that were at one time entertained by physiologists that potatoes raised from the seed might be free from the infection, had entirely vanished, and there was every reason to anticipate a failure of the plant itself. Such a failure would, in his opinion, be the worst event of the kind that had ever happened in Ireland. No antecedent calamity of a similar nature could be compared with it. He was, he said, well acquainted with the calamity of 1822, but that was as nothing compared with the one from which the people had just escaped.

Alluding to the sums of money given by Government and by private individuals, he praised the generosity of landlords, naming three or four who had given considerable subscriptions, one of them belonging to a class who had been frequently and unjustly attacked, the class of absentees. Of the aid given by Government, he said that although the funds had been administered as wisely as the machinery of the law allowed, he entirely denied that they had been economically or quickly administered for the relief of distress. To a certain extent the Board of Works must be pronounced a failure. How had it acted when the duty was confided to it of finding employment? In the county of Clare, an application was made by Lord Kenmare and himself to put them in the way of giving productive employment to the people about them, and their lordships would, he said, scarcely credit him when he stated that, up to the present time, they had not been able to obtain the preliminary survey so as to enable them to take a single step. His lordship moved that a humble address be presented to her Majesty, on the subject of encouraging industry and employment amongst the people of Ireland.

The President of the Council, the Marquis of Lansdowne, in offering some remarks on the speech of Lord Monteagle, said Ireland was poor — poor with the poverty brought upon her by wicked laws, enacted to make her poor, and keep her so; and that poverty was flung in her face by an English Minister, at a time when the effects of those laws had brought her people to the brink of one common grave — not the grave of a slaughtered army, but the vast monster-grave of a famine-slain nation.

'Was there ever heard of such a thing', wrote Lord Cloncurry, 'as the almost yearly famine of this country, abounding in all the necessaries of life, and endeavouring to beg or borrow some of its own money to escape starvation.'[13]

All relief from Government ceased, as we have seen, on 15 August. On the seventeenth, the Prime Minister went into a general statement of what had been done by Sir Robert Peel's Government to meet the Irish famine. He detailed the measures adopted by them, in a spirit of approval, like Lord Lansdowne, and dwelt, of course, with especial laudation on the celebrated purchase of Indian meal; — its wisdom, its prudence, its generosity, its secrecy — not disturbing the general course of trade; its cheapness, coming, as it did, next in price to the potato, which the Irish had lost.

Beyond doubt, there never was such a wonderful hit as that cargo of Indian meal. Sir Robert Peel flaunted it, with simpering modesty, to be sure, as his wont was, but flaunt it he did, in the face of every member who ventured to ask him what provision he had made against starvation in Ireland; and here again his successor seems to think that even he, who had nothing whatever to do with it, can take shelter under the ample protection it affords to all shortcomings with respect to the Irish Famine.

But however good and praiseworthy this purchase of Indian meal was, the precedent it afforded was not to be followed; for, said the First Minister, 'if it were to be considered as establishing a principle, for the Government to apply the resources of the Treasury *for the purchase of food in foreign countries,* and that food were afterwards to be sold by retail at a low rate, it was evident that all trade would be disturbed, *and those supplies which would be naturally a portion of the commerce of this country would be applied for the relief of the people of Ireland.'* Loud cheers hailed the announcement. 'Likewise, that portion of the local trade in Ireland, which referred to the supply of districts, would be injured, and the Government would find itself charged with that duty most impossible to perform adequately — to supply with food a whole people.'

The miserable, transparent, insulting fallacy that runs through this statement is also found in almost all Sir Robert Peel's speeches on the famine, namely, that there was not food enough in Ireland

97

for its people; and that it must be brought from foreign countries through the channels of commerce.

Let any one look at the tables of our exports of food during the famine years, and he will see how the case stood. The food was in the country, on the very ground where it was required — beside the starving peasant, but was taken away before his eyes, while he was left to travel day after day three, four, five, and in many cases six or seven miles for a pound or two of Indian meal, carried 3,000 miles to replace the wheat and oats of his own country, of which he was deprived; and there are recorded instances of men falling down dead at their own thresholds, after such journeys, without having tasted the food which they had sacrificed their lives to procure.[14]

It was a question of money also. The Government would not advance enough money to buy the wheat, oats or barley of the country; there must be a food found that was nearest in price to the potato. England could find a hundred million to spend in fighting the Grand Turk; she could find twenty million for the slave-owners of her colonies; she could find twenty million more for the luxury of shooting King Theodore, but a sufficient sum could not be afforded to save the lives of five million of her own subjects.[15]

Lord John having announced the intention of the Government, to bring in a bill empowering the Lord Lieutenant to summon baronial and county sessions, for the purpose of providing public works for the Irish people, proposed that the Commissioners of her Majesty's Treasury should issue Exchequer bills for £175,000 as a grant, and for £255,000 as a loan, to pay for the works that might be undertaken.

The fifteenth of August was fixed for the cessation of the Government works, as well as the Government relief, because it was considered that relief extended beyond that time would be, as the Chancellor of the Exchequer said, in reply to a question from O'Connell, 'an evil of great magnitude'. When the relief was withdrawn, and the blight had manifested itself in such giant proportions, the friends of the people saw nothing but famine with all its attendant horrors at their door.

At this time I find the Secretary of the Mallow Relief Committee, the Rev. C. B. Gibson, calling the urgent attention of the Commissioners of Relief, in Dublin Castle, to the state of his district, and his facts may be taken as a fair specimen of the state of a great portion of the country at the moment. He had just made a house-to-house visitation of the portion of the country over which the operations of his committee extended and, he said, the people were already starving, their only food being potatoes no larger than marbles, the blight having stopped their growth. He took some of the best of those potatoes to his house, and found that twelve of them weighed just four-and-a-half ounces merely the weight of one very ordinary sized full-grown potato. They sickened the people instead of satisfying their hunger.

In many places the children were kept in bed for want of clothing, as also to enable them to silence, to some extent, the pangs of hunger; some of them had not had any food for a day and a half. And such beds as those starving children had! Of many he described one. It consisted of a heap of stones built up like a blacksmith's fire-place (these are his words), with a little hay spread over it; bed-clothes there were none. One of the children of this family had died of starvation a fortnight before. The people in every house were pallid and sickly and to all appearance dying slowly for want of sufficient nourishment.

Mick Sullivan, a specimen of the labouring class, was the owner of a cabin in which Mr Gibson found two starved and naked children; this man was obliged to pay a rent of £1 15s. a year for that cabin and £2 5s. for half an English acre of potato garden, or rather for half an acre of mountain bog. He paid for these by his labour at 6d. a day. It took 160 days' clear work to pay for them, and of course his potato garden was no use to him this year. Mr Gibson valued the furniture in another cabin, John Griffin's, at 15d.

A week before Mr Gibson's visit, the parish priest had found in the same district a mother dividing among three of her children that nourishment which nature only intended for their infancy. And this was the moment at which the Government relief was withdrawn, because the harvest had come in. Is it not matter for wonder that the Rev. Secretary of the Mallow Relief Committee indignantly asked: 'Is not the social condition of the Hottentot, who was once thought to be the most wretched of mankind, superior to that of Mick Sullivan, or John Griffin, whose furniture you might purchase for fifteen pence? I will not compare the condition of such an Irish peasant to that of the red man of North America who, with his hatchet and gun and bearskin and soft mocassins and flashy feathers and spacious wigwam (lined with warm furs and hung about with dried deer and buffalo), may well condemn the advantages of our poor countryman's civilisation. The Irishman had neither the pleasure of savage liberty, nor the profit of English civilisation.[16]

'I think', added Mr Gibson, 'the present the proper time for noticing the panegyric passed by Lord Monteagle on the gentry of this country for their liberality.[17] He gives two or three examples of the class; and as his Lordship is one of the class he seeks to protect, his testimony cannot be received as impartial. I shall now furnish you with more satisfactory data from which to draw a conclusion. According to the Poor Law Valuation the yearly rental of Rahan, the parish a part of which I have already described, is £5,854. From those who hold the possession in fee of this pauper parish, we received £35; from a gentleman farmer we received £3; in all, £38. If this is benevolence, the inhabitants of Rahan would soon starve upon it. If it had not been for the exertions of the Mallow Relief Committee, a number of those people would not be alive this day.'

With regard to the Treasury minute, announcing the stoppage of the Government works, he expressed his conviction that if they ceased the result around Mallow would be starvation and death. In view of the facts placed before the Commissioners by Mr Gibson, which would, he said, be verified on oath by every member of the Mallow Relief Committee, he called upon them not to leave the people to starve, their only resource being their potato gardens, which are utterly destroyed.

Parliament rose on 28 August. The Queen's Speech was read by the Lord Chancellor. Her Majesty referred with thanks to the public spirit shown by the members of both Houses in their attention to the business of the nation during a laborious and protracted session. She, of course, lamented the recurrence of the failure of the potato crop in Ireland and had given, she said, her cordial assent to the measures framed to meet that calamity. After the fashion of most royal speeches, she expressed her satisfaction at the diminution of crime — not throughout the United Kingdom — but in Ireland.

6

Government 'aid'

The 9th and 10th of Victoria, cap. 107, the Act framed by the Government to provide against the Famine, sure to result in Ireland from the Potato Blight of 1846, was passed through Parliament without opposition. It was entitled An Act to Facilitate the Employment of the Labouring Poor for a limited period in distressed districts in Ireland; but it became commonly known as the Labour-rate Act. The principal provisions of that measure were:

1. On representation being made to the Lord Lieutenant of the existence of distress in any district, he was empowered to assemble an extraordinary presentment sessions for that district.

2. Such sessions were authorised to present for public works.

3. A schedule of the works presented for, was to be signed by the Chairman of the Sessions and forwarded to the Lord Lieutenant for his sanction; it should also receive the approval of the Treasury.

4. On its being approved, the Treasury was to make advances for such works to the Board of Public Works in Ireland and authorise them to be executed.

5. County surveyors were to assist in the execution of those public works.

6. The advances from the Treasury were to be repaid in half-yearly instalments; such instalments not to be less than four, or more than twenty; the tax by which they were to be repaid to be levied under grand jury presentments, according to the Poor Law valuation and in the manner of the poor rate; the occupier paying the whole but deducting from his landlord

one-half the poundage rate of the rent to which he was liable — in short, as under the Poor Law, the occupier was to pay one-half and the landlord the other. Thus, by this law, the whole expense of supplying food to the people during the remainder of the year 1846 and the entire year of 1847 was made a local charge, the Treasury lending the money at five per cent per annum, which money was to be repaid at furthest in ten years. The repayments required by the previous act, under which operations ceased on 15 August, had to be made on the principle of the grand jury cess, which laid the whole burden upon the occupier. The Labour-rate Act got rid of that evident hardship and charged the landlord with half the rate for tenements or holdings over £4 a year, and with the whole rate for holdings under that annual rent.

On 31 August, the Lords of the Treasury published a Minute explaining how the provisions of this law were to be carried out, which Minute was published to the Irish people in a letter from the Chief Secretary for Ireland.

1.   This Minute directed the Board of Works to be prepared with plans and estimates of those works in each district where relief was likely to be required, on which the people might be employed with the greatest public advantage; an officer from the Board to be present at the presentment sessions, in order to give such explanations as might be called for.

2.   It being apprehended by the Government that the public works would be calculated to withdraw from the husbandry of the country a portion of the labour necessary for the cultivation of the soil, the three following rules were laid down in the Minute which, 'in their lordships' opinion, ought to be strictly observed'. (a) No person should be employed on any relief works who could obtain employment on other public works, or in farming, or other private operations, in the neighbourhood. (b) The wages given to persons employed on relief works should, in every case, be at least twopence a day less than the average rate of wages in the district.[1] (c) The persons employed on the relief works should, to the utmost possible extent, be paid in proportion to the work actually done by them.

3.   Under the former Act, the members of Relief Committees had authority to issue tickets, which entitled persons to obtain employment on the Public Works; a system which, it was found, led to abuses, numbers having obtained employment on such tickets who did not require relief. The Treasury Minute, therefore,

confined the powers of Relief Committees to the preparation of lists of persons in need of relief by employment on the works, noting them in the order in which they are considered to be entitled to priority, either on account of their large families, or from any other cause; these lists to be supplied to the officers in charge of the works, who are to revise them from time to time. 4. With regard to donations from Government, in aid of private subscriptions, 'their lordships consider that they may be made as heretofore, where necessary, from public funds placed at the disposal of the Lord Lieutenant for that purpose, and in the proportion of from one-third to one-half of the amount of the private subscriptions, according to the extent of the destitution, and the means of the subscribers; but in consequence of such assistance, their lordships were of opinion that the proceedings of such Relief Committees should be open to the inspection of Government officers, appointed for the purpose.' 5. The Relief Committees were to exercise great care in the sale of meal or other food provided by them; such sale not to be made except in small quantities and to persons who were known to have no other means of procuring food. 6. As to the Government depots of food, their lordships 'desire that it may be fully understood that even at those places at which Government depots will be established for the sale of food, *the depots will not be opened while food can be obtained by the people from private dealers, at reasonable prices; and that even when the depots are opened, the meal will, if possible, be sold at such prices as will allow of the private trader selling at the same price with a reasonable profit.'*[2]

The rule to allow private dealers to sell at a reasonable profit, excellent in itself, required an amount of supervision which it did not receive and, in consequence, the starving poor were often obliged to pay unjustly exorbitant prices for their food supplies. Commissary-General Hewetson, writing from Limerick on 30 December 1846 said: 'Last quotations from Cork: Indian corn, £17 5s. per ton, exship; Limerick: corn not in the market; Indian meal, £18 10s. to £19 per ton. Demand excessive. Looking to the quotations in the United States markets, these are really famine prices, the corn (direct consignment from the States) not standing the consignee more than £9 or £10 per ton. The commander of an American ship, the "Isabella", lately with a direct consignment from New York to a house in this city, makes no scruple, in his trips in the public steamers up and down the river, to speak of the enormous profits the English and Irish houses are making by their dealings with the States. One house in Cork alone, it is affirmed, will clear £40,000 by corn speculation; and the leading firm here will, I should say, go near to £80,000, as they are now weekly turning out from 700 to 900 tons of different sorts of meal ..... I sometimes am inclined to think houses give large prices for cargoes imported for a market, to keep them up; it is an uncharitable thought, but really there is so much cupidity abroad, and the wretched people suffering so intensely from the high prices of food, augmented by every party through whose hands it passes before it reaches them, it is quite disheartening to look upon.'³

The Government further determined not to send any orders for supplies of food to foreign countries, as was done by Sir Robert Peel, in the case of the cargo of India meal; and their depots would be established only in those western and north-western districts where, owing to the previous almost universal cultivation of the potato (or rather owing perhaps to its universal use), no trade in corn for local consumption existed.

The system of relief thus provided was extensive and expansive enough, as it laid the entire soil of Ireland under contribution. Whether or not the country would, in the long run, be able to pay for it all, the Government acted well in making the landlords understand and feel their responsibilities in such a terrible crisis. But they should not have stopped there. Those who had mortgages on Irish estates, and their name was legion, should have been compelled to contribute their due proportion; the commercial and monied interests of the country should have been taxed, as well as the land; no one able to bear any portion of the burden should have been exempted from it, at such a moment of national calamity. Instead of taxing one species of property, namely land, to meet the Famine, the whole property of the country should have been taxed for that purpose; and this partiality was justly complained of by the landed interests.

But a much more formidable opposition than that of the landed interest, as such, rose up against the Labour-rate Act, and for a very sufficient reason. The employment to be provided under it could not and was not intended to be reproductive; the public works which it sanctioned being, as Secretary Labouchere said in his letter, only undertaken with a view of relieving the temporary distress occasioned by the failure of the potato crop.

On this account, the dissatisfaction with the measure was very general from every section of politicians; not that it was thought, except perhaps by some few, that the Government were unwilling to provide against the great Famine which all felt was already holding the Irish nation in its deadly grasp, but because it was felt and believed that the mode chosen for that purpose was the very worst possible. Under the Labour-rate Act not so much as one rood of ground could be reclaimed or improved. The whole bone and sinew of the nation, its best and truest capital, must be devoted to the cutting down of hills and the filling up of hollows, often on most unfrequented by-ways, where such work could not be possibly required; and in making roads which, as the Prime Minister himself afterwards acknowledged, 'were not wanted', but which Colonel Douglas, a Government Inspector, more accurately described 'as works which would answer no other purpose than that of obstructing the public conveyances'. This radical defect of the Act was well and happily put by Lord Devon, when he said it authorised 'unproductive work to be executed by borrowed money'.

The Act was criticised for other reasons too. It made no provision for the completion of the works taken in hand to relieve the people in 1846; and those works must be finished by 15 August of that year, or not at all, a full fortnight before the Labour-rate Act had become the law of the land. Of course many of them were unfinished at that date. Clearly this was wrong; for on the supposition that they were works of at least some utility and not mere child's-play to afford an excuse to the Government for giving the people the price of food, they should have been completed. They consisted chiefly in the making or altering or improving of roads — and everybody knows that unfinished road-work is worse than useless, it is a positive injury. Parts of innumerable roads in Ireland were impassable for years after those works had closed; and many a poor man, whose horse and dray got locked in the adhesive mud of a cut-down but unshingled hill, vented his anger against the Board of Works in the most indignant terms.

The sudden closing of the works of 1846, some even regarded as a breach of faith with the public. The Minute of 31 August, no doubt, left a course open for their completion when it ruled 'that if the parties interested desired that works so discontinued should afterwards be recommenced and completed, it was open to them to take the usual steps to provide for that object, either by obtaining loans, secured by Grand Jury presentments, or by other means.'

But this suggestion (for it was no more) did not free the Government from the charge of a breach of faith, for they called upon the country to complete works begun by themselves and to do so under new and very different conditions. Besides, it was pretty evident that Grand Juries would not present for the completion of works commenced by the Government on its own responsibility.

That the Government felt there was some ground for the charge brought against them, of a breach of faith with regard to those works, is evident from a letter from Mr Trevelyan to Lieutenant-

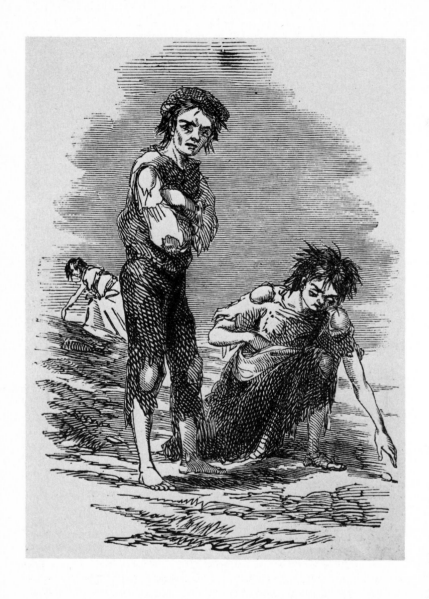

Boy and girl searching for potatoes at Caheragh.

Colonel Jones at the beginning of October. In that letter he said the works under the Labour-rate Act must, as far as the Act is concerned, come to an end on 15 August 1847; and he added that 'if Parliament should determine that the Irish proprietors shall support their poor after 15 August 1847 by payments out of the current produce of the Poor-rate, instead of by loan from Government, the transfer from one system to the other may take place without our being liable to any demands like those which have been lately made upon us to finish what we had begun, on pain of being considered guilty of a breach of faith.' This, said Mr Trevelyan, was the full mind of the Chancellor of the Exchequer.[4]

The Minute of 31 August was modified somewhat by a letter from Mr Labouchere, dated 5 September, saying that all works stopped on 15 August should be proceeded with as far as the sums which might have been so sanctioned for them respectively would admit. Should the balance not be sufficient, a presentment under 10 Vict. cap. 107, should be sought for at the Presentment Sessions, provided the work were a desirable one to undertake.

The new arrangement, under which the landlord paid one moiety of the rate, and the occupier the other, did not pass without censure. An exemption of those whose rent was under £4 a year was probably not liberal enough, but there does not seem to have been any great reason for finding fault with it. But the great and fatal blot of the Labour-rate Act was that under its provisions the people could not be employed on works capable of making a profitable return.

At the time of the Famine it was an unquestionable fact, and (to the shame of the Government be it said) it is an unquestionable fact today, that no country with any pretence to civilisation required its resources to be developed more than Ireland; in no country could a government be more imperatively called upon to foster — nay, to undertake and effect — improvements than Ireland. In a country so circumstanced, how disappointing, then, and heart-sickening must it not have been to good and thoughtful men to find the Government passing a bill for the employment of our people on unproductive labour.

Not only did the Labour-rate Act exclude productive labour from its own operations, but its direct tendency was to discourage and put a stop to improvement on the part of others. This is manifest enough. The baronies — that is, the lands of the baronies — were to be taxed to pay for all the works undertaken to give employment to the starving people. No one could foresee where or when that taxation was to end. There could be no more effectual bar to useful improvements. What landowner could afford the double outlay of paying unlimited taxation and at the same time of making improvements on his property? Then, he had to look forward to other probable years of famine, and he naturally trembled with dismay at the prospect, as well he might. So far from making improvements, the commonest prudence warned him to get together and hold fast whatever money he could, in order to maintain himself and his family when his property would be eaten up — confiscated — by taxation expended upon barren works.

Private charity, too, was paralysed; private exertion of every kind was paralysed; everything that could sustain or improve the country was paralysed, by this blind or wicked or stupid or headstrong legislation of Lord John Russell's Government, by which the energies and the capital of the country were squandered upon labour that could not, and was not intended to make any remunerative return whatever.

At this time a class of landowners, and an extremely numerous one, raised the cry of 'excessive population'. They were anxious to clear their lands, not of rocks or briars, but of human beings; and in their opinion the country could be saved only be a vast system of emigration. The Rev. Mr Moore denied that such excess existed and therefore condemned emigration. *'It is not a fact'*, he said, *'that Ireland is over-peopled*; the contrary is the fact. But the strength of Ireland, her bone and sinew, like her unequalled water-power, is either unapplied or misapplied.'[5]

Simply two things, in his opinion, were required — 'immediate occupation for the people and that that occupation shall, as far as possible, be made conducive towards providing for the exigencies of coming seasons. . . . *WE WANT EMPLOYMENT WHICH CAN BE MADE IMMEDIATELY AVAILABLE FOR THE PRODUCTION OF FOOD — and nothing will or can answer this purpose, save only to employ the people in tilling and cultivating the soil; and not a moment is to be lost!'[6]*

One is inclined to doubt the feasibility of sending the labouring population of Ireland in upon the tillage farms, to trench and dig and plough and sow; but Mr Moore had his practical plan for doing it; and although he did not go into detail, it did not seem to offer insuperable difficulties. 'The plan I would suggest', he writes, 'is briefly this: to *HIRE THE LABOURERS TO THE SMALL FARMERS ALL THROUGH THE COUNTRY, AT HALF-PRICE, TO TILL THE GROUND. The farmers would be delighted at the arrangement.'[7]*

The necessity of applying labour to the cultivation of the soil was also most strongly insisted upon by a high Government official, Sir Randolph Routh, the head of the Commissariat Relief

Office, Dublin Castle, whose experience was of the most extensive and valuable kind, he having superintended the relief works through Ireland in 1846.

These were sound views, except in so far as they threw upon landlords and people the duty of cultivating the soil; the people could do nothing, and many of the landlords had no capital: moreover, *as a class,* they were wholly disinclined to make any adequate effort. From the terms of the memorandum just quoted, it is evident that in their intercourse with Commissary Hewetson they were clamouring for emigration. If the Government were sincerely anxious to produce food, and save the country, they ought not to have leaned on such rotten reeds. They should have put their own hand more thoroughly to the work and framed an Act which would, at least indirectly, have compelled proprietors to second their efforts and discharge those duties which, as men and as Christians, they refused to attend to or acknowledge.

Meanwhile, the following requisition was put in circulation and numerously signed, both by peers and gentry: 'We, the undersigned, request a meeting of the landowners of Ireland to be held in Dublin on the ____ day of _____ next, to press upon her Majesty's Government the importance of at once adopting the necessary measures to alter the provisions of the Act, entitled the 9th and 10th Vic., chap. 107, so as to allow the vast sums of money about to be raised by presentment under it, to be applied to the development of the resources of the land, rather than in public works of an unproductive nature.'

The principle of the Labour-rate Act was doomed; no voice was raised in its defence, nor could there have been. The Government having turned a deaf ear to the call for an Autumn Session, the Repealers were anxious there should be a demonstration in Dublin that would, as far as possible, bear the similitude of an Irish Parliament. The above requisition, very probably without intending it, sustained and strengthened this idea; the Prime Minister and his colleagues became alarmed, and the Lord Lieutenant, on 5 October, suddenly and unexpectedly issued, through his Chief Secretary, the famous Proclamation known as 'Labouchere's Letter', which, if it did not entirely repeal the Labour-rate Act, changed its whole nature.

In that document the Irish public were told that the Lord Lieutenant had had under his consideration the various representations which had been made to him of the operation of the Poor Employment Act, and the difficulty of finding 'public works' upon which it would be expedient or beneficial to expend money to the extent requisite for affording employment to the people during the existence of distress; and to obviate the bad effects of a great expenditure of money in the execution of *comparatively unproductive* works he desired that the Commissioners of Public Works would direct their officers, in the respective counties, to consider and report upon such works of *a reproductive character and permanent utility,* as might be presented at any Sessions held under the above Act; and his Excellency would be prepared to sanction and approve of such of those works as might be recommended by the Board, and so presented, *in the same manner* as if they had been strictly 'public works', and presented as such in the manner required by the Act.

Never did any Government pronounce against itself a more complete verdict of ignorance and incapacity. The Government had framed the Act; every clause of it was its own handiwork; it was passed through Parliament without being modified, amended or in the slightest degree opposed and yet, before it was brought into practical operation — for a single work had not been commenced under it at the date of the Proclamation — that same Government virtually repealed it, well knowing that for such proceeding it must come before Parliament for an Act of Indemnity.

At home the fatal error of awaiting events, instead of anticipating them, and by forethought endeavouring to control and guide them, was equally pernicious. The most considerable persons in the kingdom — peers, members of Parliament, deputy lieutenants, magistrates without number — pronounced the potato crop of 1846 to be hopelessly gone early in August. But although several members of the Government expressed their belief in this, and spoke about it with great alarm, they seem not to have given it full credence, until it was too late to take anticipatory measures; in short, they regarded it, like everything Irish, as greatly exaggerated.

The most influential portion of the English newspaper press supported and encouraged this view, making, at the same time, fierce attacks on Irish landlords for not meeting the calamity as they ought, and as they were bound in duty and conscience to do. Equally bitter and insolent was their tone towards the Irish people, accusing them of many inherent vices — denouncing their ignorance, their laziness, their want of self-reliance. Whatever truth there may have been in those charges, it was not the time to put them forward. Famine was at the door of the Irish nation, and its progress was not to be stayed by invectives against our failings, or by moral lectures upon the improvement of our habits. Food, food was the single and essential requisite; let us have it at once, or we die; lecture us afterwards as much as you please.

7

Relief — of sorts!

To have met the Potato Famine with anything like complete success would have been a Herculean task for any government. The total failure of the food of a nation was a fact new in history; such being the case, no machinery existed extensive enough to neutralise its effects, nor was there extant any plan upon which such machinery could be modelled.

Great allowance must be made therefore for the shortcomings of the Government in a crisis so new and so terrible; but after making the most liberal concessions on this head, it must be admitted that Lord John Russell and his colleagues were painfully unequal to the situation. They either could not or would not use all the appliances within their reach, to save the Irish people.

Besides the mistakes they made as to the nature of the employment which ought to be given, a chief fault of theirs was that they did not act with promptness and decision. Other nations, where famine was far less imminent, were in the markets, and had to a great extent made their purchases before the Government, causing food to be scarcer and dearer for us than it needed to be.

Some of the officers connected with the relief works expressed their opinions that the failure of the potato crop and the deficiency of food in the country were both exaggerated. They threw doubts on the veracity of those with whom they conversed and warned the Government to be cautious about believing, to the full, the statements made by individuals, committees or newspapers.

Sir Randolph Routh, the head of the Commissariat Department, in a letter to Mr Trevelyan, the Assistant-Secretary to the Treasury, said: 'In the midst of much real, there is more fictitious distress; and so much abuse prevails, that if you check it in one channel, it presents itself in another.'[1] Again, Assistant Commissary-General Milliken, writing to Sir R. Routh from Galway, informed him that he met a considerable number of carts loaded with meal and other supplies; and there did not, he said, appear that extreme want and destitution that he had expected.[2]

111

More than any other did Lieutenant-Colonel Jones, Chairman of the Board of Works, keep the idea of exaggerated and fictitious distress before the mind of the Treasury. He wrote to Mr Under-Secretary Redington on 13 October, from Athlone: 'On the 11th instant I posted from Dublin to Banagher. Along the entire line of road I observed the farmyards well stocked with corn, the crop of the past harvest, unthreshed' — thus assuming that the four millions of people who lived almost exclusively on potatoes had such things as farmyards and corn to put in them.

In the same month he wrote again to Mr Trevelyan that he heard from more quarters than one that the early potatoes, which were left in the ground, now proved to be sound. Although small in size, he said, still from one-third to one-half might be considered available for food.

'On my way here from Athlone', he again wrote, 'I went into a field where a man was digging potatoes. The crop looked good, and he told me that it was an early crop and that he considered that about half were sound; and I therefore hope that there is much more food of that description than the general outcry about famine would lead strangers to suppose.'

At the end of December he reported to the Treasury a conversation he had had with an assistant-engineer from Roscommon, who told him his belief was that there were much more provisions in the country than was generally supposed. He had every day, he said, good potatoes at eight shillings a hundredweight. When the disease appeared, the people who held conacres threw them up and the potatoes remained undug. Those that were sound continued so up to the late frost; and the people had, by degrees, been taking them up. This engineer expected that a considerable quantity, serviceable for food, would be found during the ploughing of the land in spring.

But the wail of starving millions reached the Lord Lieutenant from every side and in compliance with it, he authorised the 'Extraordinary Baronial Presentment Sessions' to be held. At those sessions the tone of the speakers was, on the whole, kind and liberal, acknowledging the universality of the failure of the potato crop and the necessity of making immediate provision against its consequences.

Sometimes the presentments for the public works were very large — far beyond the entire rental of the barony; yet they may not have been too great to meet the starvation which the assembled ratepayers saw everywhere around them. At Berehaven, in the County Cork, a place certainly fearfully tried by the Famine, the presentments at the sessions — at the very first sessions held in the barony — were said to be quadruple the rental of the entire barony!

This, however, was only one district of the largest Irish county; but the presentments for the whole county of Mayo, the most famine-stricken, to be sure, of all the counties, are worth remembering; and so is their explanation. They were forwarded to the Board of Works by the County Surveyor. The number of square miles in the county is given at 2,132, the rent value being £385,100. The County Surveyor recommended to the Sessions presentments amounting in the aggregate to £228,000, nearly two-thirds of the entire rental. The Baronial Sessions, however, were far from resting contented with this. The ratepayers and magistrates assembled in their various baronies, presented for works to the amount of £388,000, nearly £3,000 in excess of the entire rental of the county; but which was finally cut down by the Board of Works to £128,456 8s. 4d.

Prudent people and political economists will at once be inclined to exclaim, 'Very right; it was most fortunate to have an authority to check such recklessness.' But, softly; let there be no hasty conclusions. Hear the end. The County Surveyor gives the population of Mayo at 56,209 families, *of whom 46,316 families*, he said, *were to be employed on the relief works!* Taking those families at the common average of five-and-a-half individuals to each, the total number would be 254,738 persons. The presentments allowed would thus give about ten shillings' worth of employment for each individual, with nine or ten foodless months before them. The conclusion is inevitable; the presentments allowed were utterly inadequate to meet the Famine in Mayo, the fearful consequences of which we shall learn as we proceed.[3]

Many of the speakers at the Presentment Sessions charged the Government with a breach of faith in not finishing the works which were prematurely closed on 15 August 1846. Those works were commenced under the law passed by Sir Robert Peel's Government, whereby the baronies or, in other words, the ratepayers, paid *one-half* the expense and the Government the other; so that even if Lord John Russell's Government took them up anew, under the Labour-rate Act, *the whole expense* should, according to the terms of that Act, fall upon the baronies.

This was looked upon as a grievance, and at the Glenquin Sessions, in County Limerick, Lord Monteagle, a friend and supporter of the Administration, put the grievance in the shape of a resolution which was adopted. The resolution was: 'That whilst we express our full approval of these works, yet the magistrates and ratepayers feel that it is also their duty to express their strong and unanimous opinion that the just construction of the arrangement between this barony and the Government for the completion of such works as have been commenced under the Act 9 Vic. c.1, requires an adherence to the terms of that contract.'

Very general discontent was manifested at the rule by which the rate of wages on the public works was to be twopence a day under the average wages of the district in which the works were being carried on. Wages were so excessively low at the time, it was felt that, with rapidly advancing markets, the labourer on the works could not get enough food for his family. The object of this rule, however, was obvious and well meant enough; it was framed to induce agricultural labourers to remain at their usual employments, in order that the crops might be sown. Had the Government been well informed of the relations subsisting between farmer and labourer in Ireland, they would have known that this arrangement could not have the desired effect, *money-wages regularly paid* being almost a thing unknown to our agricultural population at the time; whilst the Famine made money-wages, regularly paid, the first essential of existence.[4]

When the Government began to insist on task, or piecework, instead of day labour, the greatest amount of dissatisfaction that occurred during the entire Famine manifested itself. The engineers of the Board of Works reported over and over again, that an industrious man, willing to labour, could earn from fifteen to eighteen pence a day under this arrangement, yet the people rose in combination — almost in rebellion — against it, whilst daily wages ranged from eight to ten pence only. They assaulted overseers; refused to work for them; threatened their lives, and, in one instance at least, made an attempt on the life of a Government functionary.

At the village of Clare Abbey, in the county of that name, some short distance south of Ennis, the capital, this insubordination seems to have become rather formidable, as a murderous outrage was committed there on the head steward of the works, Mr W. Hennessy, half-way between Clare and Ennis. He was fired upon by one of four men whom he observed inside the road ditch, as he passed along. The weapon used was a blunderbuss. It was charged with some of the blasting powder belonging to the works, and duck shot; so that although Mr Hennessy received the contents in his right side, he was not mortally wounded, and recovered in a little time.

Captain Wynne, the local inspector, giving an account of this outrage to his Board, said the cause of the outrage was because Mr Hennessy was trying to get the men into proper training. Quite likely. But it must be taken into account that a duty of that kind might be done in such a way as neither to offend the men

114

nor lose their respect or esteem; and it might be done in an offensive, insolent manner, calculated to exasperate them, especially as they were in a state of excitement at the period.[5] Captain Wynne further said that the perpetrator of the outrage was known, but could not be brought to justice.

The Board of Works, to mark its indignation at this murderous attack upon one of its servants, stopped the works in the locality and the inhabitants, miserably off before, sank into a state of the most heartrending destitution, as was testified by Captain Wynne, writing from the same place a fortnight or three weeks after, to Colonel Jones.[6]

'I must again', he said, 'call your attention to the appalling state in which Clare Abbey is at present. I ventured through that parish this day, to ascertain the condition of the inhabitants, and although a man not easily moved, I confess myself unmanned by the extent and intensity of suffering I witnessed, more especially among the women and little children, crowds of whom were to be seen scattered over the turnip fields, like a flock of famishing crows, devouring the raw turnips, and mostly half naked, shivering in the snow and sleet, uttering exclamations of despair, whilst their children were screaming with hunger. I am a match for anything else I may meet with here, but this I cannot stand. When may we expect to resume the works?'

This letter does much credit to the feeling and manly heart of Captain Wynne. He said the wretched beings were devouring the raw turnips they found in the fields, but surely very little such was to be found among the snowdrifts in the last days of December for, sad to say, his letter was written on Christmas Eve! Such a Christmas for the people of Clare Abbey, and a thousand places besides!

Beyond doubt, the Government, and those under them, had enormous difficulties to contend against. Every new scheme, or modification of a scheme, proposed by them had its inconveniences. The opposition to task work arose from more than one cause. Lazy, unprincipled people were opposed to it because they were lazy and unprincipled; a far larger class were opposed to it because it was no secret that the works were carried on not for sake of their utility but to keep the people from being idle. Had this class been employed upon really useful works, such as reclaiming land, tilling the soil, draining, subsoiling or railroad-making, they would, no doubt, have had more heart for their daily labour.

There is a natural repugnance in the mind of a man to apply himself in earnest to what he has been told is useless — to what he sees and feels to be useless. If a labourer were hired, and even

A funeral at Skibbereen.

given good wages, for casting chaff against the wind, I make bold
to say, he would soon resign his employment from sheer inability
to work at anything so much opposed to his common sense.

A third and a very large class of the labouring population were
opposed to task work, because they were able to earn so very
little at it. 'Those who choose to labour may earn good wages',
wrote Colonel Jones to Mr Trevelyan; but he forgot, or was
ignorant of the fact, that great numbers of the working class had
been already so weakened and debilitated by starvation that they
were unable to do what the overseers regarded as a day's work;
and it is on record that task work frequently brought industrious
willing workmen less money than they would have received
under the day's work system.[7]

At the end of October a Treasury Minute was published to the
effect that such prices were to be allowed for Relief Works,
executed by task, as would enable good labourers to earn from
one shilling to one shilling and sixpence a day; the day's work
system, at the wages fixed by the Treasury Minute of 31 August,
was to be in future confined to those who were unable or
unwilling to work by task. There was some concession in this.
Under it the labourer could choose piece work or day's work as
seemed more advantageous to himself. The spirit, at least, of the
August Treasury Minute was that all should work by task.

After Skibbereen, Bantry and Schull, there was scarcely any
place in the South so famine-stricken as Ennistymon. The gentry
of the place knew the real wants of the population and pressed
them on the Government officials; while they, on the other hand,
in obedience to orders, felt bound to keep the labour lists as low
as possible. To have reduced those lists always served an
inspector at headquarters. In such cases it is no wonder that
unpleasant differences sometimes arose between committees and
inspectors.

That Ennistymon was sorely tried appears from many
communications to the Board of Works. A very short time after
Captain Wynne's unpleasant quarrel with the committee there,
I find Mr Millet, the officer, I suppose, who succeeded him,
writing to the Board from that town, that he was besieged in his
house by men trying to compel him to put them on the works,
on which account he could not get out until half-past four o'clock
in the evening. 'Some of the men make a list', he wrote, 'and
get it sent by the Committee *whether men are wanting or not*. The
people think this is sufficient authority.'[8]

From this it seems clear that the works at Ennistymon were
quite insufficient for the number of the destitute. The starving
people wanted to get employment, *whether men were wanting or*

117

not. What a complaint! Good Mr Millet, the question with the people was not whether you required workmen or not, but it was that they and their families were in the throes of death from want of food and they saw no other way of getting it but by being employed on those works. Besides, your masters began by stating that the public works were not undertaken on account of their necessity or utility, but for the purpose of rescuing the people from famine, by giving them employment.[9]

The inspectors and the local committees had such frequent differences, that the Board had it under serious consideration to dispense with those committees altogether. This idea was abandoned, but the important privilege of issuing tickets for the works was taken away from the committees, by an order of the Board, bearing date 9 December.

As before remarked, an undercurrent of feeling pervaded the minds of officials that there was not at all so much real distress in Ireland as the people pretended and that there was a great deal more food in the country than there was said to be. This was sometimes openly asserted, but more frequently hinted at and insinuated in communications to the Board of Works and the Treasury. It was founded partly on prejudice and partly on ignorance of the real state of affairs, which was far worse than the most anxious friends of the people asserted, as the event, unfortunately, too truly proved.

That there was some deception and much idleness, in connection with the public works, cannot be doubted for a moment; such works being on a gigantic and ever increasing scale, effective supervision was impossible. The mistake of many of the officials, although not of all, was that they regarded such exceptional things as an index to the general state of the country, built theories upon them and sent those theories up to their superiors, which helped to make them close-handed and suspicious.

Those officials did not and, in many cases, could not sound the depths of misery into which the country had sunk; the people were dying of sheer starvation around them, whilst they were writing reports accusing them of exaggeration and idleness. What the Rev. Jeremiah Sheahan of Glenlure, in County Cork, said of his parishioners was equally true in hundreds of other cases: 'The most peaceable have died of want in their cabins. More than twelve have done so in the last six days.'[10]

One of the proofs brought forward that the Irish people were not so badly off as they pretended — in fact that in many instances they were concealing their wealth, was *the increase of deposits in the Savings Banks.* At a superficial glance there would appear to be much truth in this conclusion; but we must remember that the millions whom the potato blight left foodless, never, in the best of times, had anything to put in Savings Banks. They planted their acre or half acre of potatoes, paid for it by their labour; they had thus raised a bare sufficiency of food; and so their year's operations began and ended.

An official of the Irish Poor Law Board, Mr Twistleton, gave a more elaborate and detailed answer to the Savings Banks argument. Writing to the Home Secretary, Sir George Grey, on 26 December, he called his attention to leaders in the *Times* and *Morning Chronicle* on the subject. One of those articles was remarkable, he said, since it 'seemed to treat the increase in the deposits as a proof of *successful swindling on the part of the Irish people*, during the present year'.

So far from this being true, an increase, in Mr Twistleton's opinion, might show 'severe distress', inasmuch as when times begin to grow hard deposits would increase for the following reasons:

1. People in employment, who were thoughtless before and did not deposit, would begin to be depositors in bad times.

2. People in employment, who were depositors before, would increase their deposits.

3. Thrifty people, who would at other times have gone into little speculations, would now be afraid to do so, and they would become depositors instead.

4. Persons of a higher class, say employers, in such times cease to be employers and become depositors.

An increase of deposits, Mr Twistelton admitted, might arise from prosperity; he only wished to show that such increase was not always a certain sign of it. We know too well now that the increase of deposits in some of our Savings Banks during the Famine was no sign whatever of prosperity; yet the journals named above at once built upon the fact a theory most damaging to the existing destitution of our people and most injurious to their moral character; basing this theory on one of those general principles of political economy, which often admits of grave exception and sometimes breaks down utterly when put to the test of practical experience.

The public works projected and carried on by the Government to meet the distress of 1845-6 were brought to a close on 15 August of the latter year. The Treasury Minute, empowering the Board to begin anew public works in Ireland under the provisions of the Labour-rate Act, was published on 31 August; so that the officials whom the Board had added to their ordinary staff, when entrusted with the management of the previous public works, were, we may assume, still in their hands when they received their new commission from the Treasury. Although numerous, they were miserably insufficient for the vast and terrible campaign now before them. Indeed, throughout those trying and marvellous times the Board was never able to secure a full supply of efficient officers; the pressure was so great, the undertakings so numerous and extensive, that this is by no means matter for surprise. A few figures selected from their accounts and reports will serve to show the sudden and extraordinary expansion of their operations.

The baronies to which loans had been issued up to 31 December 1846, under the Labour-rate Act, numbered 322 and the total sum issued up to the same time was £999,661 4s 2d. — a million of money, in round numbers. Besides this, many of those baronies (but not all) had obtained loans under previous Acts; whilst baronies which had as yet made no application for loans under the Labour-rate Act were also indebted to Government for money borrowed under previous Acts. The number of baronies which had taken out loans under the Acts of 1 Vic., cap. 21, and 9 and 10 Vic., cap. 124, was 424. The account between the baronies and the Government stood thus on 31 December 1846:

Loans to baronies under Acts passed previous

	£	s	d
to the Labour-rate Act	186,060	1	5
Grants	229,464	8	0
Loans to baronies under the Labour-rate Act ..	999,661	4	2
Making in all	1,415,185	13	7

£229,464 8s. 0d. being the amount of grants and £1,185, 721 5s. 7d. being the amount of loans; besides which there was expended by the Board of Works under various drainage Acts, for the year ending 31 December 1846 a sum of £110,022 14s. 4d.

In the week ending 3 October, there were 20,000 persons employed on the public works in Ireland; in the week ending the 31st of the same month, there were over 114,000. In the very next week, the first week of November, there were 162,000 on the works; and in the week ending 28 November, the returns give the number as something over 285,000!

A fortnight later, in a detailed account of the operations of the Board, supplied to the Treasury, this remarkable sentence occurs: 'The works at present are in every county in Ireland, affording employment to more than 300,000 persons.[11] The increase went on rapidly through December. In the week ending the fifth of that month, there were 321,000 employed; and in the week which closed on the 26th, the extraordinary figure was 398,000.'[12]

The number of persons employed was greatest in Munster and least in Ulster. At the beginning of December, they were thus distributed in the four Provinces: Ulster, 30,748; Leinster, 50,135; Connaught, 106,680; and Munster, 134,103. At the close of the month the same proportion was pretty fairly maintained, the numbers being: Ulster, 45,487; Leinster, 69,585; Connaught, 119,946; and Munster, 163,213.

According to the Census of 1841, there were in Ulster 439,805 families; in Leinster, 362,134; in Connaught, 255,694; and in Munster, 415,154. From these data, the proportion between the number of persons employed on the relief works in each province, and the population of that province, stood thus at the close of the year 1846: in Ulster there was one labourer out of every nine-and-two-thirds families so employed; in Leinster there was one out of about every five- and-a-quarter families; in Munster,one out of every two-and- a-half families; and in Connaught, one out of every two- and-one-seventh families (approx).

At the end of November, the numbers of employees superintending the public works were: 62 inspecting officers; 60 engineers and county surveyors; 4,021 overseers; 1,899 check clerks; 5 draftsmen; 54 clerks for correspondence; 50 clerks for accounts; 32 pay inspectors, and 425 pay clerks — making in all 6,913 officials, distributed over nine distinct departments.

The gross amount of wages rose, of course, in proportion to the numbers employed. At the end of October, the sum paid weekly was £61,000; at the end of November, £101,000; and for the week ending 26 December, £154,472.

The number of Relief Committees in operation throughout the country at the close of 1846 was about 1,000. Indeed, everything connected with the Public Works and the Famine tends to impress one with their gigantic proportions — even the correspondence, the state of which is thus given by the Board in the middle of December: 'The letters received averaged 800 a day, exclusive of letters addressed to individual members of the Board, on public business; the number received on the last day of November was 2,000; today (17 December), 2,500.'

All this notwithstanding, the Famine was but very partially stayed: on it went, deepening, widening, desolating, slaying,

121

with the rapidity and certainty which marked the progress of its predecessor, the Blight. The numbers applying for work without being able to obtain it, were fearfully enormous. From a memorandum supplied by the Board of Works to Sir Randolph Routh, the head of the Commissariat Department, dated 17 December, we learn that the labourers then employed were about 350,000, whilst the number on Relief Lists (for employment) was about 500,000, — that is, there were 150,000 persons on the lists seeking work, who could not, or at least who did not, get it. Those 150,000 may be taken to represent at least half a million starving people — how many more were there at the moment whose names never appeared on any list, except the death-roll!

8

The Famine worsens

Two Governmental departments were told to do battle with the Irish Famine: the Board of Works and the Commissariat Relief Office. The duty of the former was to find employment for those who were able to work, at such wages as would enable them to support themselves and their families; the latter was to see that food should be for sale within a reasonable distance of all who were necessitated to buy it, and at fair market prices; but more than this the Commissariat Office was not empowered to do.

Corn merchants, food dealers and mealmongers were not to be interfered with; on the contrary, they were to be encouraged in carrying on their trade. It was only where such persons did not exist, or did not exist in sufficient numbers, that the Commissariat depots were to sell corn or meal to the people. No food was to be given away by Government; none was to be sold under price, it being assumed that the people could earn enough to support themselves.

Government feared that if they began to undersell the merchants and dealers those classes would give up business, which, in the government's opinion, would be a very great evil. Mealmongers and food dealers are generally very shrewd men; and it was believed, with much reason, that they succeeded in raising prices when it suited them, and even in many cases, in realising large fortunes, by working on the apprehensions of the Government in respect to this very matter.

The Commissariat Relief Department was organised at the close of 1845 for the purpose of managing the distribution of Indian meal, imported at that time by Sir Robert Peel, to provide against the anticipated scarcity of the spring and summer of 1846. Its headquarters were in Dublin Castle, and its chief was a Scotch gentleman, Sir Randolph Routh — a name which, like some others, must occur pretty frequently in these pages. The Commissariat people, as is usual in such cases, began by instituting extensive inquiries. They ordered their subordinates to furnish reports of the state of the potato crop throughout the country.

The Assistant Commissaries-General and others employed in this service, in due time made their reports, which in the main agreed with the statements in the public journals and with the opinion prevalent everywhere among the people; thus differing with those officers of the Board of Works who held that there were more sound potatoes in Ireland than was generally admitted. As early as August, Mr White, writing from Galway to Assistant Commissary-General Wood, made a most unfavourable report of the state of the crop in Clare; the Blight, he said, was general and most rapid in its effects, a large quantity of the potatoes being already diseased, and a portion perfectly rotten. 'I am, therefore, clearly of opinion', he continued, 'that the scarcity of the potato last year will be nothing compared with this, and that, too, several months earlier.'[1] Commissary-General Hewetson sent specimens of diseased potatoes to the Secretary of the Treasury in the middle of August, with this information: 'The crop seems to have been struck almost everywhere by one sweeping blast, in one and the same night. I mentioned a hope that the tubers might yet rally, many of the stalks having thrown out fresh vegetation; I fear it is but a futile hope.'[2] Just about the same time, Assistant Commissary-General Dobree reported to the same quarter: 'It is superfluous to make any further report on the potato crop, for I believe the failure is general and complete throughout the country, though the disease has made more rapid progress in some places than in others. In a circuit of 200 miles, I have not seen one single field free from it; and although it is very speculative to attempt a calculation on what is not yet absolutely realised, my belief is that scarcely any of the late potatoes will be fit for human food.'[3]

Considerable stores of oatmeal and Indian corn remained in the Government depots throughout the country when they were closed in August. By a Treasury Minute these were ordered to be concentrated at six points: two in the interior, namely, Longford and Banagher, and four on the coast, Limerick, Galway, Westport and Sligo.

The depots already in existence, as well as those to be established, were only to be in aid of regular corn and meal trade; and no supplies were to be sold from them until it was proved to the satisfaction of the Assistant Commissary-General of the district that the necessity for so doing was urgent, and that no other means of obtaining food existed. This rule was, in some instances, kept so stringently that people died of starvation within easy distance of those depots, with money in their hands to buy the food that would not be sold to them.

The Treasury, rather than Commissary-General Routh or his subordinates, was to blame for this; their strong determination, many times expressed, being that food accumulated by Government should be husbanded for the spring and summer months of 1847, when they expected the greatest pressure would exist. This was prudence, but prudence founded on ignorance of the real state of things in the closing months of 1846.

The dearth of food which they were looking forward to in the coming spring and summer arose fully *five months* before the time fixed by the Government; but they were so slow or so reluctant to realise its truth that great numbers of people were starved to death before Christmas, because the Government locked up the meal in their depots in order to keep the same people alive with it in May and June!

'It is most important', said a Treasury Minute — these were the days of Treasury Minutes — 'that it should be remembered that the supplies provided for the Government depots are not intended to form the primary or principal means of subsistence to the people of the districts in which the depots are established, but merely to furnish a last resource when all other means of subsistence, whether derived from the harvest just got in or from importations, are exhausted, and the depots are, therefore, in no case to be drawn upon while food can be obtained by purchase from private parties.'[4]

This Minute is addressed to Sir Randolph Routh, who had written to the Treasury ten days before, pressing upon them the necessity of large and immediate purchases of corn. 'We have no arrivals yet announced', he said 'either at Westport or Sligo, and the remains there must be nothing, or next to nothing. The bills of lading from Mr Erichsen are all for small quantities, which will be distributed, and perhaps eaten, in twelve or twenty-four hours after their arrival. It would require a thousand tons to make an impression, and that only a temporary one. Our salvation of the depot system is in the importation of a large supply. These small shipments are only drops in the ocean.' And further on in the same letter: 'We began our operations on 1 September or thereabouts; and here, in the midst of harvest, before any Commissariat arrangement for supplies from abroad could be matured, we find the country besieging our depot for food, and scarcely a proprietor stirring in their behalf.'[5]

Government depots were only to be established where it was probable that private enterprise would not offer a sufficient quantity of food for sale. On this principle, the north, east and south were left to be supplied through the usual channels of commerce; the depot system being confined to the west coast. What was meant precisely by the west coast does not seem to have been settled at the outset, but in answer to an enquiry from Sir Randolph Routh on the subject, the Treasury, on 31 October, defined it to be the country to the west of the Shannon, with the Country Donegal to the north and Kerry to the south, with a small corner of Cork, as far as Skibbereen, because that town was on the western cost.[6]

We have seen the rapid increase of labourers on the Relief Works from October to December, yet famine was always far ahead of the Government. Their arrangements for the first famine year were made with reference to the closing of all operations at harvest time, in 1846, but there was no harvest that year *for the poor*; their crop had vanished before the destroyer, and they were actually worse off at the end of August 1846 than they had been since the beginning of the Potato Blight. In that year, the potatoes never came to maturity at all, and any that were thought worth the labour of digging were hurried to market and sold for any price they fetched before they would melt away in the owner's hands.

One of the Commissariat officers asked a farmer's wife, who was selling potatoes of this kind, what was the price of them: 'Two pence a stone, sir', she replied, 'is my price', but lowering her voice, she naively added, 'to tell you the truth, sir, they are not worth a penny.'

Even in September — it was on the 18th of that month — a resolution was passed by the Mallow Relief Committee that from information laid before them, and from the verdicts of several coroner's inquests, held during the previous few days, disease of the most fatal character was spreading in the districts around them, in consequence of the badness of the food purchasable by the working classes.

A little later, the Rev. Mr Daly announced to the ratepayers at the Fermoy sessions that, at the moment he was addressing them, numbers of persons were living on cabbage leaves, whose countenances were so altered and whose whole appearance was so changed by starvation and wretchedness that he could hardly recognise them.

Lord Mountcashel, the Chairman of the sessions, on the same occasion used these remarkable words: 'The people are starving; they have no employment; they require to be attended to immediately, for starvation will not accommodate itself to any man's convenience.' Nothing truer.

Many landlords throughout the country made similar observations; but to all such the representatives of the

Government replied, and not without a good show of reason, that whilst landlords talked in this manner they themselves, with rare exceptions, did nothing to employ the people, nor did they in any way relieve the fearful pressure upon the Public Works.

The earliest famine demonstration seems to have taken place in Westport on 22 August. On that day a large body of men marched four deep and in a very orderly manner to Lord Sligo's residence beside the town. They made their intention known beforehand to the inspector of police and asked him to be present to show they had no illegal designs. They were chiefly from Islandeady and Aughagown. Lord Sligo, accompanied by some gentlemen who were staying with him, received them at his hall door. They said they wanted food and work. His lordship assured them that he had already represented, in the strongest terms, the necessity of measures being taken to secure a supply of both, and that he would repeat his application. They seemed satisfied with this and quietly retired.

Towards the end of September, however, the state of the country became very unsatisfactory and even alarming. The low rate of wages fixed by the Government; the high price of provisions; the closing of the Government depots; the large quantities of corn which they saw sent daily to England, whilst they who raised it starved, were amongst the chief causes which excited the people to acts of intimidation.

In several instances they went in formidable bodies to the presentment sessions, apparently under the impression that the ratepayers, there assembled, had something to do with fixing the amount of wages, which of course was a popular error. On Monday 28 September, a special sessions was appointed to be held at Kilmacthomas, some fourteen miles from Dungarvan, and notices were extensively circulated the day before, by unknown hands, calling on the people to assemble at Dungarvan on that day, as the military would be away at the sessions. The avowed object of this assemblage was to seize provisions by force, or at least to lay down a scale of prices beyond which they should not be raised.

The authorities had, of course, timely notice of this movement and left a sufficient force in the town to protect it. The precaution was not an idle one, for soon after the dragoons took their departure for Kilmacthomas, about 5,000 men entered Dungarvan, led by a person named Power, well known in the locality as 'lame Pat'.

The town was guarded by sixty soldiers and fifty-four police but, in the face of such numbers, their officers considered it the best policy to stand upon the defensive and do nothing until a breach of the peace had been committed. They, however, cautioned the people and advised them to return to their houses; they did not take their advice but went round to the various places in which corn was stored and threatened the owners if they attempted to export any of the produce they had purchased. They next proceeded to the shops where Indian meal was on sale and uttered similar threats against the vendors if they charged more than one shilling a stone for it.

Meanwhile Captain Sibthorpe, the officer in command of the detachment of the 1st Royal Dragoons that had gone to Kilmacthomas in the morning, finding the number of people there assembled less than he had anticipated — only 500 or so — and being aware that a much larger body was expected at Dungarvan, asked permission from the magistrates to return to that town. At first, they were very loath to grant his request, but having at length yielded, he left forty-eight policemen for their protection and marched his men back to Dungarvan. It was a journey of three or four hours.

On their arrival they found the people under Power had concluded their preliminary business of visiting the stores and shops and, not being provided with a commissariat to supply them with rations, they were levying contributions from the bakers of the town. Seeing this Captain Sibthorpe ordered his dragoons to ride them down and drive them off, which they did. Some prisoners were taken, lame Pat Power, their leader, being of the number.

The prisoners having been secured, Mr Howley, the resident magistrate, addressed the people; he explained to them the illegality and folly of their proceedings and assured them he would forward to the Government any document detailing what they considered as their grievances, provided that it was couched in respectful language; and further that he would do all he could to have any reasonable request of theirs complied with.

Upon this they retired and drew up a statement which they handed to him and which he promised to send to the Lord Lieutenant. So far so good. The day's proceedings might be fairly supposed to have ended here — but no — what about the prisoners? The people refused to go away without them. The magistrates would not release them but assured their comrades that their punishment should be light. This did not satisfy them and they commenced to use violent language and to throw stones.

Orders were given to clear the square, which service was performed by the dragoons, who drove them into the neighbouring streets; but as the stone-throwing was continued the police were sent to drive them away; failing to do this the dragoons were ordered to advance, whereupon, it is said, a shout was raised in Irish by the people to 'kill them', which was followed by a shower of stones.

Things began to look so critical that Captain Sibthorpe asked permission from Mr Howley to order his men to fire but that gentleman refused the permission. Captain Sibthorpe then asked Mr Howley to allow him to take that responsibility upon himself but he still refused, saying that as an important trust had been reposed in him, he would retain that trust, and allow no firing until their lives were imperilled.

The stone-throwing continued; Mr Howley at length said to the other magistrates that there was no use in talking any more to the people, and that he must read the riot act, which he accordingly did. He then warned them of the dangerous course they were pursuing — a shower of stones was the response. Captain Sibthorpe now told Mr Howley that he would withdraw his men from the town, unless they were permitted to fire. The order was given; the dragoons were drawn up in sections of four — each section firing in its turn. In this manner twenty-six shots were fired, each round being answered by a volley of stones.

When the firing had continued for some time the people retired from the town; they were followed by the dragoons but, entrenching themselves behind walls and ditches, they prepared to renew the conflict under more favourable circumstances, but the opportunity was not afforded them. It grew late — the town, at any rate, was cleared and the success of the troops being by no means so certain upon this new battle ground they were withdrawn by the magistrates.

On their return to town they found two men had been wounded and, as usually happens in such cases, one of them had no connection whatever with the business, being a carter employed in carrying baggage for the troops. When asked how he came to be among the belligerents, having no interest in the matter, he replied that he was under the impression the troops had orders not to fire on the people, or if they did, it should be with blank cartridge; he was confirmed in this belief by the fact that the first four or five shots took no effect; but 'at any rate', he added, 'when I saw the fun going on, I could not resist the temptation of joining in it'.

The persons arrested on the occasion, fifty-one in number, were brought up for trial before the sitting barrister in about a month afterwards. All pleaded guilty and received merely nominal punishment, with the exception of 'lame Pat', their leader. He, poor fellow, was sentenced to one year's imprisonment although he declared he had been four days and four nights living on cabbage leaves and salt previous to his misconduct. But the saddest part of this Dungarvan tale is that the poor carrier, whose name was Michael Fleming, died of his wounds on 26 October in the Workhouse, to which he had been removed for medical treatment.

Formidable bands went about, in some portions of the country, visiting the houses of farmers and even of the gentry, warning them not to raise the price of provisions and also asking for employment. Notices continued to be distributed and posted up in public places, calling assemblies of the people in various towns of the South in order to discuss their existing state and future prospects.

A notice posted on the chapel of Carrigtwohill, calling one of those meetings, warned such as absented themselves that they would be marked men as there was famine in the parish and they should have food or blood. The priests of the place advised and warned their flocks against those illegal proceedings and the evils to themselves which must necessarily spring from them. This had the desired effect and the objects contemplated by the promulgators of the notice were entirely foiled.

At Macroom, crowds of working men paraded the streets, calling for work or food. Food they urgently required, no doubt, for two of those in the gathering fell in the street from hunger. One, a muscular-looking young man, was unable to move from the spot where he sank exhausted, until some nourishment was brought to him, which revived him.[7]

At Killarney, a crowd, preceded by a bellman and a flag of distress, paraded the streets but the leaders were arrested and lodged in the Bridewell. In the neighbourhood of Skibbereen, the people employed in breaking stones for macadamising the roads struck work and marched into the town in a body, asserting that the wages they were receiving were insufficient to support them. The overseer alleged that enough work had not been done by the men and that task work should be introduced. Their answer was that the stones given them to break, being large field stones, were as hard as anvils and they could not break more of them in a given time than they had done; and that death by starvation was preferable to the sufferings they had already endured.

Those men worked some miles from Skibbereen, at a place called Caheragh and, before their arrival, the wildest rumours were afloat as to their coming and intentions. It was Wednesday, 30 September. At twelve o'clock on that day, the principal inhabitants met to consult with Mr Galwey, the magistrate, as to what course they should adopt in the emergency. Whilst thus engaged, Dr Donovan, who had been on professional duty, rode in from the country and announced that a body of men, consisting, as far as he could judge, of from 800 to 1,000 appeared on the outskirts of the town. They were marching in regular order, ten deep.

Twenty-two years after the event, Dr Donovan thus narrated the cause of this extraordinary movement and the impression made upon his mind by the terrible phalanx, on its appearance before the trembling town of Skibbereen: 'Some difficulty', he said, 'occasionally arose in making out the pay lists and, as the people were entirely dependent for their day's support on their day's wages, great suffering and inconvenience resulted from the slightest delay. In addition to these causes of inconvenience, supplies of food had sometimes to be procured and on this particular occasion serious consequences had nearly resulted from the obstinacy of an official (a Mr H_____), a commissariat officer, who boasted of his experience in matters of the kind during the Peninsular campaigns of the Duke of Wellington and who refused to allow any food to be sold to the people, although ready money was offered on the spot.

'An additional difficulty arose when it was made known that extensive works in the neighbourhood, upon which over 1,000 persons had been employed, were stopped. Great excitement was the result and it was determined by the whole body of workmen employed upon the Caheragh relief works to march into Skibbereen, levy contributions and enforce compliance with their demands.

'About twelve o'clock in the day, a number of persons, amounting to about 1,000, marched in the direction of the town and had nearly reached their destination before the fact was made known. I believe I was, myself, one of the first who saw the approach of those once stalwart men, but now emaciated spectres; and I cannot describe adequately the interesting appearance of the body as they marched along, bearing upon their shoulders their implements of labour such as spades, shovels, etc., which, in the glitter of a blazing sun, produced a most surpassing effect.

'Immediately a most exciting scene took place. Under the apprehension that shops would be rifled, shutters were put up and doors were closed. The servants in charge of children hastened to their respective habitations and everything denoted that a serious onslaught was unavoidable. The military force in the town amounted to seventy-five men and by the sound of trumpet they were at once summoned to their post and positive directions were given that under no circumstances should the invading party be allowed to enter the town.

'The interposition of a long schoolhouse prevented the military

131

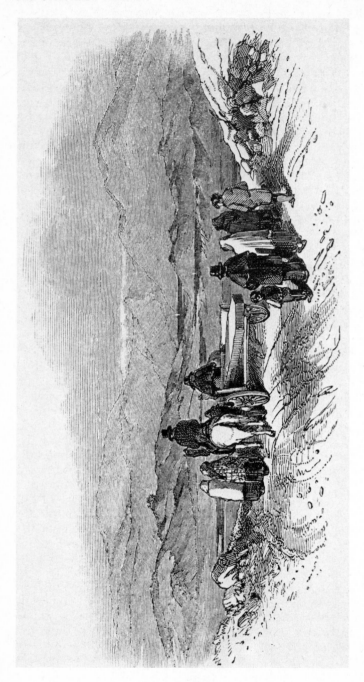

A funeral at Shepperton Lakes, near Skibbereen, Co. Cork.

from being seen until the party were within twenty yards of the school. The orders were then given to prime and load and I cannot describe what my feelings were as the clink of the ramrods clearly denoted what was likely to follow. Fortunately, the force upon this occasion was under the command of Mr Michael Galwey, JP, a gentleman remarkable for his firmness and courage, his kindness and humanity and extraordinary influence among the people.

'When a sanguinary affray was almost inevitable, he took advantage of a temporary lull and cried out in a stentorian voice: ''Three cheers for the Queen, and plenty of employment tomorrow'', a call which was immediately responded to in the best manner that the weakened vocal powers of the multitude would admit of.

'The threatening aspect of affairs was completely changed. Mr G., in his own familiar phraseology, said: ''H_____, we must get the biscuits, and we will all then go home in good humour.'' No sooner said than done. The stores were opened, the biscuits were distributed, the price was paid, the effusion of blood was avoided and this neighbourhood was saved from what in the commencement threatened to be a most fearful calamity.'[8]

It may be further mentioned that the people were four hours at the entrance to the town before they finally retired, although repeatedly called upon to do so by Mr Galwey, who had resorted to the extreme measure of reading the riot act. The people's constant reply was that they might as well be shot as not, as they had not tasted food for twenty-four hours. Several of the neighbouring gentlemen took an active part in the day's proceedings, as well as Mr Galwey, more especially Mr McCarthy Downing, the present worthy member for the county.

A body of men, numbering about 500, marched through Mallow, on their way to the Workhouse, where they began to scale the walls, at the same time exclaiming that they were starving and wanted food. Temporary relief was distributed to them outside the Workhouse, upon which they retired. It was reported that an attack had been made upon Lord Stuart de Decies, on occasion of his attending the special sessions at Clashmore, during which it was said that several persons cried out, 'Knock him down'; but his Lordship, in a letter to the newspapers, gave a complete contradiction of this report.

A deputation from the magistrates of Clonakilty, consisting of the Rev. Mr Townsend, the rector, and John O'Hea, Esq., waited on the Lord Lieutenant on 5 October. They stated they were deputed by the clergy of all denominations, the magistrates, the gentry and the people of the district, to lay before Government the utter desolation caused by the destruction of the potato crop; the poor having been for some time past living on cabbage leaves and food of that description. They pressed upon his Excellency the urgent necessity which existed for sending an immediate supply of provisions into the locality. The magistrates, they stated, had directed them to say that they would not be responsible for the peace of the district, if such a supply as would check the exorbitant price of meal were not sent forthwith.

At Youghal two ships laden with corn for exportation were stopped by the people and for some time prevented from sailing. Large numbers assembled at Macroom, with the apparent intention of making an attack upon property but, through the advice and judicious conduct of Sir David Roche, they dispersed. Horses engaged in carrying corn to the coast for exportation were sometimes shot. In a few places, especially in Connaught, convoys of meal and flour were seized and carried off.

The troops and police had a hard time of it. Detachments of either, or both, had to be despatched to those places in which disturbances had occurred, or were apprehended. Numerous arrests were made in every instance.

A very alarming symptom in those assemblages was that they occurred almost simultaneously, many of them even on the same day, although there is no trace of this being the result of previous organisation. At the moment the whole framework of society in Ireland was shaken and disjointed and, in fact, on the point of falling into utter confusion; yet there were no manifestations of reckless wickedness — the demands of the people did not go beyond the cry for food and employment at fair wages.

The Lord Lieutenant issued a proclamation against those food and labour riots, calling on magistrates and others to assist in protecting 'the lawful trade in the articles of food'. He also announced that the Government works would be stopped, wherever those employed on them manifested a disposition, 'by violence, to obtain a higher rate of wages', or to resist the arrangements made by the officers of the Board of Works. His Excellency added that he desired in an especial manner to thank the ministers of religion, of all persuasions, for their useful and exemplary conduct on the trying occasion of those riots.

The want of conveniently situated mill-power, to grind the Indian and other corn purchased by the Government, caused them great anxiety for some time. It was of the utmost importance to have the means of grinding corn as near as possible to their depots. Economy, convenience, regularity, despatch, would be secured by it. In reply to inquiries on the subject, it was found that the quantity of corn required for current demands could not be ground within reach of those depots at all. At Broadhaven and Blacksod Bay, on the western coast, both in the midwest of a famished population, there was no available mill-power whatever. Even where mills existed, a new difficulty arose. The policy of the Government was to encourage, as much as possible, private enterprise in supplying food for the people; and this private enterprise had the mills, in many places, pre-engaged.

For instance, such was the case at the important stations of Westport and Limerick. Sir Randolph Routh, pressed by this difficulty, wrote to the Treasury to say he could not altogether forego the government claim to have, at least, some corn ground at Westport. As to the mill-power at Limerick, it was so uncertain, so dependent on the weather and so very much required there by the merchants that he would make no demand upon it. Mr Lister, the official at Westport, dissuaded him however, from grinding any corn even there.

Quoting from a recent Treasury Minute, the passage about not opening the depots, while food could be obtained by the people from private dealers, at reasonable prices, he continued: 'To delay resorting to this alternative, and in order to stimulate exertion, it is, I beg to repeat, absolutely essential that the trade should have the full and exclusive benefit of all the mill-power in its own locality'.[9] In a Treasury Minute of 8 September, the head of the Commissariat was informed that, considering the limited mill-power in the neighbourhood of Westport and how important it was that private merchants who had ordered consignments of Indian corn to that port should have ready means of grinding it, 'My Lords' expressed their opinion that the supplies intended for the Government depot at Westport should, if possible, consist only of meal; and they promised to give directions that not only that depot, but all the Government depots in Ireland, should, as far as practicable, be replenished with that article.

Mr Lister, in the letter just cited, enclosed to Sir Randolph Routh, in a tabular form, an account of the mill-power in Westport, Newport and along the coast of Mayo and Connemara. He informed his Chief that there were, in the extent of country named, the ordinary mills and twenty 'gig' mills in all, capable of grinding 170 tons of oatmeal per day. Five of those mills were fit to grind Indian corn, and wheat could be ground at all except the gig mills.

The mill-power of Galway and its vicinity, taking in Loughrea, Gort, Cong and Tuam, was not so considerable. In that extent there were thirteen mills, capable of grinding about 520 tons a week, but some of these were not available for Government business. All could grind Indian corn. They were entirely dependant on the water-supply; when it failed, which generally happened about the end of September, they had to cease working.[10]

Foreseeing the great difficulty of being able to command sufficient mill-power near those places in which their depots were, the Treasury ordered a return of the mill-power at the chief government victualling establishments on the English coast, as there would be no difficulty in sending meal to Ireland from those places. It was found that the combined available mill-power of Deptford, Portsmouth and Plymouth could turn out no more than 250 quarters a day.[11] However, it was put in requisition as soon as possible. In addition, Indian corn was ground at the King's mills, Rotherhithe, and by some private mills engaged for the purpose.

There were 1,000 tons of barley ground in Essex and some even in the Channel Islands. The mill-power at Deptford was in the meantime increased by an additional engine. If anyone be curious enough to enquire how the numberless sacks necessary to carry all this meal and corn in Ireland were supplied, the answer is — the Ordnance Department undertook that service and supplied as many sacks as were required, at 1s. 7d. each.

The Treasury also put themselves in communication with the authorities in Malta, relative to its mill-power and the facilities that might exist there for purchasing grain in quantity. The Comptroller of the Victualling Department informed them that he had twenty pair of stones worked by mules and twelve pair by steam and that many private mills could be engaged for hire. All the mills, however, which were worked by mules were required for the fleet, and could not be employed for any other purpose.

Referring to the enquiry as to the purchase of grain, he reported that large quantities of wheat were generally kept on sale at Malta. As to quality, he said, Odessa wheat was hard and good, but can only be ground by 'lava stones'; Egyptian was inferior, the biscuit made from it not being liked; oats were to be had in abundance; barley scarcer, but both of good quality.

Mr Trevelyan, on the part of the Treasury, wrote back in these terms to Deputy Commissary-General Ibbotson: 'It is my wish that a considerable quantity of grain should be purchased at once, consisting altogether of Indian corn, if it is to be procured, or, if not, partly of Indian corn, and partly of barley, oats, and wheat of an inferior, but wholesome quality.'[12]

In compliance with this order, a purchase of 500 salms, or quarters, of Indian corn was at once made and the mills were set to work; but there were not such stocks of grain in Malta as reported at first and once again the Secretary of the Treasury expressed his suspicions that the French had been making food purchases in the Mediterranean.[13]

To enable the people to be, to some extent, independent of mill-power, it occurred to the authorities to revive the use of the old Irish hand-mill or quern. This very ancient and rude contrivance had been employed in many countries as well as our own; nor had it as yet fallen into complete desuetude in parts of Scotland and the Shetland Islands. Mr Trevelyan had seen it with the army in India and he hoped, by getting samples of various kinds of quern, to have one constructed that would be of considerable importance in the present crisis, especially in very out-of-the-way districts.

In September Lord Monteagle, who showed much practical good sense and kindheartedness throughout the famine, called the attention of the Treasury to this matter and requested that some steel mills and querns should be placed at the disposal of the Commissariat officer on duty in his district; for, said he, the markets are rising and the people, by buying corn and grinding it for themselves, will have food cheaper than if they bought meal; and moreover they can thus occupy old people for whom no other employment can be found. The quern, added his lordship (alluding to Matt. c.24, v. 41) is literally the Scripture mill — 'two women shall be grinding at the mill', etc.

As to the steel mills, such as those used for grinding coffee, they were considered too expensive to be brought into use, mills of this description, specially tempered to grind Indian corn, not being purchasable even in quantity at a less cost than from £4 to £5 each.

Curiously enough, the Treasury could not obtain specimens of the Scotch or Irish quern, so they procured an Indian one, from the museum of the India House. They also got a French hand-mill, which was considered superior at least to the Indian one. The attempt to revive the use of the quern had no success except in a single instance. Captain Mann, the officer in charge at Kilkee, induced a coast-guard there to take to quern making. This man turned out querns at from ten to twelve shillings each and got a ready sale for them; Mr Trevelyan recommended them to all, but it would seem their sale was confined to the locality.

The Irish mill-power given above was considerable for the extent of the district but as the machinery was worked exclusively by water, the mills, of course, were idle when the water supply failed. Towards the end of September the mills in and about Westport could not, on this account, execute the orders of the corn merchants, to say nothing of the Government business.

Captain Perceval, who had charge of the district, under the Relief Commissariat Department, called attention to this fact and suggested that whole corn should be issued from the depot, which could be cooked without being ground into meal. He says he had made a trial of this plan, by steeping the grain at night, and boiling it next morning; in this manner it made what he termed 'a very nice podge', like pease-pudding and, to his taste, preferable to stirabout.

The Treasury called Sir Randolph Routh's attention to this suggestion, deeming it important to be able to turn Indian corn into a palatable food, without being either ground or bruised. Commissary-General Hewetson prepared a memorandum on the subject and put it in circulation, especially amongst the Relief committees. How far the recommendation was acted on does not appear.[14]

9

What did the landlords do?

As events progressed, the landlords of Ireland appeared to grow more and more alarmed, not so much for the people as for themselves; and they held meetings and passed resolutions, censuring the Government for the mode which it had chosen of counteracting the Famine. The Government and its organs returned the compliment by pointing out the inaction and obstructive policy of the landlords.

At those meetings it was invariably one of the resolutions, that labour should be employed upon productive works. The common-sense principle contained in this expression of opinion could not be denied: it was, indeed, the general opinion of the country; still every one felt that it would require time to develop such works — the starving millions must be fed, or at least the attempt must be made to feed them; they could not wait for tedious preliminaries, and more tedious surveys, and no other means existed to supply their daily food except those afforded by the Labour-rate Act.[1]

But very early in the business, as soon as a famine seemed imminent, it was urged by men of weight and character that reproductive works should and could be found for their people. Yes; and it was a fatal error — it was worse than an error, it was a crime, not to have adopted, at the earliest moment, the principle of reproductive employment.

At length the Government felt the force of this logic and did, although late, make an attempt to lessen the effects of their own great blunder. On 5 October, the 'Labouchere letter' came out, authorising reproductive works, the very thing the landlords were agitating for; now that their agitation was successful, what did they do? Nothing, or next to nothing, except that they opened a new cause of disagreement with the Government about boundaries.

In the Chief Secretary's letter the Government followed the subdivisions of electoral districts, as they had been doing before; the landlords insisted on townland boundaries and would not be content with — would not act under — any other. Their opponents said that was merely to cause delay; some even asserted it was an attempt to turn the whole system of public works to their own private advantage; a contrivance of the landlords, they said, to enjoy just so many jobs unmolested.

The request about the change of boundaries was not granted and so the 'Labouchere letter' was not acted upon to the extent which it ought to have been. The entire amount presented under the letter was £380,607, of which presentments were acted on to the gross amount of £239,476. The sum actually expended was about £180,000; and the largest number of persons at any time employed was 26,961, which was in the month of May 1847.[2]

Another demand which the landlords put in the shape of a resolution was that the Government should advance loans for the construction of railways in Ireland. This the Government also refused, or rather they insisted on conditions that amounted to a refusal. They said proper security could not be had for the advancement of the money; they therefore resolved not to make any advances to Irish railways, except in the ordinary way, namely by application to the Exchequer Loan Commissioners, when fifty per cent of the subscribed capital would be paid up. Could they not have made railways themselves, as they were afterwards almost compelled to do by Lord George Bentinck, in which case they would have had something for their money?

The landlords also made a demand which must be regarded as a fair one: it was that all who received incomes from the land should be taxed for the relief of the people. This was pointed at absentees, but still more at mortgagees.

The Royal Agricultural Society of Ireland, a society mainly representing landlord and aristocratic views, of which the Duke of Leinster was president, took up, as became it, the great labour question of the moment. A deputation from that body waited on the Lord Lieutenant on 25 September and laid its views before his Excellency. Reproductive work, they said, was the only work on which the labour of the population ought to be employed and plenty of such work was to be found in every part of the country. It would improve the soil and return the ratepayers a large interest for the capital expended.

The Board of Works, they suggested, might be empowered to postpone the public works ordered by the presentment sessions, whenever they saw fit, and also to suspend the portion of money voted for that purpose on any townland, and have it applied to the carrying out of reproductive works, according to the requisition of the owners and ratepayers of such townland; such works, in every case, to be approved of by at least three-fourths of the ratepayers.

The 'Labouchere letter', authorising reproductive works, was the response to this memorial of the Royal Agricultural Society. But it received another answer, and that from the Prime Minister himself. The question of productive and non-productive labour was so important that some time after the publication of the 'Labouchere letter', Lord John Russell discussed it, in a communication addressed by him to the Duke of Leinster, as president of the Royal Agricultural Society.

After a passing allusion to the deputation that waited on the Lord Lieutenant, he at once took the landlords to task. 'It had been our hope and expectation', he said, 'that landed proprietors would have commenced works of drainage and other improvements, on their own account: thus employing the people on their own estates and rendering the land more productive for the future. The Act (the Labour-rate Act), however, was put in operation in the baronies in a spirit the reverse of that which I have described....'

It is quite true to say that the landlords should have exerted themselves far more than they did to employ the people in improving their estates, by draining, subsoiling and reclamation; which works were sure to be remunerative and at no distant time.

When Lord John said he expected it, he showed great ignorance or forgetfulness. The Irish landlords, as a class, were not improvers of their properties before the Famine — how could he expect them to become so at such a crisis, when many of them feared, with reason, that both themselves and the people would be swallowed up in one common ruin? Besides, most of the wealthy proprietors were Englishmen or absentees who, with few exceptions, never saw their tenants; took no friendly interest in them, but left them in the hands of agents, who were prized by their employers in proportion to their punctuality in sending the half-yearly remittances, no questions being asked as to the means by which they were obtained.

How could the Prime Minister pretend to think that such men would rush into the midst of a famine-stricken people, to relieve, employ and improve them? He knew, or ought to have known, they would do no such thing, except on compulsion, and there was no compulsion in the case; he being, he said, for 'willing co-operation' only.

His government had certainly a right to be credited with the praiseworthy attempt it made to turn the labour of the Irish people to profitable work, but it came too late for immediate practical purposes. Planning, surveying and laying out improvements take much time. The principle contained in the 'Labouchere letter' should have been embodied in an Act of Parliament and reclamation of waste lands made compulsory, as had been advocated by many.

Lord John was right in blaming the landlords for not making use of the powers conferred by it. They, above all others, called the loudest for reproductive employment but, when it was sanctioned, they raised new difficulties about boundaries and other matters, which looked very like a determination not to carry into practical effect the permission granted, it may be fairly said, at their own request.

Lord John spoke of the corn in the haggards of Ireland. There was, I believe, much corn in some of them at the time he addressed his letter to the Duke of Leinster. Why did not the Government buy it, instead of sending to America and Malta for Indian corn and bad wheat? Had his lordship ascertained, before he wrote, how many of the stacks in Irish haggards *had the landlord's cross upon them for the rent*, like poor Mary Driscoll's little stack of barley at Skibbereen? *It stood in her haggard* while her father, who resided with her, died of starvation in a neighbouring ditch.[3]

About the middle of November, the Royal Agricultural Society again approached the Queen's representative in Ireland by memorial. It was not this time for leave to commence reproductive works — that had been already granted; they came now to prove that reproductive works could not be undertaken under the provisions of Mr Secretary Labouchere's letter. Their opinion was that, in the majority of cases, it was 'impossible' to carry out his Excellency's views in the manner required by the letter.[4]

The memorialists prayed that each proprietor, or combination of two or more proprietors, who might be willing to charge their proportion of the rate for employing the poor upon any particular land to be improved thereby, should be relieved to that extent from the payment of the rate and that the works so to be undertaken should not be confined to drainage or subsoiling, but might include all works of a productive nature, suited to the wants of the locality for which they were proposed, provided only that such works should meet the approbation of the Board of Works.

This carefully prepared memorial was met by a refusal, the reasons given for which do not seem very cogent; the real reason, in all probability, not having been directly given at all; the impossibility of supervising townland improvements, with such care as to avoid the malversation and misapplication of funds, having, it is reasonable to suppose, great influence on the decision of the Government.

The Lord Lieutenant added a caution. He expressed an earnest hope that they would, in their various relief committees, lend their aid to the Government in resisting a practice which, he had reason to fear, had very extensively prevailed — namely, that of allowing persons, who were by no means in a destitute condition, to be employed upon the public works, thus depriving the really distressed of the benefit which was intended for them, as well as withdrawing from the ordinary cultivation of the soil the labour which was essential to the future subsistence of the people.[5]

The latter part of the answer means just this: that the landlords were already turning the public works to their private gain, by getting numbers of their well-to-do tenants, often with their carts and horses, upon those works, in order to obtain their own rents more securely; a practice of which they were repeatedly accused by the Board of Works' people; and that, therefore, if townland boundaries were conceded, the landlords would have increased power and a still greater amount of the same kind of jobbing would be the inevitable result.

It is not surprising that at this period society in Ireland was shaken to its foundations. Terror and dismay pervaded every class; the starving poor suffered so intensely, and in such a variety of ways, that it becomes a hard task either to narrate or listen to the piteous story; it sickens and wrings the heart, whilst it fills the eyes with the testimony of irrepressible sorrow. To say the people were dying by the thousand of sheer starvation conveys no idea of their sufferings; the expression is too general to move our feelings. To think that even one human creature should, in a rich and a Christian land, die for want of a little bread, is a dreadful reflection; and yet, wrote an English traveller in Ireland, the thing was happening before his eyes every day, within a few hours of London, the Capital of the Empire, and the richest city in the world.

O'Brien's Bridge is a small town on the borders of Limerick but in the County Clare. The accounts received from this place during the first half of October were that nothing could restrain the people from rising *en masse* but an immediate supply of food. On one of the admission days, 130 persons were taken into the Scariff Workhouse, out of 6,000 applicants! Scariff is the union in which O'Brien's Bridge and Killaloe are situate.

Of Killaloe, the Rev. Dr Vaughan, afterwards Bishop of the Diocese, wrote, about the same time, that there was some promise of fifty or sixty being employed out of 600. The Relief Committee, of which he was a member, had to borrow money on the stones broken by the poor labourers for macadamising the roads, in order to pay them their wages. Being paid, they were dismissed, as the

Interior of a cabin hit by the famine.

Committee could not, in any way, get funds to employ them further.

'We are a pretty Relief Committee', exclaimed the reverend gentleman, 'not having a quart of meal, or the price of it, at our disposal.' He added, with somewhat of sorrow and vexation of spirit: 'When those starving creatures ask us for bread, we could give them stones, if they were not already mortgaged.'

Employment was not and, with the appliances in the hand of the Board of Works, perhaps, could not be given rapidly and extensively enough for the vast and instant wants of the people. Hunger is impatient and the cry of all men — loudest from the South and West — was one of despair, mingled with denunciations of the Government and the Board of Works for their slowness in providing work and, if possible, still more, for their refusal to open the food depots. 'I am sorry to tell you', wrote the correspondent of a local print, 'that this town (Tuam) is, I may say, in open rebellion. They are taking away cattle in the open day, in spite of people and police.... They cannot help it; even if they had money, they could not get bread to buy.'

Works were often marked out for a considerable time before they were commenced. At a place called Lackeen, in the South, they were in that state for three weeks or more, without any employment having been given. 'If this goes on', wrote a resident of the locality, 'there must be an increase of coroners and a decrease of civil engineers.' 'It is coffins', said another, 'must now be sent into the country. I lately gave three coffins to bury some of the poor in my neighbourhood.' This was bad enough; but a time was at hand when the poor had to bury their dead without coffins.

Three weeks had scarcely elapsed from the day on which the labourers engaged on the Caheragh road had shouldered their spades and picks and marched to Skibbereen, when an inquest upon one of them laid open a state of things that no general description could convey.

A man named Denis M'Kennedy was employed on those works. He was found dead on the side of the road one day and a coroner's inquest was held upon his remains in the historic graveyard in Abbeystrowry. The evidence will tell the rest.

Johanna M'Kennedy, the wife of the deceased, was the first witness examined. She said her husband died on Saturday, 24 October, and had been at work on the Caheragh road the day he died. He had been so engaged for about three weeks before his death. He did not complain of being sick. She explained to the coroner and the jury what they had had to support them during the week, on the Saturday of which her husband died.

Her family was five in number. She had nothing, she said, to give them on Monday; and then the poor woman varied her mode of expression by saying they had nothing at all to eat on Tuesday. On Wednesday night she boiled for her husband and her family one head of cabbage, given to her by a neighbour, and about a pint of flour, which she got for a basket of turf she had sold in Skibbereen. On Thursday morning her husband had nothing to eat. She did not account for Friday, but on Saturday morning she sent him for his breakfast less than a pint of flour baked.

Poor creature! She had but a pint for the whole family but, in her loving anxiety to sustain her husband, who was trying to earn for them, she only kept 'a little' for the children. 'The rest was sent to him', said Mrs M'Kennedy, through her choking grief, 'but it was too late; before it arrived he was dead.'

Thus, through the whole of that, to her, dreadful week, she had for her family of five persons about half a weight of potatoes,[6] small and bad, which were given to her by a kind neighbour, Mick Sweeney (God bless him, she said, for he often relieved us), two pints of flour and one head of cabbage.

It is no great marvel that the man who was trying to work on his share of such provision was dead on Saturday. In M'Kennedy we have a specimen of the people to whom the Board of Works insisted on giving task work. 'For the three weeks he was at work', said his wife at the inquest, 'he got two shillings and sixpence, being one week's pay.' There was a fortnight's wages due to him the day he died. 'Even if his hire was regularly paid', she added, 'it would not support the family; but it would enable us to drag on life, and he would be alive today.'

Jeremiah Donovan, the steward of the works at Caheragh, deposed that M'Kennedy was at work the morning of the day on which he died. On that morning he saw the deceased leave his work and go to the ditch-side; seeing him stop so long, he told him to return to his work. He did not return, but said to deponent, 'How can a man work without food? — a man that did not eat anything since yesterday morning.' Deponent then handed him a bit of bread. He took it in his hand and was putting it to his mouth when it fell from him. He died two or three hours after. His pay was eight pence a day.

The Rev. Mr Webb, incumbent of Caheragh, then volunteered a statement — hear it, ye rich, who have not that mercy and compassion for His poor, which the God of all so strictly requires at your hands — 'I have been told by some on the road', said the reverend gentleman, 'that this poor man had frequently divided amongst the labourers his own scanty food.'

There were two physicians at the inquest, of whom Dr Donovan was one; having made a post-mortem examination, no disease was discovered that could account for death. There was no food in the stomach or small intestines but a portion of raw, undigested cabbage. The physicians said they had seen hundreds of dead bodies but declared they had never seen one so attenuated as that of M'Kennedy.

The representative of the Board of Works, when asked to explain why it was that a fortnight's wages was due to M'Kennedy, said that the money was sent to the wrong pay-clerk. It had really come but, through some mistake, had been sent to Mr Notter and was by him expended in payment of his own district, when it should have been paid on the Caheragh line. 'But these stories', he added, 'received in gossip, are turned against the Board of Works.'

It is not very clear what this official meant by stories, but there is one thing plain enough in the matter: Mr Notter's men must have been in arrears of their pay as well as those on the Caheragh works, or there could be no opportunity of expending the Caheragh money upon them. If Mr Notter had got his own money together with the Caheragh money, he certainly would not require both remittances. There is another thing pretty obvious too: if the money had been directed to the overseer of the Caheragh works, Mr Notter would not be justified in paying it away to his workmen.

In reference to the flippant pertness of the Board's officials, the Rev. Mr Townsend, the incumbent of Abbeystrowry, said: 'We have here M'Kennedy's death and the cause of it sworn to. That evidence proves that our people are dying by the ditch-side for want of payment of their hire. We take no such statements, sir, on gossip, nor shall we be told we do.' The jury returned the following verdict: 'We find that the said Denis M'Kennedy, on 24 October, in the year aforesaid, at Caheragh, in the county aforesaid, died of starvation, owing to the gross negligence of the Board of Works.'

Turning over the public journals during this period is the saddest of sad duties. It is like picking one's way over a battle-field strewn with the dead and dying. 'Starvation and death in Dingle'; 'Deaths at Castlehaven'; 'Death of a labourer on his way to the Workhouse'; 'Four more deaths on the roads at Skibbereen'. Such are specimens of the ghastly headings that lie before us.

One of those deaths at Skibbereen calls for more than a passing word; it is that of Jeremiah Hegarty. As in M'Kennedy's case we have here what is seldom attainable, an account of the evidence given at the inquest upon his remains. He was a widower and

147

lived with his married daughter, Mary Driscoll, at Licknafon.
Driscoll, his son-in-law, was a small farmer. He had a little barley
in his haggard, some of which he was from time to time taking
privately out of the stack to keep himself and his family from
dying of starvation, although Curley Buckley, his landlord's
driver,[7] *had put a cross and keepers on it.*

Mary Driscoll, daughter of the deceased, being examined,
deposed that her father ate a little barley stirabout on Saturday
morning, but had not enough; 'None of us', she said, 'had
enough. We all lived together — nine in family, not including the
infant at my breast. My father went to work; my husband worked
with him; three pints of barley meal was the only thing we had
from Thursday before. I had no drink for the infant', she said;
by which, I suppose, the wretched being meant the nourishment
which nature supplies to infants whose mothers are not in a state
of starvation; 'It ate nothing. On Thursday we had nothing but
a quarter weight of *croshanes*.[8] We had but a little barley — about
a barrel and, God help us, we could not eat any more of that same,
as the landlord put a cross on it, I mean it was marked for the
rent.'

She here gave the name of the landlord, on being asked to do
so. He wanted, she said, to keep the barley for the last rent, £2
17s. She simply and frankly acknowledged they had been taking
some of it but their condition was such that it melted the heart
of the landlord's driver, Curley Buckley, who told them 'to be
taking a little of it until the landlord would come'.

The poor Driscolls were not bad tenants, they owed their
landlord *the last rent only* but they were responsible for another
debt. 'We owed', Mary Driscoll said, 'ten shillings for the seed
of the barley; we would sooner die, all of us, than not to pay.
Since a fortnight past', continued this wretched woman, in her
rude but expressive English, 'there was not one of us eat enough
any day.'

Driscoll, the husband of the last witness, was examined. He
said: 'If he [the deceased] was paid the wages due to him for
working on the road, it would have relieved him, and he might
be now alive; but', he added, 'even if we had received the money,
it would be hardly sufficient to keep us alive.' Referring to his
own case, he said he was but one day working on the road and
that he was six weeks looking for that same.

Dr Donovan had made a post mortem examination. He found
the stomach and upper part of the intestines totally devoid of
food. There was water in the stomach but nothing else. Want,
the doctor said, was the remote — exposure to the cold the
immediate — cause of death. The jury found that the deceased,

Jeremiah Hegarty, met his death in consequence of the want of sufficient sustenance for many days previous to his decease; and that this want of sustenance was occasioned by his not having been paid his wages on the Public Works, where he was employed for eight days previous to the time of his death.

Instead of providing employment for the tenants on their estates, which the Premier, and his commentator, the *Times*, looked upon as a mere ordinary duty, many Irish landlords began to evict for non-payment of rent. The parish priest of Swinford concluded a letter, detailing the sufferings of his people, thus: 'One word as to the landlords. There are several owners of land in this parish (Kilconduff), but not one of them resident. We made an effort to create by subscription a fund for the purpose of keeping a supply of provisions in Swinford, to be sold to the poor in small quantities. The non-resident landlords were applied to, but not one of them responded to the call. They are not, however, idle. Their bailiffs are on the alert, distraining for rent, and the pounds are full.'[9]

In County Sligo, thirty families were evicted together by one landlord; they must have been 150 individuals in all. They were somewhat in arrears. But in other cases the corn was distrained at the beginning of October for rent falling due the previous May. This, in the second year of the Famine, meant eviction, purely for the sake of clearing the soil of its human incumbrances.

As the year 1846 wore on to its close, the Famine deepened in intensity and every day extended itself more and more. The cold, which was very severe in December, became its powerful auxiliary. Wherever the blame is to rest — at headquarters in Dublin or with the clerks at the works — the irregularity with which wages were paid by the representatives of the Government caused terrible suffering and innumerable deaths. Many of those recorded at this period occurred from the taking of food by persons who had been without it for a long time. 'Carthy swallowed a little warm milk and died', is the simple announcement of one man's death from starvation; but, with slight variations, it might be given as the record of thousands of deaths as well as Carthy's.

The means of providing coffins for the victims of famine was becoming a serious question, as the survivors in many a poor family could not now attempt to purchase them, as the outlay of a small sum for a coffin might be the cause of further deaths from starvation in the same family.

At a meeting in Skibbereen, in the beginning of December, Dr Donovan said that, since his return from Glandore that morning, he had been followed by a crowd of applicants, seeking coffins for their deceased friends; and he had, he said, just visited a house in the Windmill,[10] where he saw two dead bodies lying, awaiting some means of burial. His opinion was that they were on the eve of a pestilence that would reach every class. 'And', said a gentleman, interrupting, 'when I asked a presentment for coffins at the session, I was laughed at.'

Dr Donovan continued: 'The case of a man named Sullivan was a most melancholy one. His children began to drop off without any apparent disease, after they had entered the Workhouse. From scarcity of beds, the father and son — the latter being sick and weakly — had to sleep together; and one morning the son was found dead alongside of his father, while another child died in the mother's arms next day. He [Dr Donovan] had asked Sullivan why he did not tell him his children were sick. His answer was, ''They had no complaint''.'

Mr D. McCarthy said it would be for the meeting to consider whether they should not pronounce their strong condemnation upon the conduct of an official in the town who, with starvation staring them in the face, would not give out a pound of food except at famine price, though he had stores crammed with it. 'He'd give you', said Mr Downing, 'for £17 a ton what cost our paternal Government £7 10s.'

Dr Donovan, writing to one of the provincial journals at this time, said: 'Want and misery are in every face; and the labourers returning from the relief works look like men walking in a funeral procession, so slow is their step and so dejected their appearance.'

The South and West were the portions of the country in which the Famine committed its earliest ravages; but before the close of 1846 considerable parts of Leinster and Ulster were invaded by it and deaths from starvation began to be recorded in those comparatively wealthy provinces.

In Maryborough, a man named William Fitzpatrick died of starvation at the beginning of December. He and his family were in a state of destitution for a considerable time. He tried to earn or obtain food for them but without success. At the inquest, his wife said that when she pressed him to eat such scanty food as they could occasionally procure, he often said to her, 'Eat it yourself and the children.' A kind neighbour, having heard how badly off this poor family was, gave an order for some bread; but, as occurred in so many cases, this act of Christian charity came too late. Fitzpatrick was unable to eat, and so he died.

At Enniskillen, a poor girl who had been sent for Indian meal fell down near her dwelling and expired. She had not gone out more than eight or nine minutes when she was discovered lifeless and clutching a small parcel of Indian meal tied up in a piece of cloth.

In parts of Ulster, the applications for employment on the Government works were very numerous; in one parish alone [Ballynascreen] there were 1600 such applications. In West Innishowen, within twelve miles of Londonderry, twelve people died of starvation in one week.

Thus had the great Famine seized upon the four provinces before the end of 1846; Munster and Connaught, however, enduring sufferings which, in their amount and terrible effects, were unknown to Leinster or Ulster. In the West, Mayo up to this time had suffered most, which, from its previously known state of destitution, was to be expected; in the South, Cork seems to have been the county most extensively and most fatally smitten. This, however, may not have been actually the case.

Clare and Kerry suffered greatly from the very beginning, but their sufferings were not brought so prominently before the public as those of Cork. This county had many and faithful chroniclers of her wants and afflictions — a fact especially true of Skibbereen. That devoted town and its neighbourhood were amongst the earliest, if not the very earliest, of the famine-scourged districts; and their story was well and feelingly told by special correspondents and, above all, by Dr Donovan, the principal local physician, whose duties placed him in the midst of the sufferers.

There can be no doubt that even at this comparatively early period of the famine, parts of Connaught, especially Mayo, suffered as much as Skibbereen, but the results were commonly told in briefer terms than in parts of the South. 'More deaths from starvation in Mayo'; 'Dreadful destitution in Mayo.' 'Coroners' inquests in Mayo'. Such were the headings of brief but suggestive paragraphs, during the latter part of November and all through December.

Many of the Mayo inquests may have been the occasion of more dreadful revelations than even those of Skibbereen, but they did not receive the same extensive and detailed publicity. Here are two or three starvation cases from that county. Patrick McLoughlin, in the parish of Islandeady, was ordered by the Relief Committee a labour-ticket, in consequence of earnest representations as to his starving condition. He did not get the ticket for five days, he, his wife and five children not having a morsel of food in the interval.

Having at length obtained the ticket, he produced it and went to labour on the Public Works. He got no pay for the first three days, and in the meantime his wife died from actual starvation. Being unable to purchase the timber for a coffin in which to bury her, poor McLoughlin held over the remains for upwards of forty-eight hours; but yet anxious to earn what would give her decent burial and at the same time procure food for his children, he went each of the two days her remains were in his cabin to labour and spent the night in sorrowing over his departed wife. At length the story came to the ears of the parochial clergy, one of whom immediately furnished the means of interment and she was consigned to the grave *at night,* in order that the survivors might not lose the benefit of McLoughlin's toil on the following day.[11]

Bridget Joyce, a widow with four children, was found dead in a little temporary building which had been erected in a field to shelter sheep. One of the children was grown enough to give some attention to her dying mother but had nothing to moisten her parched lips but a drop of water or a piece of snow. The woman died, and so poor were the people of the locality that for want of a few boards to make a coffin she remained uninterred for eight days.

There is a melancholy peculiarity in the case of a young lad named Edmond McHale. When he had been a considerable time without food, he became, or seemed to become delirious. As his death approached he said from time to time to his mother, 'Mother, give me three grains of corn.' The afflicted woman regarded this partly as the mental wandering of her raving child, and partly as a sign of the starvation of which he was dying. She tried to soothe him with such loving words as mothers only know how to use. '*Astore*', she would say, 'I have no corn yet awhile — wait till by-and-by'; 'Sure if I had all the corn in the world I'd give it to you, *avourneen*'; 'You'll soon have plenty with the help of God'.

A neighbouring woman who was present at the touching scene searched the poor boy's pockets after he had died, and found in one of them three grains of corn, no doubt the very three grains for which, in his delirium, he was calling. Many of the deaths which happened are too revolting and too horrible to relate; no one could travel any considerable distance in Mayo at this period without meeting the famine-stricken dead by the roadside.

Still it would be hard to surpass Skibbereen in the intensity and variety of its famine horrors. Dr Donovan, writing on 2 December, said: 'Take one day's experience of a dispensary doctor. It is that of a day no further off than last Saturday — four days ago.' He then proceeds with the diary of that day: his first case was that of Mrs Hegarty, who applied to him for a subscription towards burying her husband and child; the doctor had not prescribed for them, and he asked why he had not been applied to; the answer was as in other cases — they had no disease and he could be of no use to them.

His second case was that of a boy named Sullivan, who came to him for some ointment for his father. This application was somewhat out of the usual course, ointment being a peculiarly useless thing as a remedy against famine. There was, however, need of it. The boy's grandmother had died of fever some days before and his father and mother, with whom she had resided, took it from her.

The neighbours were afraid to go into the fever-house but some of them, kindly and charitably, left food outside the door and candles to wake the corpse. The mother struggled out of bed to get the candles in order to light them. She succeeded in doing so but from weakness she was unable to stand steadily, so she reeled and staggered towards where the corpse was laid out and with the lighted candles set the winding sheet on fire: the thatch caught the flame; the cabin was burned down and the parents of this miserable boy were rescued with the utmost difficulty. They got more or less burned, of course, and the ointment was therefore required for them. Having escaped death from fire, they almost suffered death from cold, as they were left four hours without the shelter of a roof on a bitter December day, all being afraid to admit them lest they should catch the contagion.

The doctor's third case happened at midnight, being called on duty to the Workhouse at that hour. It was about a mile from the town. Halfway on his journey he found a man trying to raise a poor woman out of the dyke. He went to his assistance and found the woman paralysed with cold and speechless. Locked in her arms, which were as rigid as bars of iron, was a dead child, whilst another with its tiny icy fingers was holding a death-grip of its mother's tattered garment. Her story was short and simple, which she was able to tell next day: she had made an effort to reach the Workhouse, but sank exhausted where she was discovered.

After a while the effects of famine began to manifest themselves in the sufferers by a swelling of the extremities. Perhaps the severe cold caused this or increased it. However that may be, experience soon taught the people that this puffy unnatural swelling was a sure sign of approaching dissolution.

When the cold weather had fairly set in, it frequently happened that the straw which composed the bed, or the excuse for a bed, occupied by members of a family dying of fever or hungry, or both combined, was, piecemeal, drawn from under them and burned on the hearth to keep up a scanty fire. It was felt, we may presume, that the dying could not require it long and those who had still some hopes of life were famishing as much from cold as from hunger.

An eye-witness, describing such a family in Windmill Lane, Skibbereen, one of whom had already died, thus wrote: 'The only article that covered the nakedness of the family, that screened them from the cold, was a piece of coarse packing stuff which lay extended alike over the bodies of the living and the corpse of the dead; which seemed as the only defence of the dying, and the winding sheet of the dead!'

The same writer said: 'In this town have I witnessed today, men — fathers, carrying perhaps their only child to its last home, its remains enclosed in a few deal boards patched together; I have seen them, on this day, in three or four instances, carrying those coffins under their arms or upon their shoulders, without a single individual in attendance upon them; without mourner or ceremony, without wailing or lamentation. The people in the street, the labourers congregated in town, regarded the spectacle without surprise; they looked on with indifference, because it was of hourly occurrence.[12]

The statements in the public journals about the effects of the famine in and about Skibbereen were so new and appalling that many people thought them greatly exaggerated. Finding this feeling to exist, and perhaps to some extent sharing in it, Mr Cummins, a magistrate of Cork, proceeded to Skibbereen to examine for himself the state of things there. He was not only convinced but horrified.

He published the result of his visit in a letter to the Duke of Wellington, in which he begged that exalted personage to call the Queen's attention to the fearful sufferings of her people. Convinced that he was destined, at least, to witness scenes of real hunger and starvation, Mr Cummins informed us that he took with him as much bread as five men could carry.

He began his inquiries at a place called South Reen, in the parish of Myross, near Skibbereen.[13] Being arrived at the spot, he was surprised to find the wretched hamlet apparently deserted. There was no external appearance of life — silence reigned around. On entering some of the cabins he soon discovered the cause. He was at once confronted with specimens of misery which, he said, no tongue or pen could give the slightest idea of.

In the first cabin he entered he found six famished, ghastly skeletons, to all appearance dead, huddled in a corner on a little filthy straw, their sole covering being what seemed a piece of ragged horsecloth; their miserable shrivelled limbs were hanging about as if they did not belong to their bodies. He approached them in breathless horror and found by a slow, whining moan

A soup kitchen run by the Society of Friends in Cork.

that they were alive — four children, a woman and what had once been a man — all in fever. Mr Cummins met other cases as fearful, more especially one similar to that described by the writer quoted above, where a corpse was lying amongst the surviving members of the family, sharing their straw bed and their scanty covering. At a meeting of the Killarney Relief Committee, the Earl of Kenmare being in the chair, the parish priest, the Rev. B. O'Connor, made a statement which, except as an illustration of the unprecedented misery to which the people had sunk, I would hesitate to reproduce. He said: 'A man employed on the public works became sick. His wife had an infant at her breast. His son, who was fifteen years of age, was put in his place upon the works. The infant at the mother's breast', said the reverend gentleman, amid the sensation of the meeting, 'had to be removed, in order that this boy might receive sustenance from his mother, to enable him to remain at work.'

Another poor woman, the mother of eight children, when dying of want, was attended by the Rev. Mr O'Connor. She made her last request to him in these words: 'O Father O'Connor, won't you interfere to have my husband get work, before the children die?

'In December 1846, matters seemed to have come to a climax, and on Christmas Eve I witnessed a scene which scarcely admits of description. On that day a board was held at the Workhouse, for the admittance of paupers. The claims of the applicants were, in many cases, inquired into, but after some time the applicants became so numerous that any attempt to investigate the different cases was quite useless and an order was then given by the members of the Board present, to admit all paupers and at least to give them shelter, as but little food was to be had. I shall never forget the scene which I that night witnessed: mothers striving, by the heat of their own persons, to preserve the lives of their little ones; women stretching out their fleshless arms, imploring for food and shelter; old men tottering to the destination where they were to receive shelter. The odour from the clothes and persons of those poor people was dreadfully offensive and the absence of active complaints clearly showed that in many the hope of restoration was not to be accepted. On my visiting this scene next morning, eleven human beings were dead.'[14]

Some twenty years after the famine-scourge had passed away, and over two million of the Irish people with it, I visited Skibbereen. Approaching the town from the Cork side, it looks rather an important place. It is the seat of the Catholic bishop of Ross and attention is immediately arrested by a group of fine ecclesiastical buildings, on an elevated plateau to the left, just beside the road, or street, I should rather say, for those buildings are the beginning of the town; they consist of a cathedral and a convent, with very commodious schools and a pretty Gothic chapel.

On the other side of the way is the schoolhouse, in the shade of which the military were concealed on the day the Caheragh labourers invaded Skibbereen.

The town of Skibbereen consists chiefly of one long main street, like a horse-shoe, or rather a boomerang, in shape. One of its sections, Bridge Street, leads directly to the suburb known as Bridgetown, in which the poorest inhabitants resided and where the famine revelled — hideous, appalling and triumphant.

Bridgetown is changed now. In 1846 it contained a large population, being not much less than half a mile in length, with a row of thatched houses on each side; when the Famine slaughtered the population, those houses were left tenantless in great numbers and, there being none to reoccupy them, they fell into ruins and were never rebuilt. Hence, instead of a continuous line of dwellings at either side, as of old, Bridgetown now presents only detached blocks of three or four or half-a-dozen cabins here and there.

Coming towards the end of it, by a gradual ascent, I accosted a man who was standing at the door of his humble dwelling: 'I suppose you are old enough', I said to him, 'to remember the great Famine?' 'Oh! indeed I am, sir', he replied, with an expressive shake of his head. 'Were there more people in Bridgetown and Skibbereen at that time than now?' 'Ay, indeed', he replied, 'I suppose more than twice as many.' 'And where did they all live — I see no houses where they could have lived?' 'God bless you, sure Bridgetown was twice as big that time as it is now; the half of it was knocked or fell down, when there were no people to live in the houses. Besides, great numbers lived out in the country, all round about here. 'Come here', he said earnestly; and we ascended the road a little space. 'Do you see all that country, sir?' and he pointed towards the north and west of the town. 'It was all belonging to farmers and it was full of farmers' houses before the famine; now you see there are only a couple of gentlemen's places on the whole of it. The poor all died, and of course their houses were thrown down.'

'And where were they all buried', I enquired. 'Well, sir', he replied, 'some of them were buried in the old chapel yard, near the windmill; a power of them were buried in Abbeystrowry, just out there a bit, where you are going to, but', he suddenly added, as if correcting himself, 'sure they were buried everywhere — at the Workhouse over — in the cabins where they died —

157

everywhere; there was no way, you see, to bring them all to Abbeystrowry, but still there were a power of them, sure enough, brought to it.'

My informant was quite right about my going to Abbeystrowry. The churchyard of Abbeystrowry was the spot in which a generation of the people of Skibbereen was buried in a year and a half! Immediately inside the gate, a little to the right, are those monster graves called by the people 'the pits', into which the dead were thrown coffinless in hundreds, without mourning or ceremony, hurried away by stealth, frequently at the dead of night, to elude observation and to enable the survivors to attend the public works next day and thus prolong for awhile their unequal contest with the all-conquering famine.

A difficulty arose in my mind with regard to the manner of interment in those pits. Great numbers, I knew, were interred in each of them; for which reason they must have been kept open a considerable time. Yet, surely, I reflected, something resembling interment must have taken place on the arrival of each corpse, especially as it was coffinless. The contrivance, as I afterwards learned, was simple enough. A little sawdust was sprinkled over each corpse, on being laid in the pit, which was thus kept open until it had received its full complement of tenants.

To trace one's steps, slowly and respectfully, among the graves of those who have reached the goal of life in the ordinary course, fills one with holy warnings; to stand beside the monument raised on the battle-field to the brave men who fell there, calls up heroic echoes in the heart, but here there is no room for sentiment; here, in humiliation and sorrow, not unmixed with indignation, one is driven to exclaim:

O God! that bread should be so dear,
And human flesh so cheap.

Although thus cast down by earthly feelings, divine faith raises one up again. Divine faith! The noblest and brightest, and holiest gift of God to man; always teaching us to look heavenward — *Excelsior* in its theme for ever. And who can doubt but the God of all consolation and mercy received the souls of his famine-slain poor into that kingdom of glory where he dwells and which he had purchased for them at so great a price. Even in their imperfections and sins, they were like to him in many ways; they were poor, they were despised, they had nowhere to lay their head; they were long-suffering, too; in the deepest pangs which they had suffered from hunger and burning thirst (the last and most terrible effect of hunger), they cursed not, they reviled not; they only yearned for the consolations of their holy religion, and looked hopefully to him for a better world.

It is one of the sweetest consolations taught us by holy faith that the bones now withered and nameless in those famine pits, where they were laid in their shroudless misery, shall one day, touched by his almighty power, be reunited to those happy souls, in a union that can know no end, and can feel no sorrow.

10

Committees and resolutions

About the middle of December, there was formed in Dublin a committee of landlords which assumed the name of the Reproductive Works Committee. Its objects were excellent. It was to be the beginning of a real Irish party, whose members were to lay aside their differences, political and religious, that, by a united effort, they might carry the country through the death-struggle in which it then was, and lay the foundation of its future progress to prosperity.

Many of the best men in the whole nation were active promoters of this movement; but, viewed as a whole, it was little more than the embodied expression of the fears of the landlords that they would be swamped by the rates levied to feed the people, and of their hopes that, by uniting for the occasion with the popular leaders, they would be able to compel the Government so to shape its course that, at any rate, they would come forth safe from the ordeal. Neither the Committee, nor the landlords who met in Dublin at their call, intended to form a permanent Irish party; in fact, it could not be done in the sense indicated by them.

The Committee instructed their secretaries to call a meeting of the peers, Members of Parliament and landed proprietors of Ireland, in the Rotunda, on 14 January, for the consideration of the social condition of the country, all political and extraneous topics to be strictly excluded. They published at the same time the resolutions they proposed submitting to the meeting, one series of which referred to temporary measures which, in the opinion of the Committee, were necessary for the immediate wants of the country; another suggested those required for her future prosperity.

The great meeting of Irish peers, Members of Parliament and landlords, as it was called, was held in the Rotunda on the above day. The attendance on the occasion was large and the meeting was what might be termed a great success. Tickets of admission were issued to fourteen peers, twenty-six Members of Parliament and about 600 provinces. So great, however, was the influx of country gentlemen who were anxious to take a part in the proceedings that it became necessary to issue a further supply of tickets in the forenoon of that day, notwithstanding which a considerable number were sold at the entrance door.

Every phase of Irish politics was represented at the meeting. Amongst the peers were the Marquis of Ormond, the Earl of Erne, Lord Cloncurry and Lord Farnham; the MPs reckoned, amongst others, O'Connell, Frederick Shaw, William Smith O'Brien, Anthony Lefroy, John O'Connell and Edward Grogan. The Marquis of Ormond was chairman.

The resolutions prepared by the Reproductive Works Committee were proposed and unanimously adopted. They had, the chairman said, been considered by a committee composed of gentlemen of all shades or parties. Great differences occurred upon almost every word of every resolution. However, personal opinions had been sacrificed with a view of having perfect unanimity at the present meeting — a meeting, as he truly said, of peculiar construction — perhaps the only one of the kind ever assembled in the Rotunda before.

The resolutions went very fully into the state of the country, its evils and their remedies. They contained much that was wise and well intended and some of the measures suggested in them would be found in the programme of the Government or, as their plan was called by their friends, the 'group of measures', by which the present and future of Ireland were to be settled to the satisfaction and advantage of all parties.

One thing the landlords who met in the Round-room had evidently set their hearts on — there was to be an extensive emigration, the land was to be cleared. If half the improvements suggested in the resolutions were undertaken, instead of a surplus population, labour enough could not be had for the purpose of carrying them out: if piers and harbours were taken in hand, and if the earthworks of the projected railways were commenced, and if the reclamation of the waste lands were seriously taken up, the labour wasted on the barren road-making would be found insufficient for such gigantic undertakings: but the piers were not built; the harbours were not deepened or improved; the waste lands were not reclaimed; the railway earthworks were left to private enterprise but *Emigration* — Oh! that darling object was always in favour with the ruling class, and most effectively promoted by wholesale eviction.

The people were sent to benefit the colonies, as the fourteenth resolution suggested, by their labour; sent 'to increase the supply of food throughout the world (except in Ireland), to bring fresh land under cultivation', and above all to 'largely extend the

161

market for home manufacture'. Yes, that last was a happy hit to secure the willing ear of the 'mother country'; as for the poor 'sister island', from which all those people were to emigrate, she had no manufactures to open a market for.

But the Rotunda people would send away another class too. The last clause of the twelfth resolution read thus: 'That as there must be a large amount of population dependent for subsistence, during the year, upon public or private charity, provision should be made for assisting those to emigrate, with their families, who cannot be supported in this country by the exercise of independent labour'!

This is no slip of the pen. Almost every word of every resolution, the noble chairman said, was carefully discussed. The suggestion, then, is that those who are *unable to work*, from age, weak health or who, having got chronic coughs, asthma or rheumatism, by working for 6d. or 8d. a day, 'wet and dry', on the land that gave them birth and are now unfit to work any longer; or, in rosewater phrase, 'who cannot be supported in this country by the exercise of independent labour', are to be 'shot', like so much rubbish, upon the shores of the western hemisphere provided the crazy barques into which they are to be huddled do not go down with them bodily in the middle of the Atlantic.

Surely, of all other people, such were unfit for emigration, being unfit to earn their bread; but they were a burden, a real burden on the soil here and, so that the clearance took place, the manner of it and its results to the exiled were held to be a small account indeed.

Parliament was opened by the Queen in person, on Tuesday, 19 January. She read the speech from the throne, about two-thirds of which related to Ireland exclusively. No wonder. The state of that country had become the theme of public writers, politicians and philanthropists in both hemispheres. England was on her trial before the civilised world. Could not she, the richest nation of the earth, whose capitalists searched the globe for undertakings in which to invest their vast and ever accumulating wealth — could not she — or would not she — save the lives of those starving Irish, who were her subjects, and who, if not loved by her like others of her subjects, were at least useful in giving size and importance to the empire, and in fighting those battles which helped her to keep her place among first-class nations; useful in opening up, with the bayonet's point, those foreign markets so essential to her iron and cotton lords — nay, to all her lords? England was on her trial; England's Government was on its trial; and the Queen's speech was to shadow forth their line of defence for past legislation and to indicate those future measures which were to stay the famine and prevent its recurrence.

Here is the portion of the speech relating to Ireland: 'It is with the deepest concern that, upon your again assembling, I have to call your attention to the dearth of provisions which prevails in Ireland, and in parts of Scotland.

'In Ireland, especially, the loss of the usual food of the people has been the cause of severe sufferings, of disease, and of greatly increased mortality among the poorer classes. Outrages have become more frequent, chiefly directed against property, and the transit of provisions has been rendered unsafe in some parts of the country.

'With a view to mitigate these evils, very large numbers of men have been employed, and have received wages, in pursuance of an Act passed in the last session of Parliament. Some deviations from the Act, which have been authorized by the Lord Lieutenant of Ireland, in order to promote more useful employment, will, I trust, receive your sanction. Means have been taken to lessen the pressure of want, in districts which are most remote from the ordinary sources of supply. Outrages have been repressed, as far as it was possible, by the military and police.

'It is satisfactory to me to observe, that in many of the most distressed districts, the patience and resignation of the people have been most exemplary.

'The deficiency of the harvest in France and Germany, and other parts of Europe, has added to the difficulty of obtaining adequate supplies of provisions.

'It will be your duty to consider what further measures are required to alleviate the existing distress. I recommend to you to take into your serious consideration whether, by increasing, for a limited period, the facilities for importing from foreign countries, and by the admission of sugar more freely into breweries and distilleries, the supply of food may be beneficially augumented.

'I have also to direct your earnest attention to the permanent consideration of Ireland. You will perceive, by the absence of political excitement, an opportunity for taking a dispassionate survey of the social evils which afflict that part of the United Kingdom. Various measures will be laid before you, which, if adopted by Parliament, may tend to raise the great mass of the people in comfort, to promote agriculture, and to lessen the pressure of that competition for the occupation of land, which has been the fruitful source of crime and misery.'

In the House of Commons, one of the earliest speakers on the address was Smith O'Brien. He said he was asked, by assenting to the address, if he was prepared to say that the Government had been altogether guiltless of having produced that frightful state of things; and if he were called upon to affirm, that everything had been done by the Government, which might have been done by them, he would answer, that *he believed it was in their power, to prevent one single individual from dying of starvation in Ireland.* He did not impute to them the wilful intention of bringing about a state of things so disastrous, but it was his opinion, and the opinion of others in Ireland, that they had not introduced those measures which were suitable to the condition in which Ireland was placed, and had thus brought about the state of things which was now witnessed.

To the declaration of the Prime Minister, last session, that there was to be no legislative interference with the price of food, he believed they owed many of the disasters which had taken place in Ireland, he said. This sentiment was received with cheers.

Smith O'Brien made a point in favour of the Irish landlords; saying it was most unreasonable that the Irish landlords should be called upon to bear the whole expense of the Famine. But it is equally true that, as a body, they made no effort worth the name to stay or mitigate the Famine until it had knocked at their own hall doors in the shape of rates, present and prospective, that threatened them with the confiscation of their properties.

Mr Labouchere, the Irish Chief Secretary, as was to be expected, was put up to defend the Government and to foreshadow the future measures of relief. His line of defence was a strange one for an English minister to adopt. It was that the agricultural population of Ireland, vast in its numbers, was always on the brink of starvation; so that when the potato blight swept the country from sea to sea, it was impossible for the Government to meet the disaster fully.

An English journal of high repute,[1] whose words have been already quoted in these pages, truly said that for 500 years Ireland had been completely in the hands of England, to mould and fashion her as she pleased; and now at the end of those five centuries, a British statesman did not blush to urge, as an argument in favour of the Government of which he was a member, that the normal state of Ireland was to be on the brink of starvation.

This defence, weak and inconclusive from every point of view, served his colleagues and himself, of course, but little, while it was calculated to cover his nation with shame and confusion. He went on to prove the fact, alas! too easily proved; he went to Lord Devon's Commission and told us from it that it was no exaggeration to say that the people of Ireland were the worst housed, the worst clothed, and the worst fed of any people in Europe.

'It is a country', said the Secretary, 'of which I find an account given from a most unexceptionable source, the Commission of Poor Law Enquiry in 1835. From this Report it appeared that Ireland then contained 1,131,000 agricultural labourers, whose average earnings did not exceed from two shillings to two shillings and six pence a week; and that of these one-half were destitute during thirty weeks of every year. This is the ordinary condition of Ireland, and it is upon such a country as this that the calamity has fallen — a calamity which I believe to be without a parallel in modern times.'

Such was the defence of the Irish Chief Secretary. And here it is worth while remarking that in the earlier stages of the Famine it was the practice of the government organs to throw doubt on the extent of its ravages which were published, and the Government, apparently acting on these views, most culpably delayed the measures by which the visitation could be successfully combated. *Now* their part was to admit to the fullest extent the vastness of the Famine, and make it the excuse for their want of energy and success in overcoming it.

On the same principle, Mr Labouchere, relying on figures supplied by Mr Griffith, went into what appeared to be a fair statement of the actual money value of the loss Ireland suffered from the potato blight. The money value of the potatoes destroyed by the Blight of 1846, he estimated at £11,250,000: the loss of the oat crop of that year he calculated to be £4,666,000, making the whole loss in oats and potatoes £15,916,000.

Still this sum, he said, was under the actual loss; the money value of the loss not at all representing the real loss to the people; and the House, he added, would form a very inadequate notion of the nature and extent of the loss which had befallen Ireland, if they merely considered the money value of the crop which had failed or the stock of human food which had been supplied.

The chronic poverty and misery of Ireland, as set forth in the Report which the Poor Law Commissioners published in 1835, seemed to have been the favourite armoury whence Mr Labouchere loved to draw his logical weapons, for the defence of the Government on this occasion. In that Report he found it stated that 'Mayo alone would furnish beggars to all England'.[2]

Be it remembered that the Poor Law Commissioners had published their Report eleven years before Mr Labouchere made his speech but he did not inform us what measures the British Government had in the meantime adopted, or if they had adopted any, to raise the people out of such a state of misery and degradation; but he clearly thought he had brought forward a clever argument in his own and his colleagues' defence, when he stated that one of the thirty-two counties of Ireland had such abundant and redundant pauperism. Yet this was in the 'sister country' — the sister of that great and wealthy and enlightened England of which, no doubt, the Irish Secretary felt proud to be a native.

Lord George Bentinck read a letter from the Rev. Mr Townsend, of Skibbereen, in which it was stated that in one month, from 1 December to 1 January, there were 140 deaths in the Workhouse of that town; the people having entered the Workhouse, as they said, 'that they might be able to die decently under a roof and be sure of a coffin.' The Rev. Mr Townsend also mentioned that in the churchyard of his parish there were, at one time, fourteen funerals waiting whilst the burial of a fifteenth corpse was being completed. In the next parish to his there were nine funerals at once in the churchyard and in two other adjoining ones there were six together in each.

To prove his assertion that the Government should have done more in supplying food to the people, his lordship said: 'At this moment, we know that there are between 300,000 and 400,000 quarters of corn in stock on hand in the different ports of London, Liverpool and Glasgow. I want to know, then, what was to have prevented ministers from sending any part or all of this food to the West of Ireland, to feed the starving people there? ... It would have kept the retailers and forestallers in order and prevented them from availing themselves of the Famine to obtain undue prices. What do we see with regard to Indian meal? Why Indian corn is, at this moment, selling in New York at three shillings and at Liverpool and in Ireland at nine shillings per bushel.'

The Prime Minister spoke towards the close of the debate. The reason he gave for not having summoned Parliament in the Autumn, as O'Connell and many others had suggested, or rather demanded, was a striking proof of the evils of absenteeism. 'We had to consider', he said, 'that if we did meet in Parliament we should be acting against the opinion of the Irish Government and against the opinion of almost every one I saw who was connected with Ireland, who thought that to take away at that time — at the commencement of the severe pressure — every person connected by property with Ireland, would inflict a very great injury upon that country and that, consequently, Parliament should not be called together at that time'

If it could be looked upon as a great injury to Ireland to have the comparatively few proprietors who are resident there absent for even one short month, doing important business for Ireland, how terrible the evil must be of having the owners of £4,000,000 of her rental continually absent and to have her representatives in both Houses of Parliament absent, not merely for a month, but for about seven months out of every twelve!

The First Minister made no unnecessary delay in bringing the state of Ireland formally before Parliament. On 25 January, six days after the opening of the session, he rose in a full house; expressed his sense of the great responsibility under which he laboured, and claimed its indulgence whilst he endeavoured to explain what had been already done to counteract the disastrous results of the potato blight in Ireland; to call their attention to those measures which the Government considered necessary to meet the existing emergency and, finally, to submit to its consideration other measures which, in the opinion of her Majesty's advisers, were calculated to improve the general condition of that country, and lay the foundation of its permanent improvement.

He then proceeded to develop a somewhat pretentious programme.

Through all the Famine time, there is nothing more remarkable than the manner in which the expounders of the views of Government, as well as many others, managed, when it suited them, to confound two things which should have been kept most jealously distinct — 1. What was best for the Famine crisis itself; 2. What was best for the permanent improvement of the country. The confounding of these two questions led to conclusions of the most unwarrantable and deceptive kind. In the present instance, the Prime Minister himself seemed to fall into the same mistake; or he went into it with his eyes open, that he might be able to draw conclusions to suit his purpose. The proposition laid down by him was by no means unreasonable in itself; in fact it might be accepted as true: the fallacy was, that he kept out of sight the peculiar circumstances of the case, and put his proposition stripped of those circumstances, which should greatly modify it, when applied to Ireland, as she then was.

The simple question: 'Was it better to employ the labour of the country on productive rather than on non-productive works during the Famine?' became involved and obscured by the enunciation of principles which applied only to an ordinary state of society. It is an amusing commentary on the line of argument adopted by the First Minister, that he concluded this speech with two distinct sets of measures for Ireland, one temporary, to meet the Famine, and another permanent.

The first great means he proposed for arresting the progress of the Famine was to establish soup-kitchens and to give the people food without any labour test whatever. Was the townsland boundary system, which he had just condemned, half so demoralising to the labourer as this? Certainly not; but this had the excuse that there was now no time for anything but the immediate supply of food: exactly so; but, when there was time, it was wasted in needless delay and misused in barren discussions about questions of political economy, and the probable extent of the Famine, when its real extent was already well known.

He then laid his new scheme before the House:

1. His first proposal was to form the country into districts, with a relief committee in each, empowered to receive subscriptions, levy rates and receive donations from the Government. By these means the committees were to purchase food and establish soup-kitchens in the different districts, where food was to be distributed without any labour test; the labourer, however, was to be allowed to work on his own plot of ground, for the next harvest.

2. As soon as circumstances would permit, by an easy transition and without disturbing existing arrangements, no further presentments would be made and no new public works undertaken.

Lord John next proposed a loan of £50,000 for one year, to enable landed proprietors to furnish seed for land. The loan was not to be made to the small tenants themselves, which he considered would be disadvantageous, but to the proprietors, which course he thought would be safe and beneficial.

The Premier next proceeded to lay before the House other measures which the Government considered would be of permanent as well as immediate benefit to Ireland. These measures were three in number:

1. An improved drainage act

2. An act for the reclamation of waste lands

3. A system of outdoor relief, at the discretion of the guardians of the poor.

During the delivery of the speech here summarised, Lord John Russell was frequently interrupted with an amount of applause very unusual in the House of Commons, and at its close he is reported to have sat down amidst vociferous and continued cheering.

And no wonder, for never did an English Minister touch the grievances of Ireland with a bolder or truer hand than he did on

The village of Moveen in west Clare — roofless houses, deserted hearths.

this occasion; but amongst his proposals, that which was of the greatest value, the reclamation of the waste lands, was abandoned — in fact, was never brought forward.

May we not well ask: why were not the permanent measures, now proposed, thought of long before, and passed into laws? Statesmen appear to have understood them well enough: why then did it require a famine to have them brought officially before Parliament? Because it seemed to be the rule with successive Governments to do nothing for Ireland until they were forced to it by agitation, rebellion, famine or some abnormal state of things, which would not be passed over or resisted.

Here we have a plan sketched for the reclamation of the waste lands of Ireland which, if in operation for twenty years before, would have gone far to make the famine transient and partial, instead of general and overwhelming, as it was. Still the plan was very welcome when it came, as it offered the prospect of great future prosperity for this country; everybody felt this, and hence it was hailed with the most unusual marks of approbation by the House of Commons.

But, the turning point of the famine crisis over, one of the most valuable measures ever proposed for the benefit of Ireland was shamefully abandoned. One is inclined to suspect that the Government never really intended to carry the measure — it was good, too much to the advantage of the people, too great a boon to this country. Mr Labouchere, as Irish Secretary, had charge of it; he never seemed in any hurry to bring it forward, and after a notice or two, followed by postponements, it ceased to be heard of.

After further considerable discussion and many modifications, 'The Poor Relief (Ireland) Bill', granting outdoor relief and establishing soup kitchens, became law on 16 April. The name of William Henry Gregory, then member for the City of Dublin, and afterwards for the County of Galway, must remain for ever associated with this measure, on account of two clauses which he succeeded in having incorporated with it. The first was to this effect: that any tenant, rated at a net value not exceeding £5 and who would give up to his landlord the possession of his land, should be assisted to emigrate by the Guardians of his Union, the landlord to forego any claim for rent, and to provide two-thirds of such fair and reasonable sum as might be necessary for the emigration of such occupier and his family; the Guardians being empowered to pay to the emigrating family any sum not exceeding half what the landlord should give, the same to be levied off the rates. This clause, although not devoid of redeeming features, was proposed and carried in the interest of the landlord-clearing-system, yet it was agreed to without what could be called even a show of opposition.

It was, however, on the second clause — the renowned quarter-acre clause — that Mr Gregory's enduring fame, as an Irish legislator, may be said to rest.

By this clause the head of a family who happened to hold a single foot of ground over one rood was put outside the pale of relief, with his whole family. A more complete engine for the slaughter and expatriation of a people was never designed. The previous clause offered facilities for emigrating to those who would give up their land — the quarter-acre clause compelled them to give it up or die of hunger.

In the fullness of his generosity Mr Gregory had, he said, originally intended to insert 'half an acre' in the clause but, like many well-intentioned men, he was overruled; he had, he said, been lately in Ireland and people there who had more knowledge of the subject than he could lay claim to, told him half an acre was *too extensive*, so he made it a quarter of an acre. It is not hard to conjecture who his advisers were on this occasion.

Mr Gregory, in defence of his clause, used these words: 'Many honourable members insisted that the operation of a clause of this kind would destroy all the small farmers. If it could have such an effect, he did not see of what use such small farmers could possibly be'; because, I suppose, they could not survive a famine that threatened the lords of the soil with bankruptcy or extinction, as they were constantly proclaiming. Mr Gregory's words — the words of a liberal, and a pretended friend of the people — and Mr Gregory's clause are things that should be for ever remembered by the descendants of the slaughtered and expatriated small farmers of Ireland.

On a division, there were 119 for the clause and nine against it. Here are the nine who opposed the never-to-be-forgotten quarter-acre Gregory clause: William Sharman Crawford, B. Escott, Sir De Lacy Evans, Alderman Humphrey, A. McCarthy, G.P. Scrope, W. Williams. Tellers: William Smith O'Brien and J. Curteis.

11

The railway scheme

No effort of statesmanship to overcome the Famine is remembered with such gratitude in Ireland as Lord George Bentinck's generous proposal to spend £16,000,000 in the construction of railways, for the employment of its people.

In the autumn of 1846, when the Potato Blight had become an accepted fact by all except those who had some motive for discrediting it, he began to think that to finish the railways, already projected in Ireland, would be the best and promptest way of employing its people upon reproductive works. He was a great enemy to unprofitable labour. To the Labour-rate Act, which became law at the close of the session of 1846, Lord George was conscientiously opposed; because, whilst millions were to be spent under it, the labour of the people was to be thrown away upon profitless or pernicious undertakings.

His was an eminently practical mind and, being so, he did not rest satisfied with reflections and speculations upon the plan he had conceived. He took counsel with men who were the most eminent, both for scientific and practical knowledge, with regard to the construction of railways. Among them, of course, was Robert Stephenson. The result of his conference with those gentlemen was that two engineers of acknowledged ability were despatched by him to Ireland, to examine and report upon the whole question of Irish railways.

Many years before, in 1836, a commission had been issued to enquire into the expediency of promoting the construction of railways in Ireland. The Commissioners, in their report, recommended that a system of railway communication should be established there by Government advances. Ten years had passed; but, of course, nothing was done. Yes, another commission! The noted Devon one was, I should have said, issued some years after the former by another Government, which confirmed all the recommendations of the Railway Commissioners of 1836, and pointed to those new methods of communication, by the assistance of loans from the Government, as the best means of providing employment for the people.[1]

Had the recommendations of those Commissioners been carried out or even begun within a reasonable time there could have been no Irish famine in the sense in which we are now obliged to chronicle it. There must have been extensive employment at wages that would have afforded great numbers other and better food than the potato. As it was, all that resulted from those commissions and countless others of the like kind were the ponderous Blue Books, which contained their reports and the evidence upon which they were founded. And, indeed, so many tons of those had been, from time to time, produced and stowed away in Government vaults and rubbish stores that, had they contained some of the nutritive qualities which go to sustain human life, they would have been an appreciable contribution towards feeding the starving Irish people during the Famine.

No new Acts were necessary to be passed through Parliament to authorise the construction of railways in Ireland, in order to justify the Government in advancing the necessary funds. When Lord George Bentinck brought his plan before the House of Commons, there were Acts in existence authorising the construction of more than 1,500 miles of railway in this country, some of those Acts having been passed so far back as eleven years before; yet, at the close of 1846, only 123 miles had been completed.

Here, then, was the field in which Lord George had made up his mind that the superabounding but wasted labour of the famishing people should find profitable employment. After taking the advice of his political friends and securing their approval and support, he, on Thursday, 4 February, introduced his Bill to the House of Commons.

The Government had made up their mind, however, to oppose Lord George Bentinck's bill. But seeing that he had a large following and that the Irish members, and many independent English members too, would support him, they had recourse to the stale trick of weak governments — the threat of resignation.

The affairs of the country were at the moment in a most critical position and every hour's delay in sending relief to Ireland would add hundreds to the deaths from starvation. The confusion which would be caused by resignation would inflict serious injury on the country that Lord George Bentinck was so anxious to serve: Lord John knew this well and, therefore, he knew his threat of resignation had a certain coercive power in it.

Moreover, the Tory party was split in two; Lord George was at the head of the Protectionists, who had deserted Peel, or rather, who had been deserted by him; Sir Robert had still many adherents, but a fusion of the two sections of the party was, at the moment, next to impossible, so that there could be no Tory Government framed to succeed Lord John Russell's. What Bernal Osborne prophesied at the time would in all likelihood have happened, that if the noble lord went out by one door he would come in by another.

Many thought the risk of breaking up the Government too great, considering the state of Ireland; and many Irish liberal members were but too glad of an excuse to keep it in office. If we assume that no action of the Irish representatives would affect any votes but the votes of those returned by Irish constituencies, the division shows that it was beyond their power to secure a majority for the second reading; but it is not unreasonable to suppose that had the Irish members maintained a united and determined opinion in favour of the Bill, English members would see the wisdom and necessity of yielding to them.

On the day fixed for the second reading of the Bill, the Premier called a meeting of his party at his private residence. Nearly 200 obeyed the summons. He spoke, on the occasion, against the Irish railway scheme; but his arguments were devoid of force and solidity. He said the money could not be raised, which nobody believed. He said it was generally admitted that only twenty-five per cent of the money spent in the construction of railways went for labour; an assertion for which neither he nor the Chancellor of the Exchequer gave any authority, and which Mr Hudson triumphantly refuted in his speech on the Bill next day. But Lord John further said that he was resolved to meet the second reading with a direct negative, and that he would resign if the Government were out-voted; an announcement which, although it lacked argument, had force and meaning in it.

Several of those present at the meeting expressed their views for and against the Bill. The Irish members, especially the Liberal members, felt they were in a dilemma. They knew Lord George's proposal was popular in Ireland — regarded, in fact, as a great boon. They did not at all desire the resignation of the Government, from which they had received many favours and expected many more. What was to be done? They hit upon a plan, which they considered would lift them out of their dilemma: they resolved to ask Lord George to postpone the second reading of his Bill, for a time, by which arrangement the Premier would not be bound to carry out his threat of resignation; and Ireland eventually might have the benefit of the railway scheme proposed by the Protectionist leader.

There was no postponement: the second reading was proceeded with that evening as originally intended. When it came on, Smith O'Brien, who was probably appointed by the Irish party for the purpose, immediately rose and appealed to the noble lord to postpone the second reading, saying (as the resolution had said) that the constituents of the Irish members had not had time to express their opinions on the Bill — a most delusive plea, as if the Irish people would at such a moment, or at any time, object to the outlay of £16,000,000 on the improvement of their country. Besides, they were known to be favourable to the Bill.

Mr O'Brien gave the true reason when he asked Lord George to postpone the second reading because the Government had staked their existence upon it. A change of ministry, he truly said, would throw into confusion legislation which was of pressing necessity for Ireland. He tendered his support to the noble lord but he was anxious to consider the question apart from a change of ministry; and he knew that many members, like himself, wished for a postponement, at least for a few days.

The following passage of a speech, delivered at a public meeting some years afterwards, lets in the light upon the motives which actuated many of the Irish members in their conduct with regard to this famous measure: 'I went into a certain room in London', said the speaker, 'where some thirty Irish members sat in conclave, after the intimation from Lord John Russell that he would resign if the Bill passed the second reading. The question raised at that private conference was, what was the state of each man's constituency? and it was agreed that, wherever there was a constituency that would not book a sale, its representative must vote against the Government; but wherever there was an inactive clergy, and local leaders who sought places, and instructed their representatives in making a traffic of the votes of the people, for the purpose of getting cousins, nephews, and other connections appointed to places of emolument and gain, in these cases the representatives were required to vote against the people, and to sacrifice them; because there was a consciousness, on their part, that there were none amongst those they ought to fear, who would call them to account, before God and man, for their treachery and baseness (tremendous cheers). We are dealing here tonight, not so much with theories as facts; and I, therefore, tell you of those things which I have seen, my statements in reference to which I can vouch'.[2]

Before the second reading of his Bill came on, Lord George Bentinck knew it was a doomed measure. The meeting at Lord John Russell's, the threat of resignation, the treachery of many Irish members, the opposition of Sir Robert Peel and his followers, left no doubt that the majority against the second reading would be a large one.

It was well into the small hours of the morning before the division bell rang, after three nights' debate. In a house of 450, the Bill was supported by only 118 votes. A majority of 214 for the Government left them secure in their places.

Of the 105 members returned from Ireland, sixty-six voted — thirty-nine with Lord George Bentinck, and twenty-seven against him. There were Liberals and Tories at both sides. The noble proposer of the Irish Railway Scheme proclaimed — and, no doubt, intended — that it should not be regarded as a party question. After his very effective speech on introducing it, the common opinion was that it would be carried. It was popular in the House and out of it. Everybody in England and in Ireland was sick of spending money on unprofitable work. Lord John Russell saw but one way of defeating the measure, and that was to make it a party question; and so he made it one. We find some of the most decided Irish Tories voting for the Bill, whilst many Whigs and professing patriots voted against. For some days before the division it was known the Bill would be defeated, but few, if any, thought the majority against it would have been so large. After his seven or eight months of hard work, in preparing and maturing his Railway Scheme, its rejection touched Lord George keenly; but his lofty spirit would not stoop to manifest his feelings.

He had, however, the gratification to see himself vindicated, not to say avenged, a few weeks afterwards. The Chancellor of the Exchequer, the great opponent and decrier of Lord George's Bill, actually brought in a Railway Bill himself of a similar character. Lord George Bentinck had proposed to employ 110,000 men with £6,000,000 but the Chancellor of the Exchequer then told the House that £6,000,000 laid out in railways would only furnish employment for 45,000 labourers. Now, the Chancellor of the Exchequer told the House that £600,000 would employ 15,000 labourers; so that, upon his calculations, £6,000,000 would afford employment not merely for 110,000 as Lord George Bentinck had formerly stated, but for 150,000 able-bodied labourers.

The Chancellor of the Exchequer's Bill was carried by a large majority. It is a pity that noble-hearted Englishman, Lord George Bentinck, did not live long enough to see how enduring the gratitude of the Irish people has been for the friendly and bounteous hand he endeavoured to stretch out to them, in their hour of sorest need. Seven-and-twenty years have passed away since then; yet that gratitude still survives, nor is it likely soon to die out amongst a people noted for warm hearts and long memories.

12

Black '47

1

The year 1846 closed in gloom. It left the Irish people sinking in thousands into their graves under the influence of a famine as general as it was intense and which trampled down every barrier set up to stay its desolating progress. But the worst had not yet come. It was in 1847 that the highest point of misery and death had been reached.

Skibbereen, to be sure, ceased to attract so much attention as it had been previously doing but the people of that devoted town had received much relief; besides there were now fewer mouths to fill there, so many were closed in death, at the Windmill Hill, in the Workhouse grounds, and in the churchyard of Abbeystrowry. Instead of one, Ireland had now many Skibbereens. In short, the greater part of it might be regarded as one vast Skibbereen.

In the Autumn of 1846, the famine, which all saw advancing, seized upon certain districts of the South and West; but as ulcers, which first appear in isolated spots upon the body, enlarge until, touching each other, they become confluent, so had the famine, limited in its earlier stages to certain localities, now spread itself over the entire country.

Hence, it is not in any new forms of suffering amongst the famine-stricken people that its increasing horrors are to be looked for: it is in its universality and in the deadly effects of a new scourge — fever — which was not only manifesting itself throughout the land at this time but had already risen to an alarming height — a thing not to be wondered at, because it is the certain offspring, as well as the powerful auxiliary, of famine.

In the fall of 1846 several parts of Clare were in a very wretched condition; but at the opening of the new year the most prosperous localities in that county had been sucked into the great famine vortex. Writing at this period from Ennis, the chief town, Captain Wynne said: 'The number of those who, from age or exhaustion and infirmity, are unable to labour, is becoming most alarming; to those the public works are of no use; they are, no doubt, fit subjects for private charity and the exertions of relief committees, but it is vain to look to these sources for relief at all commensurate with the magnitude of the demand. Deaths are occurring from famine and there can be no doubt that the Famine advances upon us with giant strides.'

Several of the officials who had written to Sir Randolph Routh and others, from different parts of the country, blamed the people for their listlessness, their idleness and the little interest they seemed to take in cropping their land in order to secure a future supply of food. Addressing himself to this point, Captain Wynne said: 'It is in vain to direct their (the people's) attention to the prosecution of those agricultural operations which can alone place any limit to to their present deplorable condition. Agricultural labour holds out a distant prospect of reward — their present necessities require immediate relief. Such is their state of alarm and despair at the prospect before them, that they cannot be induced to look beyond tomorrow; *thousands never expect to see the harvest*. I must say the majority exhibit a great deal of patience, meekness and submission.'

Again, in the same letter: 'The effects of the Famine are discernible everywhere: not a domestic animal to be seen — pigs and poultry have quite disappeared. The dogs have also vanished, except here and there the ghost of one, buried in the skeleton of one of those victims of cruelty and barbarity, which have been so numerous here within the last two months — I allude to the horses and donkeys that were shot. It is an alarming fact that, this day, in the town of Ennis, there was not a stone of breadstuff of any description to be had on any terms, nor a loaf of bread.'[1]

In the chief cities, the pressure of the Famine, day by day, became greater. In Belfast, the flourishing seat of the linen trade, one of the gentlemen appointed to visit the different districts with the view of ascertaining the real amount of distress amongst the poor wrote in the following terms to the *Northern Whig*: 'There is not any necessity that I should point out individual cases of abject want, though in my visitations, I have seen many of whose extreme destitution I could not possibly have formed a true estimate had I not seen them. Let it suffice, however, to state that in many of our back lanes and courts there are families in the veriest wretchedness, with scarcely enough of rags to cover their shivering emaciated bodies; they may be found huddled together around a handful of dying cinders, or endeavouring to fan into flame a small heap of damp smoking sawdust. Perhaps when they have not been happy enough to procure even that scanty fuel, they will be found, to the number of five or six — some well, some ill, and all bearing the aspect of pinching hunger — endeavouring to procure warmth by crouching together upon a scanty heap of filthy straw, or mouldering wood shavings, their only covering an old worn-out rag of a blanket or a coverlet, that has been so patched and re-patched that its original texture or colour it would be impossible to discern. On looking around this miserable dwelling, nothing meets the eye save the damp floor and the bare walls, down which the rain, or condensed vapour, is plentifully streaming. Not a stool, chair or seat of any description, in many instances, is to be seen, nor commonest utensil; and as for food, not so much as would satisfy the cravings of even a hungry infant. Let not this picture be deemed overdrawn. If any one suppose it exaggerated, had that individual been with me, on Sunday last, I could have shown him some instances of suffering that would have removed all doubt regarding the reality of distress in Belfast. I will merely mention one of them: I entered a house to which my attention had been directed; in the kitchen there was not a single article of furniture — not even a live cinder on the cold, deserted-looking hearth. In the inner room I found a woman, lately confined, lying upon a heap of chopped-up rotten straw, with scarcely a rag to cover her; beside her nestled two children, pictures of want, and in her bosom lay her undressed babe that, four days before, had first seen the light. She had no food in the house, nor had she nor her children had anything since her confinement, save a little soup procured from the public kitchen. Such was her statement; and the evidence of her wretched dwelling bore but too ample testimony to her melancholy tale.'

Large numbers were in a state of utter destitution in the city of Cork. As happened in other cities and important towns, the country people flocked in to swell the misery; and roaming in groups through the streets, exhibiting their wretchedness and imploring relief, they gave them a most sad and deplorable appearance. Even the houses of once respectable tradesmen, denuded of every article of furniture, and without fuel or bedding, presented a most affecting spectacle of want and misery.

So impressed were the committee of the Society of Friends in Cork with the sufferings of this class that a separate subscription was raised for supplying them with straw beds and some fuel. The apparatus which this committee had erected for the making of soup was, they thought at first, on too extensive a scale, but it was soon found to be insufficient to meet the calls which were daily made upon it.

Their Report of 1 February said: 'Our distribution of soup is rapidly increasing; during the past week it averaged 1,016 quarts a day, and on the seventh day it reached the extent of 1,268 quarts.' It went on increasing until it had, a fortnight later, reached 1,400 quarts a day.

Besides the distribution of soup by the Society of Friends, there were four district soup houses, supplying over 6,000 quarts of soup daily; so that, at this time, 48,000 quarts of soup were made and distributed weekly in the city of Cork. There was a nominal charge of a penny or so a quart for some of this soup but much of it was given away gratuitously.

Speaking of the accounts from different parts of the county Cork, the Report said: 'Where the potato crop was most completely annihilated — in the far west — the Famine first appeared but other quarters were also invaded as the remnant of the crop became blighted or consumed. Hence, in localities which until recently but slightly participated in this afflictive visitation, distress and destitution are now spreading and the accounts from some of these are presenting the same features of appalling misery as those which originally burst upon an affrighted nation from the neighbourhood of Skibbereen.'

In the postscript of a letter to the *Cork Examiner*, Rev. James O'Driscoll, PP, writing from Kilmichael, said: 'Since writing the above a young man named Manley, in fever at Cooldorahey, had to be visited. He was found in a dying state, without one to tend him. His sister and brother lay dead quite close to him in the same room. The sister was dead for five days, and the brother for three days. He also died, being the last of a large family. The three were interred by means of a sliding coffin.'

The Cork Workhouse was crowded to excess and the number of deaths in it, at this time, was simply frightful: they were 174 in a single week — more than one death in every hour.[2] In one day, at the beginning of February, there were forty-four corpses in the house; and on the tenth of that month 100 bodies were conveyed for interment to a small suburban burial place near Cork. Several persons were found dead in the streets; numbers of bodies were left unburied for want of coffins. Under a shed at the Shandon guard-house lay some thirty-eight human beings; old and young men, women and infants of tenderest age, huddled together like so many pigs or dogs, on the ground, without any covering but the rags on their persons.[3]

The *Limerick Examiner*, in giving an account of the state of the poor in that city, published a day's experience of one of the Catholic priests in the parish of St John. In one day he was called to officiate at the death-beds of seven persons who were dying of starvation, the families of which they were members comprising, in all, twenty-three souls. The wretched abodes in which he found them were much of the same character — no beds, scarcely any clothing, no food, the children quite naked. In one of those miserable dwellings he could not procure a light to be used whilst administering the Sacraments to a dying woman; and such was the general poverty around that the loan of a candle could not be obtained in the neighbourhood. His last visit was to a girl in fever, who had had three relapses. He found her father and mother tottering on their limbs from want. The father said he had a dimness in his eyes and he thought he would become mad from hunger before night.

Dublin, notwithstanding its many advantages, did not escape the all-pervading scourge. In the month of December 1846 there were 700 persons under treatment for dysentery in the South Union Workhouse, besides convalescents. The disease proved more fatal than cholera. Parochial meetings were held and committees appointed to collect funds for the relief of the starving people; besides which a meeting of the citizens was convened at the Music Hall, on 23 December, to form a general committee for the whole city.

In the unavoidable absence of the Lord Mayor, it was presided over by Alderman Staunton, Lord Mayor-elect. The meeting was very numerously attended by leading citizens and clergymen of various denominations. Amongst the latter were the Most Rev. Dr Murray, Archbishop of Dublin and the Provost of Trinity College. A committee was formed, whose duties were to raise funds and 'by a due disbursement thereof', for the relief of the necessities, to endeavour to mitigate 'the alarming and unparalleled distress of the poor of the city', and so arrest the progress of 'a train of evils that must otherwise follow in the track of famine'.

Four days later 'The General Central Relief Committee for all Ireland' sprang into existence, under the chairmanship of the Marquis of Kildare, the Duke of Leinster. This became a very important and useful body, having disbursed, during the year of its existence, over £70,000. Greater still were the results achieved by a committee formed on 13 November 1846 by the Society of Friends. That admirably managed body sent members of the Society to the most distressed parts of the country in order to investigate on the spot the real state of things and report upon them. This committee received from various parts of the world the very large sum of £198,326 15s. 5d., £2,700 of which remained unappropriated when they closed their glorious labours in the cause of benevolence.

But of all the charitable organisations produced by the Famine, the most remarkable was 'The British Association for the Relief of Extreme Distress in Ireland and Scotland'.⁴ This association received in subscriptions, at home and abroad, over £600,000. The balance in hands, when they drew up their report, was the very trifling one of £1,400; whilst so many of those immediately connected with this gigantic work laboured gratuitously, the whole expense of management was only £12,000, barely two per cent. Further on I shall have an opportunity of speaking more in detail of charitable committees.

There is one curious fact regarding the Government in connection with those committees. It is this: The Government seemed anxious to have it understood that it was not the money outlay which concerned or alarmed them but the difficulty of procuring food and the probability of not being able to procure it in sufficient quantity, by any amount of exertion within their power.

The Government, as we have already seen, allowed the French, Belgians and Dutch, who were in far less need than we, to be in the food markets before them and to buy as much as they required — even in Liverpool, which they cleared of Indian corn in a single day. If food were the difficulty, and not money, it is not easy to see what great advantage there was in those charitable associations, formed to receive money subscriptions for the purchase of food. Of what use was money, if food were not procurable with it?

The aid of such bodies, in investigating cases of destitution and distributing food, would, no doubt, be very valuable; but this service they could render the Government as well without subscriptions as with them.

The Government, it may be fairly said, should not refuse any aid proffered to them. Certainly not; but they did more. They showed a decided anxiety to receive aid in money, not only from landlords, who were bound to give it, but from any and every quarter — even from the Great Turk himself, who subscribed £1,000 out of his bankrupt treasury to feed the starving subjects of the richest nation in the world.

The noblemen and gentlemen who signed the Address of Thanks to the Sultan Abdul Medjid Khan, for his subscription, amongst other things, said to his majesty that 'it had pleased Providence, in its wisdom, to deprive this country suddenly of its staple article of food and to visit the poor inhabitants with privations, such as have seldom fallen to the lot of any civilised nation to endure. In this emergency, the people of Ireland *had no other alternative but to appeal to the kindness and munificence of other countries* less afflicted than themselves, to save them and their families from famine and death.'⁵

182

Besides making the Famine a money question, this address contains the blasphemous attack upon Divine Providence, so current at the time among politicians. William Bennett, one of those praiseworthy gentlemen whom the Society of Friends sent to distribute relief in the far west was, however, of opinion that the responsibility of the Irish Famine should not be laid at the door of Divine Providence, at least without some little investigation.

In his letters to his committee, he endeavoured to give a bird's-eye view of the distressed portions of Ireland, drawn upon the spot, with the vivid delineation of truth, but without exaggeration or colouring. And what is the picture? he asked.

'Take the line of the main course of the Shannon continued north to Lough Swilly and south to Cork. It divides the island into two great portions, east and west. In the east there are distress and poverty enough, as part of the same body suffering from the same cause; but there is much to redeem. In the west it exhibits a people, not in the centre of Africa, the steppes of Asia, the backwoods of America, not some newly-discovered tribes of South Australia or among the Polynesian Islands, not Hottentots, Bushmen or Esquimaux, neither Mahommedans nor Pagans, but some millions of our own Christian nation at home, living in a state and condition low and degraded to a degree unheard of before in any civilised community; driven periodically to the borders of starvation; and now reduced by a national calamity to an exigency which all the efforts of benevolence can only mitigate, not control; and under which thousands are not merely pining away in misery and wretchedness, but are dying like cattle off the face of the earth, from want and its kindred horrors! *Is this to be regarded in the light of a Divine dispensation and punishment? Before we can safely arrive at such a conclusion, we must be satisfied that human agency and legislation, individual oppressions, and social relationships have had no hand in it.'*[6]

Was it not a money question, when a labourer at task work could earn only 8d. or 8.25d. a day? — not enough to buy one meal of food for a moderate sized family. No, no, answered the Government people; this low rate of wages is fixed, in order not to attract labour from the cultivation of the soil. Now, in the famine time, the labourer, as a rule, could not obtain *money wages* for the cultivation of the soil — a fact well known to the Government; so that *money wages* of almost any amount must withdraw him from agriculture, from the absolute necessity he was under of warding off immediate starvation. If, therefore, the Government wished the labour of the country to be employed in cultivating and improving the soil, why did they not, instead of spoiling the roads, so employ that labour at fair money wages and subject to just and proper conditions? They were often urged to do it, but in vain. They yielded at last, but at an absurdly late period of such a concession.

Further: if it were solely a food question, the Government should have used all the means in their power to bring food into the country, which they did not do; because they refused to suspend the navigation laws and thus deliberately excluded supplies from our ports. By the navigation laws, merchandise could be brought to these countries only in British ships, or in ships belonging to the nation which produced the merchandise. The importation of corn fell under this *protective* regulation. If those laws were suspended in time, food could be carried to British ports in the ships of any nation; and, in fact, whilst a great outcry was raised by our Government about the scarcity of food, and the want of ships to carry it, Odessa and other food centres were crowded with vessels, *looking for freights to England, but could not obtain them,* in consequence of the operation of the navigation laws.

The immediate effect was a great difficulty in sending food to those parts of Ireland where the people were dying of sheer starvation. But a second effect was the enrichment, to an enormous extent, of the owners of the mercantile marine of England; freights having nearly doubled in almost every instance, and in a most important one, that of America, nearly trebled. The freights from London to Irish ports had fully trebled.

The Prime Minister came down to Parliament at the end of January 1847 and proposed the suspension of the navigation laws until the first of September following; in order, he said, that freights might be lowered and food come in more abundantly; but, as one of the members said in the debate that followed, the proposal, good in itself, came too late, being made at a time when the surplus of the harvest of 1846 was, to a great extent, disposed of.

Yet, at the very time it was written, President Polk's message to Congress, delivered in Washington on 8 December, arrived in England, containing the following passage: 'The home market alone is inadequate to enable them (the farmers) to dispose of the immense supplies of food which they are capable of producing, even at the most reduced prices, for the manifest reason that they cannot be consumed in the country. The United States can, from their immense surplus, supply not only the home demand, but the deficiency of food required by the whole world.' Was it a money question or a food question?

There was, naturally enough, a mournful sameness in the news from every part of the country: starvation, famine, fever, death; such are the commonest headings in the newspapers of the time. Seven deaths from starvation near Cootehill was the announcement from a locality supposed not to be at all severely visited. In Clifden, County Galway, the distress was fearful; 5,000 persons there were said to be trying to live on field roots and seaweed.

A Catholic priest who was a curate in County Galway during the Famine but who now occupies, as he well deserves to do, a high position in the Irish Church, has kindly supplied the author with some of his famine experiences. There are five churchyards in the parish where he then ministered. Four of these had to be enlarged by one half during the Famine and the fifth, an entirely new one, became also necessary that there might be ground enough wherein to inter the famine-slain people.

This enlargement of burial accommodation took place, as a rule, throughout the South, West and North-west. One day as this priest was going to attend his sick calls — and there was no end of sick calls in those times — he met a man with a donkey and cart. On the cart there were three coffins, containing the mortal remains of his wife and his two children. He was alone — no funeral, no human creature near him. When he arrived at the place of interment, he was so weakened by starvation himself that he was unable to put a little covering of clay upon the coffins to protect them.

When passing the same road next day, the priest found ravenous, starved dogs making a horrid meal on the carcasses of this uninterred family. He hired a man, who dug a grave, in which what may be literally called their remains were placed.

On one occasion, returning through the gray morning from a night call, he observed a dark mass on the side of the road. Approaching, he found it to be the body of a man. Near his head lay a raw turnip, with one mouthful bitten from it.

In several of the reports from the Board of Works' inspectors and other communications, it was said that as the Famine progressed the people lost all their natural vivacity. They looked upon themselves as doomed; and this feeling was expressed by their whole bearing. The extent to which it prevailed amongst all classes is well illustrated by a circumstance related by the same clergyman. When the Famine had somewhat abated in intensity, he was one day in a field which was separated from the public road by a wall. He heard a voice on the road; it was that of a peasant girl humming a song. The tears rushed to his eyes. He walked quickly towards her, searching meanwhile for some coin to give her. He placed a shilling in her hand, with a feeling somewhat akin to enthusiasm. 'It was', said he to the author, 'the first joyous sound I had heard for six months.'

From Roscommon the brief but terrible tidings came that whole families, who had retired to rest at night, were corpses in the morning and were frequently left unburied for many days for want of coffins in which to inter them. And the report added: 'The state of our poorhouse is awful; the average daily deaths in it, from fever alone, is eighteen; there are upwards of 1,100 in it, and of these 600 are in typhus fever.'[7]

'In a circumference of eight miles from where I write', said a correspondent of the *Roscommon Journal*, 'not less than sixty bodies have been interred without a coffin'. In answer to queries sent to a part of Roscommon, I received the following replies from a reliable source: Query. 'What other relief was given during the Government works by private charity, committees, etc.?' Answer. 'There was considerable relief given by charitable committees.' Query. 'What did the wealthy resident landlords give?' Answer. 'Considerable.' Query. 'What did the wealthy non-resident landlords give?' Again the answer was, 'Considerable.' But I am sorry to add that the two latter queries were almost uniformly answered from various parts of the country by the expressive words 'Nothing whatever.'

The same correspondent said, in reply to another query, that the aged and infirm did not live more than a day or two after being sent to hospital. They died of dysentery. The two following anecdotes are given on the best authority: a family, consisting of father, mother and daughter were starving; they were devotedly attached to each other; the daughter was young and comely. Offers of relief were made by a wealthy person but they were accompanied by a dishonorable condition and they were therefore indignantly spurned. 'Fond as I am of my life', said the starving girl, 'and much as I love my father and mother, for whose relief I would endure any earthly toil, I will suffer them as well as myself to die rather than get them relief at the price of my virtue'.

A Roscommon man thus wrote in the query sheet sent to him: 'Years after the Famine and when in another part of the country, I was obliged, on my way to my house, to pass the house of a poor blacksmith; and often at night, as I passed, I heard him and his family reciting the Rosary. I told him one day how much edified I was at this. The poor fellow replied with great earnestness: "Sir, as long as I have life in me I'll say the Rosary, and I'll tell you why. In the Famine times, my family and myself were starving. One night the children were crying with the hunger, and there was no food to give them. By way of stopping their cries they were put to bed but, after a short sleep, they awoke with louder cries for food. At length, I recommended that all of us, young and old, should join in saying the Rosary. We did; and before it was ended a woman came in, whose occupation was to deal in bread and she had a basketful with her. I explained our condition to her and asked her to give me some bread on credit. She did so and from that day to this we never felt hunger or starvation; and from that day to this I continue to say the Rosary and will, please God, to the end of my life.'''

The news came from Sligo, through the public journals, that the Famine was carrying off hundreds and thousands there and that the work left undone by the Famine would be finished by pestilence. The Workhouse was described as a pesthouse and the guardians in terror had abandoned it. The following short note will give a better idea of the state of this part of the country than any lengthened description:

Riverston, 8 Feb.

Sir, — Half-a-dozen starvation deaths have been reported to Mr Grant this evening and he directs me to write to you to request you will attend here early tomorrow morning to hold inquests.

James Hay, Head Constable
Alexander Burrows, Esq.

But things were much worse than was revealed by this note. Mr Burrows was quite unequal to the work he had to do. In one day, although he tired three horses, he succeeded in holding only five inquests. Poor progress indeed, inasmuch as there were forty dead bodies in the district of Managharrow alone awaiting him!

One of the cases, that of Owen Mulrooney, was a moving one. He was a young, muscular man in the prime of life. He had a wife and five young children. Here is the substance of his wife's depositions at the inquest held upon his remains. She sold all her little furniture for ten shillings and with this sum she and her five children left home to make her way to England, as she thought her husband would be able to support himself, if unencumbered by her and the family. The weather became cold and rainy; and when she had got as far as Enniskillen the children took cramps and she had to retrace her steps by slow degrees, and seek again her desolate home.

Meanwhile, the public works, upon which her husband had been employed, were stopped and he was at once reduced to starvation. A neighbour gave him one meal of food and a night's

A typical cabin at the time of the famine.

lodging. He was revived by the food and had strength enough to make up two loads of turf, which he sold and bought an ass, which he killed and tried to cook and eat. He partook of some portion of the ass's flesh twice or thrice but his stomach refused the food, as it always brought on great retching.

When his wife and children returned he was dying and she was only in time to see him and give the above sorrowful evidence.

We select this case, said the local journal, out of dozens; because it has some remarkable features in it. Many, it further adds, who were sent to purchase food, died of starvation on the journey. The family of Mary Costello were in a state of starvation for three weeks and she herself had not had food for two days. Previous to her death, one of her brothers procured the price of half-a-stone of meal, for which she was sent to town; and on the following morning she was found dead by the roadside, with the little bag of meal grasped tightly in her hand.

Although it is notorious that some districts in the South, especially Skibbereen, were the first to attract a large share of public attention, County Mayo, so populous, so large, so poor, was from the beginning marked out for suffering; but it lacked an organ so faithful and eloquent as the *Southern Reporter*, through whose columns Skibbereen and Bantry and Schull became as well known to the Empire as Dublin, Paris or London. Poor Mayo suffered intensely from end to end, although it suffered in comparative silence.

In the beginning of January, what may be termed a monster meeting of the county was held in Westport. Forty thousand persons were said to have assembled on the occasion. The Very Rev. Dean Burke, who presided, complained that as far back as September a presentment of £80,000 was passed for the county, £12,000 of which was allotted to their barony, Murrisk; but from that time to the period of the meeting only £7,000 had been expended.

Resolutions were passed, calling for a liberal grant of money to save the people from death; expressive of deep regret at the uncultured state of the corn lands of the county; calling for the establishment of food depots in the remote districts; and recommending the completion of the roads then in progress.

More than one speaker hinted that there existed an undercurrent for preventing the employment of the people and that this undercurrent emanated from the landlords, who were opposed to the taxing of their proportion for such a purpose.

At the close of the meeting, one of the gentlemen present, Mr John C. Garvey, made the following observations: 'It has been said that an under-current exists to prevent the employment of the people. In my opinion the landlords would be working against their own interest in preventing the employment of the poor. (Cries of 'No, no.') Well, I, as one of the landlords, do declare most solemnly, before my God, that I have not only in public, but in private, done everything that I could do to extend the employment of the people (loud cheers); and I now brand every landlord that does not come forward and clear himself of the imputation.'

A great number of coroners' inquests were reported from Mayo but those inquests were no real indication of the number of deaths which occurred there from starvation; there were not coroners enough to hold inquests and four-fifths of those that were held were not reported. Besides, inquests were not and could not be held unless in cases where the death was somewhat sudden or had some specialty about it. The effects of the Famine were not usually very sudden. People dragged on life for weeks, partly through that tenacity of life which is one of the characteristics of human nature; partly through chance scraps of food obtained from time to time, and in various ways. Families have gone on for many weeks on boiled turnips, with a little oatmeal sprinkled over them; often on green rape, and even the wild herbs of the fields and seaweed; such things kept prolonging life whilst they were destroying it. After a while they brought on dysentery: dysentery brought on death. But no one thought of a coroner in such cases, which were by far the most numerous class of cases until fever became prevalent, and even then dysentery commonly came in to close the scene.

'During that period', wrote Mr James H. Tuke, 'the roads in many places became as charnel-houses and several car and coach drivers have assured me that they rarely drove anywhere without seeing dead bodies strewn along the road side and that, in the dark, they had even gone over them. A gentleman told me that in the neighbourhood of Clifden one inspector of roads had caused no less than 140 bodies to be buried, which he found scattered along the highway. In some cases it is well known that where all other members of a family have perished, the last survivor has earthed up the door of his miserable cabin to prevent the ingress of pigs and dogs, and then laid himself down to die in this fearful family vault.'[8]

In January 1847 a Protestant gentleman, now a colonial judge, well known for his ability and integrity, gave, through the columns of a Dublin newspaper, an account of the state of Mayo as he saw it. He found great dissatisfaction, in fact indignation, existing with regard to the unaccountable delay of the public works which had been presented for in that county; and this not merely amongst the starving people but amongst the most respectable and intelligent persons with whom he conversed. He — a man not likely to take a narrow or prejudiced view of any subject — was of the opinion that those complaints were not groundless.

The officials, he said, instead of extending the works in Mayo, and feeding the people, 'are employed in diverting public attention by prating of subscriptions, paltering about Queen's letters and English poor-boxes, and frittering away the strength of public opinion and the efficiency of all public action, by engaging private charity in a task that can be met only by the Herculean efforts of a whole nation, knit into a single power, and bound into concentrated exertion by all the constraining forces that the constitution of political society affords'.[9] And then the starving people are blamed for finding fault and for being suspicious. What else, he asked, can they be? How can a man dying of starvation have patience?

The chief places he visited were Balla, Claremorris, Ballyhaunis and Hollymount. The scenes he witnessed were, he said, scarcely if at all less harrowing than those which had been reported from the locality of Skibbereen. This writer, a Protestant, conversed, amongst others, with the priests of the districts which he visited, and of them he said: 'The Catholic clergy are the only persons who can form a tolerably correct estimate of the numbers of persons who are now dying of starvation. The Catholic clergy know all the people of their respective parishes — *no one else does*; the Catholic priest knows them as the shepherd does his sheep; he knows them individually; he knows not only every lineament of every individual face, but he knows, too, every ailment of body — every care of mind — every necessity of circumstances from which he is suffering. The Catholic clergy of the West attend every death-bed: the poor there are all Catholics. The Catholic clergy know, then, to what it is that the extraordinary mortality now prevalent is owing — *and they set it down as the immediate consequence of want and starvation.*'[10]

One of the priests of whom W.G. asked information told him his whole time, and that of his assistant, was unceasingly occupied in administering the last comforts of religion to the victims of starvation. It would, he said, be an endless task and, he feared, a useless one to record his sad experience.

People died in Connaught whilst in full employment on the public works just as they did in Munster. Of such cases, the following is one of which W.G. collected some particulars: James Byrne, of Barnabriggan, Brise, parish of Balla, was employed up to his death on the public works. The last food of which he had partaken was obtained by his wife pledging her cloak. There was an inquest upon this poor man's remains, at which his wife deposed that up to the time of his death he was employed on the public works and as they had no food she was obliged to pledge her cloak for one stone of meal. Deceased often said he would do well if he had food or nourishment. Deponent stated to the best of her belief that her husband died for the want of food. She and her four children were now living on rape, which she was allowed to gather in a farmer's field.

James Browne, MD, being sworn, said he found, on examination, all the internal organs of the deceased sound. There was no food whatever in his stomach or in any part of the alimentary canal. There was a small quantity of thin faeces in the lower portion of the large intestine. Was of opinion that deceased came by his death from inanition, or want of food. Verdict: 'James Byrne came by his death in consequence of having no food for some days; and died of starvation.'

'With every disposition', wrote WG, 'to make allowances for the difficulties of their position, let me ask, Sir, how have the gentry acted? They have seemed to think that the whole relief question just split itself into two sides, one of which belonged exclusively to the Government, the other exclusively to them. One side comprised the duty of providing for the lives of the people and this was left to the Government; the other, the duty of providing for the safety of the estates and this the gentry took upon themselves. They [the landlords] have complained much of the character of the works; they have strongly urged the Government to undertake something else; *at all events to give up what they were doing at the moment*; but when did their indignation take the shape of complaining that what the Government was doing was inadequate for coping with the starvation that was abroad?'

The penetrating mind of W.G. led him to forecast tremendous results from the potato failure, exclusive of its immediate effect — death by starvation. Having expressed his opinion that the extent of the destitution was fearful, he made the following observations, which time has completely verified. 'As regards the effect', said he, 'of the present calamity upon the relations of landlord and tenant, believe me, that terrible as are the immediate and direct effects of the calamity, you will find a set of collateral results springing out of it, tending to the *extermination* of the smaller tenantry by the landlords, that may lead you, ere many months, to regard the secondary stage of this scourge as scarcely less terrible to our unhappy peasantry that the first.'

And again: 'Symptoms of a *wide-spread systematic extermination* are just beginning to exhibit themselves. I am not speaking under the influence of any prejudice against the landlord class. Let none of your readers set down to the account of such a feeling my present warning as to the wholesale system of ejectment that is now in preparation. The potato cultivation being extinguished, at least for a time, the peasant cultivators can pay no rents; sheep and horned cattle *can* pay rents, and smart rents too; therefore the sheep and cattle shall have the lands and the peasants shall be ousted from them; a very simple and most inevitable conclusion, as you see. I repeat it, a universal system of ousting the peasantry is about to set in. Whether this results from the fault or from the necessities of the landlords it matters not.'

The following extract from the *Roscommon Journal* was emphatically cited by W.G. in support of his views. *'The number of civil bills served by landlords for the approaching sessions of this town will treble those ever sent out for the last ten years.'* [11]

More than twenty years after W.G. wrote those letters, I had a conversation relative to the Famine with a gentleman who knew the Midland counties and portions of the West well. I asked him what was the effect of the Famine in his district. 'My district', he answered, 'was by no means regarded as a poor one but the Famine swept away more than half its population. The census of '41 gave the families residing in it as 2,200; the census of '51 gave them at 1,000.'

Did the landlords, I enquired, come forward liberally to save the lives of the people? 'Only one landlord', he replied, 'in the whole locality with which I am connected did anything to save the people, F_____ O'B_____. He asked no rent for two years and he never afterwards insisted on the rent of those two years; although I must say he was paid it by many of his tenants, of their own free will; but, for the rest, he cancelled those two years' rent and opened a new account with them, as with men owing him nothing'. And what, I further asked, were the feelings of the landlords with regard to their tenants dying of starvation? He answered with solemn emphasis, *'Delighted to be rid of them.'*

'I shall never forget', said Rev. Mr F_____ to W.G. 'the impression made on my mind a few days ago by a most heartrending case of starvation. It was this: the poor mother of five children, putting them to bed one night, almost lifeless from hunger, and despairing of ever again seeing them alive, took her last look at them and bade them her last farewell. She rose early in the morning, and her first act was to steal on tiptoe to where they lay. She would not awake them but she must know the truth — are they alive or dead? And she softly touched the lips of each to try and discover if there was any warmth in them and she eagerly watched to see if the breath of life still came from their nostrils. Her apprehensions were but too well founded, she had lost some of her dear ones during the night.'

The mournful poetry of this simple narrative must touch every heart.

Ass and horse flesh were anxiously sought for, even when the animals died of disease or starvation. In the middle of January it was recorded that a horse belonging to a man near Claremorris, having died, was flayed and the carcass left for dogs and birds to feed upon; but, says the narrative, before much of it was consumed it was discovered by a poor family (whose name and residence are given) and used by them as food. Father, mother and six children prolonged life for a week upon this disgusting carrion and even regretted the loss of it when the supply failed; and the poor mother said to the person who made the fact public, 'the Lord only knows what I will now do for my starving children, since it is gone!'

A fortnight earlier a most circumstantial account of the eating of ass flesh was given by a commercial gentleman in a letter addressed to the Premier, Lord John Russell, and dated 'Ballina, Christmas-eve' (!) In this case the poor man killed his ass for food, the skin being sold to a skin dealer for 8d. The writer of the letter visited the skin dealer's house in order to make sure of the fact. It was quite true and the skin dealer's wife told him this could not be a solitary case, 'as she never remembered so many asses' skins coming for sale as within the month just past.'[12]

Mr Forster, in his report to the Society of Friends, said of the conditions of Westport in January 1847 that it was a strange and fearful sight, like what we read of beleaguered cities; its streets crowded with gaunt wanderers, sauntering to and fro, with hopeless air and hunger-struck look; a mob of starved, almost naked women were around the poor house, clamouring for soup-tickets; our inn, the headquarters of the road engineer and pay clerks, was beset by a crowd of beggars for work.[13]

The agent of the British Association, Count Strezelecki, writing from Westport at this time, said no pen could describe the distress by which he was surrounded; it had reached such an extreme degree of intensity that it was above the power of exaggeration. 'You may', he added, 'believe anything which you hear and read, because what I actually see surpasses what I ever read of past and present calamities.'[14]

The weather in March became mild and even warm and sunny; some little comfort, one would suppose, to those without food or fuel. But no; they were so starved and weakened and broken down that it had an injurious effect upon them and hurried them rapidly to their end. A week after the passage quoted above was written, Count Strezelecki again wrote and said he was sorry to report that the distress had increased; a thing which could be hardly believed as possible. Melancholy cases of death on the public roads and in the streets had become more frequent. The sudden warmth of the weather and the rays of a bright sun accelerated prodigiously the forthcoming end of those whose constitutions were undermined by famine or sickness.

'Yesterday', he wrote, 'a countrywoman, between this and the harbour (one mile distance), walking with four children, squatted against a wall on which the heat and light reflected powerfully; some hours after two of her children were corpses and she and the two remaining ones taken lifeless to the barracks. Today, in Westport, similar melancholy occurrences took place.'[15]

Some years ago, during a visit to Westport, I received sad corroboration of the truth of these statements. I met several persons who had witnessed the Famine in that town and its neighbourhood and their relation of the scenes which fell under their notice not only sustained but surpassed, if possible, the facts given in the above communications.

A priest who was stationed at Westport during the Famine was still there at the period of my visit. During that dreadful time the people, he told me, who wandered about the country in search of food frequently took possession of empty houses, which they easily found, the inmates having died, or having gone to the Workhouse, where such existed. A brother and sister, not quite grown up, took possession of a house in this way in the parish of Westport. One of them became ill; the other continued to go for the relief where it was given out but this one soon fell ill also. No person heeded them. Everyone had too much to do for himself. They died. Their dead bodies were only discovered by the offensive odour which issued from the house in which they died and in which they had become putrefied. It was found necessary to make an aperture for ventilation on the roof before anyone would venture in. The neighbours dug a hole in the hard floor of the cabin with a crowbar to receive their remains. And this was their coffinless grave!

This same priest administered in one day the last Sacrament to thirty-three young persons in the Workhouse of Westport; of these there were not more than two or three alive next morning.

Mr Egan, who at the date of my visit was Clerk of the Union, held the same office during the Famine. The Workhouse was built to accommodate 1,000 persons. There were two days a week for admissions. With the house crowded far beyond its capacity, he had repeatedly seen as many as 3,000 persons seeking admission on a single day. Knowing, as we do, the utter dislike the Irish peasantry had in those times to enter the Workhouse, this is a terrible revelation of the Famine; for it is a recorded fact that many of the people died of want in their cabins and suffered their children to die rather than go there. Those who were not admitted — and they were, of course, the great majority — having no homes to return to, lay down and died in Westport and its suburbs.

Mr Egan, pointing to the wall opposite the Workhouse gate, said: 'There is where they sat down, never to rise again. I have seen there of a morning as many as eight corpses of those miserable beings, who had died during the night. Father G_____ [then in Westport] used to be anointing them as they lay exhausted along the walls and streets, dying of hunger and fever.'[16]

The principal aim of the Society of Friends was to establish soup-kitchens and give employment to the women in knitting. As soon as their committee was in working order they sent members of their body to various parts of the country — more especially to the West — to make inquiries and to see things with their own eyes. Their reports, made in a quiet, unexaggerated form, are amongst the most valuable testimonies extant as to the effects and extent of the Famine.

The delegate who was the first to explore portions of the West wrote that, at Boyle (a prosperous and important town), the persons who sought admission to the Workhouse were in a most emaciated state, many of them declaring that they had not tasted food of any kind for forty-eight hours; and he learned that numbers of them had been living upon turnips and cabbage-leaves for weeks. The truth of these statements was but too well supported by the dreadfully reduced state in which they presented themselves, the children especially being emaciated with starvation and ravenous with hunger.

At Carrick-on-Shannon he witnessed what he calls a most painful and heartrending scene — poor wretches in the last stage of famine begging to be received into the house; women, who had six or seven children, imploring that even two or three of them might be taken in, *as their husbands were earning but 8d. a day,* which, at the existing high price of provisions, was totally inadequate to feed them. Some of those children were worn to skeletons; their features sharpened with hunger and their limbs wasted almost to the bone. Of course, he said, among so many applicants (110), a great number were necessarily refused admittance, as there were but thirty vacancies in the house. Although the guardians exercised the best discrimination they could, it was believed that some of those rejected were so far spent that it was doubtful if they could reach their homes alive — those homes, such as they were, being in many cases five or six Irish miles away.

This kind-hearted gentleman, having expressed a wish to distribute bread to those poor creatures, that they might not, as he said, 'go quite empty-handed', forty pounds of bread were procured, all that could be purchased in the town of Carrick-on-Shannon. They devoured it with a voracity which nothing but famine could produce. One woman, he said, was observed to eat but a very small portion of her bread and, being asked the reason, said she had four children at home to whom she was taking it, as without it there would not be a morsel of food in her cabin that night.

What struck him and his fellow-traveller in a special manner was the effects of famine on the children; their faces were so wan and haggard that they looked like old men and women; their sprightliness was all gone; they sat in groups at their cabin doors, making no attempt to play.

Another indication of the Famine noticed by them was that the pigs and poultry had entirely disappeared. To numberless testimonies as to the spirit in which the poor people bore their unexampled privations, this good man added his: 'To do the poor justice', he wrote, 'they are bearing their privations with a remarkable degree of patience and fortitude, and very little clamorous begging is to be met with upon the roads — at least, not more than has been the case in Ireland for many years. William Forster' (his fellow-traveller), he added, 'has completely formed the opinion that the statements in the public newspapers are by no means exaggerated.'[17]

Although Donegal is in the Ulster division of the kingdom, in the famine time it partook more of the character of a Connaught than an Ulster county. A gentleman was deputed by the Society of Friends to explore it, who gave his views upon the Irish Famine with a spirit and feeling which do him honour as a man and a Christian. Writing from Stranorlar he said: 'This county, like most others in Ireland, belongs to a few large proprietors, some of them, unhappily, absentees, whose large domains sometimes extend over whole parishes and baronies, and contain a population of 8,000 to 12,000. Such, for instance, is the parish of Templecrone, with a population of 10,000 inhabitants; in which the only residents above small farmers are the agent, the Protestant clergyman, the parish priest, a medical man and perhaps a resident magistrate with the superintendent of police and a few small dealers'.[18]

Writing from Dunfanaghy in the midst of snow, he said: 'A

portion of the district through which we passed this day, as well as the adjoining one, is, with one exception, the poorest and most destitute in Donegal. Nothing, indeed, can describe too strongly the dreadful condition of the people. Many families were living on a single meal of cabbage and some even, as we were assured, upon a little seaweed.

'A highly respectable merchant of the town called upon this gentleman and assured him that the small farmers and cottiers had parted with all their pigs and their fowl; and even their bed clothes and fishing nets had gone for the same object, the supply of food. He stated that he knew many families of five to eight persons, who subsisted on 2.5lb. of oatmeal per day, made into thin water gruel — about 6oz. of meal for each!'

'Dunfanaghy is a little fishing town situated on a bay remarkably adapted for a fishing population; the sea is teeming with fish of the finest description, waiting, we might say, to be caught. Many of the inhabitants gain a portion of their living by this means, but so rude is their tackle and so fragile and liable to be upset are their primitive boats or coracles, made of wicker-work, over which sailcloth is stretched, that they can only venture to sea in fine weather; and thus with food almost in sight the people starve, because they have no one to teach them to build boats more adapted to this rocky coast than those used by their ancestors many centuries ago.[19] This is but one among many instances of the wasted industrial resources of this country which, whether in connection with the water or the land, strike the eye of the stranger at every step'.[20]

To Glenties Mr Tuke and his companions made their journey through a succession of wild mountain passes, rendered still wilder by the deep snow which covered everything. They put up at Lord George Hill's Gweedore hotel and endorsed all they had previously heard about the admirable zeal and enlightened benevolence of that nobleman, who had effected great improvements both in the land and in the condition of the inhabitants of one of the wildest portions of Donegal.

'We started at daybreak', he wrote, 'for Glenties, thirty miles distant, over the mountains; and after leaving the improved cottages and farms on the Gweedore estate, soon came upon the domain of an absentee proprietor, the extent of which may be judged by the fact that our road lay for more than twenty miles through it. This is the poorest parish in Donegal and no statement can be too strong with respect to the wretched condition, the positive misery and starvation in which the cottiers and small farmers on this immense domain are found. We baited at Dungloe. A more miserable and dilapidated village or town I never saw. What a contrast did its dirty little inn present to the hotel at Gweedore.'

There was not a single pound of meal, Indian or oat, to be purchased in this miserable place, whilst thousands were depending on it for their supplies. It was crowded with poor people from the surrounding country and from the island of Arranmore, who were crying with hunger and cold; the next market town was thirty miles from them, and the nearest place where food could be obtained was Lord George Hill's store at Bunbeg, some twenty miles distant. Surely this extreme wretchedness and neglect must be, to a great extent, attributed to the want of a resident proprietor.

'Leaving Dungloe,' said Mr Tuke, 'we proceeded to Glenties, still on the same property; and throughout our journey met with the most squalid scenes of misery which the imagination can well conceive. Whilst thousands of acres of reclaimable land lies entirely neglected and uncultivated, there are thousands of men both willing and anxious to obtain work but unable to procure it.'

On the following morning, William Forster had an interview with the resident magistrate, as well as with the rector of the parish and some other gentlemen, who gave distressing accounts of the poverty existing around them. Their attention was directed to the necessity for the immediate establishment of soup-kitchens, the employment of women in knitting and the formation of local committees for their relief, extending over several parishes.

'We visited the poorhouse at Glenties, which is in a dreadful state; the people were in fact half starved and only half clothed. The day before they had but one meal of oatmeal and water; and at the time of our visit had not sufficient food in the house for the day's supply. The people complained bitterly, as well they might, and begged us to give them tickets for work, to enable them to leave the place and work on the roads. Some were leaving the house, preferring to die in their own hovels rather than in the poorhouse. Their bedding consisted of dirty straw, in which they were laid in rows on the floor; even as many as six persons being crowded under one rug; and we did not see a blanket at all. The rooms were hardly bearable for filth. The living and the dying were stretched side by side beneath the same miserable covering! No wonder that disease and pestilence were filling the infirmary, and that the pale haggard countenances of the poor boys and girls told of sufferings which it was impossible to contemplate without the deepest commiseration and pity.'

The carelessness and neglect of their duty by Irish landlords have so often come before us during the progress of the Famine, that it is a pleasure to meet with something worth quoting on the other side. 'Throughout Donegal we found', said Mr Tuke, 'the resident proprietors doing much for their suffering tenantry; in many cases, all that landlords could do for their relief and assistance. Several of them had obtained loans under the late Drainage Act, and with this or private resources are employing large numbers of labourers for the improvement of their estates. We met with several who had 100 men employed in this manner. Many of these landlords, as well as the clergy, are most assiduously working in all ways in their power. They have imported large quantities of meal and rice which they sell at prime cost, there being in many districts no dealers to supply those articles; and are making soup at their own houses, and dispensing daily to their famishing neighbours'.[21]

In the South, after Skibbereen, Schull, its neighbour, seems to have suffered most. To cross from Cape Clear to Schull — partly rowing, partly sailing — in a stiff breeze is very exciting and might well cause apprehension but for the crew of athletic Cape men or Capers, as the people of the mainland call them, in whose hands you have placed your safety. With them you are perfectly secure. Those hardy, simple-minded people are as used to the sea as a herdsman is to green fields. Even when they are not actually upon its stormy bosom, they are usually to be seen in groups about the little harbour, leaning against the rocks, quietly smoking their pipes, watching the tide and the weather, and discussing the proper moment for 'going out'.

It is some five miles from Cape Clear to the town of Schull. The distance is not long, but without skill and local knowledge the passage is dangerous, for what seems only a light gale elsewhere makes the sea almost tempestuous among the bluffs and rocky islands of this wild coast, where many a foundering barque has been rescued from destruction by the brave and trusty oarsmen of Cape Clear. Leaving Roaring-water Bay to the north-east and getting in shelter of the land, a church tower, humble in design and proportions, rises in the midst of a graveyard, crowded in one part with tombstones, and almost entirely devoid of them in the other. There rest the mortal remains of many generations of the people of Schull; but it is especially worthy of notice as the burial-ground which had to be doubled in size in order to receive upwards of half the population within its bosom in a single year; and yet all were not interred there: many found a grave in the fields nearest to which they died; many others, among the ruins of their dismantled cabins.

The parish of Schull is situated in the barony of West Carbery, in County Cork, and is very large, containing no fewer than 84,000 acres. The town, a small one, is on the shore in the portion of

A visitor in the cabin of the Mullins family at Schull.

the parish called East Schull; West Schull runs inland towards Skibbereen, and in this division is the village of Ballydehob. The town of Schull is built upon a piece of low level ground, a short distance from which, in the direction of Ballydehob, there is a chain of hills, the highest of which, Mount Gabriel, rises 1,300 feet above sea level.

A correspondent of the *Southern Reporter*, writing from Ballydehob during the first days of January, gave the most piteous account of that village; every house he entered exhibited the same characteristics — no clothing, no food, starvation in the looks of young and old. In a tumbledown cabin resembling a deserted forge, he found a miserable man seated at a few embers, with a starved-looking dog beside him that was not able to crawl. The visitor asked him if he were sick; he answered that he was not, but having got swelled legs working on the roads, he had to give up; he had not tasted food for two days; his family had gone begging about the country and he had no hope of ever seeing them again.

Efforts were still being made at this place to get coffins for half the people; many were tied up in straw and so interred. This writer mentioned what he seems to have regarded as an ingenious contrivance of the Galeen relief committee, namely the use of the coffin with the slide or hinged bottom, but such coffins had been previously used in other places.

He related a touching incident which occurred at Ballydehob, at the time of his visit. Two children, the elder only six years, went into a neighbour's house in search of food. They were asked where their father was and they replied that he was asleep for the last two days. The people became alarmed and went to his cabin, where they found him quite dead, and the merest skeleton. The mother of those children had died some weeks before and their poor devoted father sacrificed his life for them, as the neighbours found some Indian meal in the place, which he was evidently reserving for his infant children, whilst he suffered himself to die of starvation.

But a common effect of the Famine was to harden the hearts of the people and blunt their natural feelings. Hundreds, remarked this correspondent, were daily expiring in their cabins in the three parishes of this neighbourhood, and the people were becoming so accustomed to death that they had lost all those kindly sympathies for the relatives of the departed, which formerly characterised their nature. Want and destitution had so changed them that a sordid avarice and a greediness of disposition to grasp at everything in the shape of food, had seized hold of the souls of those who were considered the most generous and hospitable race on the face of the earth. As happened in other places, no persons attended the funerals; those who were still alive were so exhausted that they were unable to inter the dead, and the duty of doing so was frequently left to casual passers-by.

About the middle of February, Commander Caffin, of her Majesty's ship *Scourge,* visited Schull, in company with the rector, the Rev. Robert Traill Hall. After having entered a few houses, the Commander said to the reverend gentleman: 'My preconceived ideas of your misery seem as a dream to me compared with the reality.'

And yet Captain Caffin had only time to see the cabins on the roadside in which the famine was not so terrible as it was up among the hills and fastnesses where, in one wretched hovel, whose two windows were stuffed with straw, the Rev. Mr Hall found huddled together sixteen human beings. They did not, however, belong to one family — three wretched households were congregated into this miserable abode. Out of the sixteen, two only could be said to be able to work; and on the exertions of those 'two poor pallid objects' had the rest to depend. Eight of the others were crowded into one pallet — it could not be called a bed, being formed of a little straw — which scarcely kept them from the cold mud floor. A poor father was still able to sit up but his legs were dreadfully swollen and he was dead in two or three days after the Rev. Mr Hall's visit. Beside him lay his sister and at his feet two children — all hastening to eternity.

Captain Caffin wrote to a friend an account of his visit to Schull and his letter was published in many of the public journals. 'In the village of Schull', he wrote, 'three- fourths of the inhabitants you meet carry the tale of woe in their features and persons, as they are reduced to mere skeletons, the men in particular, all their physical power wasted away; they have all become beggars. Having a great desire to see with my own eyes some of the misery which was said to exist, Dr Traill Hall, the rector of Schull, offered to drive me to a portion of his parish. I found there was no need to take me beyond the village, to show me the horrors of famine in its worst features. I had read in the papers letters and accounts of this state of things, but I thought they must be highly coloured to attract sympathy; but I there saw the reality of the whole — no exaggeration, for it does not admit of it — famine exists to a fearful degree, with all its horrors. Fever has sprung up consequent upon the wretchedness; and swellings of limbs and body, and diarrhoea, from the want of nourishment, are everywhere to be found.'

Again: 'In no house that I entered was there not to be found the dead or dying; in particularising two or three they may be taken as the picture of the whole — there was no picking or choosing, but we took them just as they came.' A cabin which he entered had, he said, the appearance of wretchedness without, but its interior was misery. The Rev. Mr Hall, on putting his head inside the hole which answered for a door, said: 'Well, Phillis, how is your mother today?' Phillis answered, 'O Sir, is it you? Mother is dead.' Captain Caffin adds — 'And there — fearful reality — was the daughter, a skeleton herself, crouched and crying over the lifeless body of her mother, which was on the floor, cramped up as she had died, with her rags and her cloak about her, by the side of a few embers of peat.'

They came to the cabin of a poor old woman, the door of which was stopped up with dung. She roused up, evidently astonished. They had taken her by surprise. She burst into tears and said she had not been able to sleep since the corpse of the woman had lain in her bed. The circumstance which destroyed her rest happened in this way: Some short time before, a poor miserable woman entered the cabin and asked leave to rest herself for a few moments. She got permission to do so. She lay down, but never rose again. She died in an hour and in this miserable hovel of six feet square the body remained four days before the wretched occupant could get any person to remove it. It is not much to be wondered at that she had lost her rest.

'I could', said Captain Caffin, 'in this manner take you through thirty or more cottages that we visited, but they, without exception, were all alike — the dead and the dying in each; and I could tell you more of the truth of the heartrending scene, were I to mention the lamentations and bitter cries of each of those poor creatures, on the threshold of death. Never in my life have I seen such wholesale misery, nor could I have thought it so complete. All that I have stated above', he concluded 'I have seen with my own eyes, and can vouch for the truth of. And I feel I cannot convey by words the impression left on my mind of this awful state of things. I could tell you also of that which I could vouch for the truth of, but which I did not see myself, such as bodies half eaten by the rats; of two dogs last Wednesday being shot by Mr O'Callaghan whilst tearing a body to pieces; of his mother-in-law stopping a poor woman and asking her what she had on her back, and being replied it was her son, telling her she would smother it; but the poor emaciated woman said it was dead already, and she was going to dig a hole in the churchyard for it. These are things which are of everyday occurrence'.[22]

Taking Ballydehob as a centre, there were, at this time, in a radius of ten or twelve miles around it, twenty-six soup kitchens — at Skibbereen, Baltimore, Sherkin and Cape Clear (three);

Creagh, Castlehaven (two); Union Hall, Aghadown (two); Kilcoe (three); Schull (two); Dunmanus, Crookhaven (two); Caheragh (two); Durrus, Drimoleague, Drenagh, Bantry, Glengariff, Adrigoole, Castletown, Berehaven, and Ballydehob. They were making and distributing daily about 17,000 pints of good meat soup. They did great good but it was of a very partial nature. Mr Commissary Bishop tells us 'they were but a drop in the ocean'. Hundreds, he said, were relieved, but thousands still wanted. And he added that soup kitchens had their attendant evils: an important one in this instance was that the poor small farmers were selling all their cows to the soup kitchens, leaving themselves and their children without milk or butter.

There seems to have been an understanding among the employers that the true state of things, in its naked reality, was not to be given in their communications to Government. It was to be toned down and modified. Hence the studied avoidance of the word 'famine' in almost every official document of the time. Captain Caffin's letter was written to a friend and marked 'private'; but having got into the newspapers, it must, of course, be taken notice of by the Government. Mr Trevelyan lost no time, but at once wrote, enclosing it to Sir John Burgoyne. To use his own words on the occasion, the receipt, from the Commander of the 'Scourge', of 'the awful letter, describing the result of his personal observations in the immediate neighbourhood of Schull', led him (Mr Trevelyan) to make two proposals on the part of the Treasury. And indeed, it must be said, well meant and practical they were.

The first was to send two half-pay medical officers to Schull to try and do something for the sick, many of whom were dying for want of the commonest care; and also to combine with that arrangement, the means of securing the decent interment of the dead. The second proposal was to provide carts for the conveyance of soup to the sick in their houses in and around Schull; a most necessary provision, inasmuch as the starving people were, in numerous cases, unable to walk from their dwellings to the soup kitchen; besides which, in many houses, the whole family were struck down by a combination of fever, starvation and dysentery.

Sir John Burgoyne, as might be expected, picked holes in both proposals. In the carriage of soup to the sick Sir John saw difficulty on account of the scarcity of horses which were, he said, diminishing fast. He added that several, if not all of the judges, who were then proceeding on circuit, were obliged to take the same horses from Dublin throughout, as they would have no chance of changing them as usual.

Then, with regard to the decent burial of the dead, Sir John thought there were legal difficulties in the way and that legislation was necessary before it could be done. He failed to produce any objection against the appointment of the medical officers. In a fortnight after, a Treasury Minute was issued to the effect that Relief Committees should be required to employ proper persons to bury, with as much attention to the feelings of the survivors as circumstances would admit, the dead bodies which could not be buried by any other means. How urgently such an order was called for appears from the fact that, at that time in the neighbourhood of Schull, none but strangers, hired by the clergy, could be found to take any part in a burial.[23]

The incumbent of Schull, the Rev. Robert Traill Hall,[24] a month after Captain Caffin's letter was published, said 'the distress was nothing in Captain Caffin's time compared with what it is now'. On reading Captain Caffin's letter, one would suppose that destitution could not reach a higher point than the one at which he saw it. That letter fixed the attention of the Government upon Schull and yet, strange result, after a month of such attention the Famine was intensified there, instead of being alleviated.

Mr Commissary Bishop had charge of the most famine-visited portion of Co. Cork (Skibbereen always excepted), including West Carbery, Bantry and Bere. He seems to have been an active, intelligent officer and a kind-hearted man; yet his communications, somehow, must have misled the Government, for Mr Trevelyan starts at Captain Caffin's letter, as if suddenly awakened from a dream.

Its contents appeared to be quite new, and almost incredible to him. No wonder, perhaps. On 29 January, a fortnight before the publication of Captain Caffin's letter, Mr Bishop wrote to Mr Trevelyan: 'The floating depot for Schull arrived yesterday and has commenced issues; this removes all anxiety for that quarter.'

On the day before Captain Caffin's letter was written, Mr Bishop said: 'At Schull, in both east and west division, I found the distress, or rather the mortality had pretty well increased.' And this, notwithstanding the floating depot. Yet in the midst of the famine-slaughter described by Captain Caffin, Mr Bishop was still hopeful, for he said: 'The Relief Committees at Schull and Crookhaven exert themselves greatly to benefit the poor. There is an ample supply of provisions at each place'.[25]

How did they manage to die of starvation at Schull? — one is tempted to ask. Yet they did, and at Ballydehob too, the other town of the parish; for, three weeks after the announcement of the 'ample supply of provisions', the following news reaches us from the latter place, on the most reliable authority. A naval officer, Mr Scarlet, who was with the *Mercury* and *Gipsey* delivering provisions in the neighbourhood of Schull, on his return to Cork, wrote on 8 March, to his admiral, Sir Hugh Pigot, in these terms: 'After discharging our cargoes in the boats to Ballydehob, we went on shore and, on passing through the town we went into the ruins of a house and there were two women lying dead, and two, all but dead, lying along with them. When we enquired how it was that they did not bury them, a woman told us that they did not know and that one of them had been dead for five days. As we were coming down to the boat, we told the boat's crew if they wanted to see a sight to go up the street. When they went, there were four men with hand-barrows there and the men belonging to the boats helped to carry the corpses to the burial ground, where they dug holes, and put them in without coffins.'

At this period of the Famine, things had come to such a pass that individual cases of death from starvation were seldom reported and, when they were, they failed to attract much attention, deaths by wholesale had become so common. To be sure, when Dr Crowley wrote from Skibbereen that himself and Dr Donovan had interred, in a kitchen garden, the corpse of a person eleven days dead, the case, being somewhat peculiar, had interest enough to be made public; but an ordinary death from hunger would be deemed a very ordinary affair indeed.

I will here give a specimen or two of the way in which the progress of the Famine was chronicled at the close of 1846 and through the winter and spring of 1847.

The correspondent of the *Kerry Examiner*, writing from Dingle on 8 February said: 'The state of the people of this locality is horrifying. Fever, famine and dysentery are daily increasing, deaths from hunger daily occurring, averaging weekly twenty — men, women and children thrown into the graves without a coffin — dead bodies in all parts of the country, being several days dead before discovered — no inquests to inquire how they came by their death, as hunger has hardened the hearts of the people. Those who survive cannot long remain so — the naked wife and children of the deceased, staring them in the face — their bones penetrating through the skin — not a morsel of flesh to be seen on their bodies — and not a morsel of food can they procure to eat. From all parts of the country they crowd into the town for relief, and not a pound of meal is to be had in the wretched town for any price.'

'This parish (Ventry, Dingle) contained, six months since, 3,000 souls; over 500 of these have perished and three-fourths of them interred coffinless. They were carried to the churchyard, some on lids and ladders, more in baskets — aye, and scores of them thrown beside the nearest ditch and there left to the mercy of the dogs, which have nothing else to feed on. On the 12th instant I went through the parish to give a little assistance to some poor orphans and widows. I entered a hut and there were the poor father and his three children dead beside him and in such a state of decomposition that I had to get baskets, and have their remains carried in them'.[26]

A hearse piled with coffins — or rather rough, undressed boards slightly nailed together — each containing a corpse, passed through the streets of Cork, unaccompanied by a single human being save the driver of the vehicle. Three families from the country, consisting of fourteen persons, took up their residence in a place called Peacock Lane, in the same city. After one week the household stood thus: Seven dead, six in fever, one still able to be up.

The apostle of temperance, the Rev. Theobald Mathew, gave the following evidence before a Committee of the House of Lords on 'Colonisation from Ireland':

Question 2,359: 'You have spoken of the state of things [the Famine] as leading to a very great influx of wretchedness and pauperism into the city of Cork. Will you yourself describe what you have seen and known?'

Answer: 'No tongue can describe — no understanding can conceive — the misery and wretchedness that flowed into Cork from the western parts of the country; the streets were impassable with crowds of country persons. At the commencement they obtained lodgings and the sympathies of the citizens were awakened; but when fever began to spread in Cork they became alarmed for themselves and they were anxious at any risk to get rid of those wretched creatures. The lodginghouse keepers always turned them out when they got sick. We had no additional fever hospitals; the Workhouse was over full and those poor creatures perished miserably in the streets and alleys. Every morning a number were found dead in the streets; they were thrown out by the poor creatures in whose houses they lodged. Many of them perished in rooms and cellars, without its being known, and without their receiving any aid from those outside. It may appear as if the citizens of Cork and the clergy of Cork had neglected their duty; but they did not. The calamity was so great and so overwhelming, that it was impossible to prevent those calamities. As one instance, I may mention that one Sunday morning I brought Captain Forbes, who came over with the *Jamestown*, United States' frigate, and Mr William Rathbone and several other persons, to show the state of the neighbourhood in which I resided and to show them the thousands whom we were feeding at the depot. While we were going round a person told me, 'There is a house that has been locked up two or three days.' It was a cabin in a narrow alley. We went in and we saw seventeen persons lying on the floor, all with fever and no one to give them assistance. Captain Forbes was struck with horror; he never thought there could be in any part of the world such misery. That was in the south suburbs. A poor, wretched widow woman resided there; she let it out for lodgings, and received those people as lodgers, who all got the fever. We three gave what relief we could, and got them conveyed to the hospitals; but they all died.'

Question 2,365: 'Can you form any judgment what proportion of the population, which is thus added at present, bears to the ordinary population of the City of Cork?'

Answer: 'Those poor creatures, the country poor, are now houseless and without lodgings; no one will take them in; they sleep out at night. The citizens of Cork have adopted what I consider a very unchristian and inhuman line of conduct. They have determined to get rid of them. Under the authority of an Act of Parliament, they take them up as sturdy beggars and vagrants, and confine them at night in a market-place, and the next morning send them out in a cart five miles from the town; and there they are left, and a great part of them perish, for they have no home to go to. When they fled from the country, their houses were thrown down or consumed for fuel by the neighbours who remained and those poor creatures have no place to lay their heads'.[27]

It would be a useless and a harrowing task to continue such terrible details. I therefore close this chapter with some account of Bantry, that town having had the misfortune to be the rival of Schull, Skibbereen and Mayo during the Famine-slaughter.

The deaths at Bantry had become fearfully numerous before they attracted any great share of public sympathy, or even, it would seem, of Government attention. The *Southern Reporter* of 5 January published this curt announcement from that town: 'Five inquests today. Verdict — Death by starvation.' The jury having given in its verdict, the foreman on their part proceeded to say that they felt it to be their duty to state, under the correction of the court, that it was their opinion that if the Government of the country should persevere in its determination of refusing to use the means available to it, for the purpose of lowering the price of food, so as to place it within the reach of the labouring poor, the result would be a sacrifice of human life from starvation to a fearful extent and endangerment of property and the public peace. This remonstrance was committed to writing and signed E. O'Sullivan, foreman; Samuel Hutchins, JP; Richard White, JP.

One of the five cases was that of Catherine Sheehan, a child two years old. She had been a strong healthy child, never having complained of any sickness till she began to pine away for want of food. Her father was employed on the public works and earned ninepence a day, which was barely enough to purchase food for himself to enable him to continue at work. This child had had no food for four days before her death, except a small morsel of bread and seaweed. She died on the evening of Christmas day.

The case of Richard Finn was another of the five. He went into a house where they were making oatmeal gruel. He begged so hard for a little that the woman of the house took up some of it for him, when it was about half boiled. The food disagreed with him and he was able to take only a small portion of it. He soon got into a fainting state and was lifted into a car by four men, in order to be carried to the Workhouse. One of the priests, Rev. Mr Barry, PP, was sent for. He was at the Relief Committee but left immediately to attend Finn. In his examination before the coroner, he said he found him in a dying state but quite in his senses. He would not delay hearing his confession till he reached the Workhouse but heard it in the car. Finn was then removed to the House and laid on a bed in his clothes, where he received the sacrament of Extreme Unction. 'I feared', said the Rev. Mr Barry, 'the delay of stripping him.' And the reverend gentleman was right, for he had scarcely concluded his ministrations when Finn expired.

Every Catholic will understand how severely the physical and mental energies of priests are taxed during times of fever, cholera, smallpox and the like; but all such epidemics combined could scarcely cause them such ceaseless work and sleepless anxiety as the Famine did, more especially in its chief centres. To those who are not Catholics, I may say that every priest feels bound, under the most solemn obligations, to administer the last sacraments to every individual committed to his care, who had come to the use of reason.

What, then, must their lives have been during the Famine? Not only had they to attend the dying but they were expected, and they felt it to be their duty, to be present at Relief Committees, to wait on officials, write letters and do everything they thought could in any manner aid them in saving the lives of the people. Their starving flocks looked to them for temporal as well as spiritual help and, in the Famine, they were continually in crowds about their dwellings, looking for food and consolation. The priest was often without food for himself and had not the heart to meet his people when he had nothing to give them.

An instance of this occurred in a severely visited parish of the West. The priest one day saw before his door a crowd — hundreds, he thought — of his parishioners seeking relief. He had become so prostrate and hopeless at their present sufferings and future prospects that, taking his breviary, he left the house by a private way and bent his steps to a neighbouring wood. On reaching it, he knelt down and began to recite his office aloud, to implore Almighty God to have mercy on his people and himself. He did not expect to leave that wood alive. After a time he heard a voice not far off: he became alarmed, fearing his retreat had been discovered. Strange as the coincidence seems, it is perfectly true; the voice he heard was that of a neighbouring priest, a friend of his, who had taken the very same course and for the same reason. Gaining strength and consolation from having met, and giving each other courage, they returned to their homes, resolving to face the worst.

A physician, an excellent, kind-hearted man who had been sent on duty to Bantry in the later stages of the Famine, said one day to a priest there: 'Well, Father —, how are you getting on these times?' 'Badly', was the reply, 'for I often remain late in bed in the morning, not knowing where to look for my breakfast when I get up.'[28]

At this same time, there was a charitable lady in or near Bantry who had discovered that another of the priests was not infrequently dinnerless; so she insisted on being permitted to send him that important meal, ready-cooked, at a certain hour every day, begging of him to be at home, if possible, at the hour fixed. This arrangement went on for a while to her great satisfaction, but news reached her one day that Father _____ seldom partook of her dinner. Such dreadful cases of starvation came to his door that he frequently gave the good lady's dinner away. She determined that he must not sink and die; and to carry out her view she hit upon an ingenious plan. She gave the servant, who took the dinner to Father _____, strict orders not to leave the house until he had dined; the reason to be given to him for this was that her mistress wished her to bring back the things in which the dinner had been carried to him. That priest, I am glad to say, is still among us and, should these lines meet his eye, he will remember the circumstances and the honest and true authority on which it is related.

A short time after the five inquests above referred to were held, the *Cork Examiner* published the following extract from a private letter: 'Each day brings with it its own horrors. The mind recoils from the contemplation of the scenes we are compelled to witness every hour. Ten inquests in Bantry — there should have been at least *200 inquests*. Every day, every hour produces its own victims — holocausts offered at the shrine of political economy. Famine and pestilence are sweeping away hundreds, but they have now no terrors for the people. Their only regret seems to be that they are not relieved from their sufferings by some process more speedy and less painful. *Since the inquests were held here on Monday, there have been twenty-four deaths from starvation;* and, if we can judge from appearances, before the termination of another week the number will be incredible. As to holding any more inquests, it is mere nonsense; *the number of deaths is beyond counting.* Nineteen out of every twenty deaths that have occurred in this parish, for the last two months, were caused by starvation. I have known children in the remote districts of the parish, and in the neighbourhood of the town, too, live, some of them for two, some three, and some of them for *four days on water!* On the sea shore, or convenient to it, the people are more fortunate, as they can get seaweed, which, when boiled and mixed with a little Indian corn, or wheaten meal, they eat, and thank Providence for providing them with even that, to allay the cravings of hunger.'

Although the writer of the above letter said, and with reason it would seem, that the holding of any more inquests at Bantry was useless, the very week after it was written a batch of inquests were held there, one of which bids fair to be, for a long time, famous on account of the verdict returned. There were forty deaths, but from some cause, perhaps for want of time, there were only fifteen inquests. A respectable jury having been sworn, the first of these was upon a man named John Sullivan.

One of the witnesses in the case said a messenger came and announced to him that a man was lying on the old road in a bad state. Witness proceeded to the place but, in the first instance, alone; finding the man still alive, he returned for help to remove him. He got a servant boy and a cart; but on going again to where Sullivan was lying, he found life was extinct.

The jury having consulted, the foreman announced their verdict in these terms: 'From the multitude of deaths which have taken place in the locality and the number of inquests which have already been held, without any good resulting, he thought, with his fellow-jurors, that they ought to bring in a general verdict, inculpating Lord John Russell as the head of the Government. That Minister had the power of keeping the people alive and he would not do so. Notwithstanding the fatal consequences which had attended his policy, he had expressed his determination to persevere in the same course and therefore he (the foreman) thought that he was guilty of this death and of the rest. He would bring in no other verdict but one of *wilful murder* against Lord John Russell.'

The Rev. Mr Barry suggested that the verdict should simply record the immediate cause of death — starvation; and the jury might append their opinion as to how far it was attributable to the neglect of Lord John Russell in yielding to the interests of a class of greedy monopolists. The foreman said he wished it should be remembered that the opinion which he had expressed with reference to the conduct of the Government was that of men upon their oaths. A verdict was ultimately given of death from starvation, with the addition mentioned.

The inquest was held in the court-house, in the presence of three magistrates, assisted by the Catholic clergy of the town and the officers of the Constabulary.

Other verdicts of the same tendency, although not so decided in tone as this one, were recorded in different parts of the country. At Lismore an inquest was held on a man, also named Sullivan, and the jury found that his death was caused by the neglect of the Government in not sending food into the country *in due time*. In this town fourteen horses died of starvation in one week.

Whilst Bantry was in the condition described above, Dr Stephens was sent by the Board of Health to examine the Workhouse there. He found it simply dreadful. Here is an extract from his report, which duty compels me, however unwillingly, to quote: 'Language', he said, 'would fail to give an adequate idea of the state of the fever hospital. *Such an appalling, awful and heart-sickening condition as it presented I never witnessed*, or could think possible to exist in a civilised or Christian community. As I entered the house the stench that proceeded from it was most dreadful and noisome; but, oh! what scenes presented themselves to my view as I proceeded through the wards and passages: patients lying on straw, naked and in their excrements, a light covering over them — in two beds living beings beside the dead, in the same bed with them and dead since the night before. There was no medicine — no drink — no fire. The wretched creatures, dying from thirst, were constantly crying 'Water, water', but there was no Christian hand to give them even a cup of cold water for the love of God.'

Towards the end of April, the Rev. Mr Barry estimated the deaths from famine, in Bantry alone, at 4,000.

Some time ago, speaking with a gentleman, a distinguished public man, about the hinged coffin, he said: 'At the time of the Famine I was a boy, residing not far from Bantry. I have seen one of those hinged coffins, which had borne more than 300 corpses to the grave. I have seen men go along the roads with it, to collect dead bodies as they met them.'

Good God! — picking up human forms, made to his image and likeness, and lately the tenements of immortal souls, as fishermen may sometimes be seen on the seashore, gathering the debris of a wreck after a storm!

With such specimens of the Irish Famine before us, we cannot but feel the justice, as well as the eloquence, of the following passage: 'I do not think it possible', wrote Mr A. Shafto Adair, 'for an English reader, however powerful his imagination, to conceive the state of Ireland during the past winter, or its present condition. Famines and plagues will suggest themselves, with their ghastly and repulsive incidents — the dead mother — the dying infant — the feast of cannibals — Athens — Jerusalem — Marseilles. But these awful facts stand forth as dark spots in the illuminated chronicles of time; episodes, it may be, of some magnificent epoch in a nation's history — tragedies acted in remote times, or in distant regions — the actors, the inhabitants of beleaguered cities, or the citizens of a narrow territory. But here the tragedy is enacted with no narrower limits than the boundaries of a kingdom, the victims — an entire people — within our own days, at our own thresholds.'[29]

13

Expansion of public works

The expansion of the system of Public Works, under the Labour-rate Act, was as unparalleled as it was unexpected by the Government. The number of persons employed rose, in less than three months, from 20,000 to 400,000; the return for the week ending 5 October was just 20,000; for the week ending 26 December, 398,000! there being at the latter period at least 150,000 on the books of the officers of the works, who either would not or could not be employed; the famine- stricken were, meanwhile, hastening to their shroudless and coffinless graves by the thousand.

During its progress the terrible scourge was checked more or less by the various means made use of, but it was never stayed. The Government was not only astonished — they were profoundly alarmed at the magnitude to which the public works had grown. Almost the sole object of those works was *to apply a labour test to destitution;* but the authorities now felt that they must dismiss that pet theory of theirs and try to feed the people in the most direct way possible.

At the opening of Parliament the Prime Minister brought forward, as we have seen, a new Irish Relief Act, the 10th Vic., c. 7. It was called an Act for the temporary relief of destitute persons in Ireland. It was framed according to the views expressed by the Prime Minister in his speech of 25 January, and became law on 26 February. Its chief provisions were: That Relief Committees should be formed by order of the Lord Lieutenant, and their powers were to extend to November 1847, on which day they were to cease. Those Committees were to consist of the Justices of the district, the Poor Law Guardians and one of the Inspectors appointed by the Relief Commissioners. A Finance Committee was to be selected from the General Committee, but the Lord Lieutenant was empowered to add others to it.

A chief duty of Relief Committees was to make out lists of persons requiring relief, but the Finance Committees had authority to examine such lists and correct them if necessary. The money required for this new system of relief was to be levied and collected as a poor-rate and the Guardians of any Union who refused to do this could be dissolved by the Poor Law Commissioners who were also empowered to appoint paid Guardians in their place. The Treasury, on being applied to by the Relief Commissioners, was authorised to make advances to enable them to grant loans in aid of rates, but no such grant or loan was to be made after 1 October 1847.

Immediate preparations were made to carry this Act into effect. Commissioners were appointed; a General Order was issued by the Lord Lieutenant, and in due time that most potential of documents, a Treasury Minute, was published. The following were the Commissioners appointed under the Act: Sir John F. Burgoyne, Thomas N. Redington, Under Secretary; Edward T.B. Twistleton, Colonel Duncan McGregor, Commissary-General Sir Randolph J. Routh and Colonel Harry D. Jones.

In virtue of the powers conferred on him, his Excellency, in his General Order, declared that besides the Justices, Poor Law Guardians and Relief Inspector, archbishops and bishops of every denomination, the principal officiating clergy of the three denominations, and the three highest ratepayers of the district should be members of Relief Committees.

The Treasury Minute repeats the numbers on the public works during the month of February. They were, in the

Week ending 6	615,055
Week ending 13	605,715
Week ending 20	668,749
Week ending 27	708,228

It also gives the outlay for three months, not including the expenses of the Commissariat Department, which were by no means inconsiderable.

For December 1846....................	£545,054
For January 1847	£736,125
For February 1847	£944,141

being nearly a million pounds for that month. Besides excluding the expenditure of the Commissariat, this amount did not, of course, take in the very large sums disbursed by charitable bodies and by private individuals.

The new Relief Act came into force on 27 February and the Government obtained, without any difficulty, the permission of Parliament to borrow £8,000,000 to carry out its provisions. As this Act was to supersede the Public Works, it was decreed by the Treasury Minute that on Saturday, 20 March the labourers on those works should be reduced by not less than twenty per cent. The remainder were to be dismissed by successive reductions at such times and in such proportions as would be determined by the Board. The order in which dismissals were to be carried out was that persons holding ten acres of land and upwards were to be discharged on 20 March, even if they should exceed the twenty per cent; if they fell below it .the persons holding the next largest quantity of land should be discharged in order that the full twenty per cent should be dismissed. In districts where rations of soup could be supplied by the Relief Committees, the Relief Works were to be entirely suspended.

As soon as the Relief Commissioners entered upon their duties they drew up a code of rules for the information and guidance of Relief Committees.

The following are the principal:

1. Relief Committees to be under the regulating control of a Finance Committee for each Union.

2. As to funds: local or other subscriptions, with donations from Government and moneys in hand of Poor Law Guardians, to be regarded as appropriated rates on electoral divisions, where needed.

3. The funds in hands of existing Relief Committees were to be generally available for Committees under the new Act.

4. Relief to be given exclusively in food; gratuitously to the absolutely desolate; by reasonable prices to such as were in employment, or had the means of purchasing.

5. There was to be a Government Inspector of every Union, who was to be an ex-officio member of every Committee under the Act in the Union.

6. Persons requiring relief were to be classed under four heads, namely: 1. Those who were destitute, helpless or impotent; 2. Destitute able-bodied persons not holding land; 3. Destitute able-bodied persons who were holders of small portions of land; 4. The able-bodied employed at wages insufficient for their support, when the price of food was very high.

7. The first three classed to get gratuitous relief, but the fourth to be relieved by the sale of food of a cheap description: and it was specially laid down that there were to be 'no gratuitous

supplies of food to them'. 'This', said the Instructions, 'is to be a fixed rule.'

Yet it was afterwards modified with regard to class 4: the clause saying 'they were to be relieved by the sale of food of a cheap description' did not, it would seem, mean that such food was to be sold under its value. This was represented as a hardship, and on 11 May the Relief Commissioners ruled, that with regard to the price of food to class 4, 'any food cooked in a boiler might be sold under first cost.'

8. Persons receiving wages, or refusing hire, to be excluded from gratuitous relief.

9. To entitle holders of land to gratuitous relief, it should be absolutely required of them to proceed with the cultivation of their land.

The relief lists were to be revised every fortnight; the food best suited to each district, and the most easily obtained *there*, to be at once taken into consideration.

As to rations, it was considered that the most nourishing and economical food was soup made after some of the approved recipes, with a portion of bread, meal or biscuit.

The twenty-sixth rule fixed the quantity and quality of a ration. It was to consist of

1 lb. of bread;or
1 lb. of biscuit;or
1 lb. of meal or flour of any grain; or
1 quart of soup thickened with a portion of meal, according to the known recipes, and one quarter ration of bread, biscuit or meal, in addition.

Persons above nine years of age to have one full ration; those under that age half a ration. These rules were promulgated from the Relief Commission Office, in Dublin Castle, on 8 March.

A difficulty having arisen as to what could be strictly considered 'soup', the following definition of it was issued by the Relief Commissioners to the Inspecting officers of each Union.

'Sir, As the term "Soup" in the Instructions seems to have created an impression with many parties that only the liquid ordinarily so called is meant and that meat must necessarily form an ingredient, the Relief Commissioners beg that the general term "soup," in their Instructions, may be understood to include any food cooked in a boiler, and distributed in a liquid state, thick or thin, and whether composed of meat, fish, vegetables, grain or meal.'

The Commissioners published their first report on 10 March,

eleven days after the Relief Act came into force; an exceedingly short time in which to have done anything worth reporting; but this is explained by the fact that the Commissioners and their officers had been set to work a considerable time before the Relief Act had become law; the Government assuming that it would meet with no real opposition in its passage through Parliament.

From this Report we learn that there were, at the time, 2,049 electoral divisions in Ireland; and from a later one that Blackrock, near Dublin, was the smallest electoral division, consisting only of 257 acres; that the largest was Belmullet, in County Mayo, which contained 145,598 acres. The extremes in the valuation of electoral divisions were, — Mullaghderg, in Glenties Union, £331 10s. 0d.; South Dublin, £402,516 3s. 4d. So that a shilling rate levied off Mullaghderg would produce just £16 12s. 6d., which in all probability would not pay for the time necessary to collect it.

The Commissioners reported that two conditions laid down by them had called forth several remonstrances, namely, 1. The prohibition of administering relief under the Act *in aid of wages;* and 2. The restriction to the sale of food under cost price, with the exception of soup.

The quantity of stationery necessary for the carrying out of the Relief Act is certainly worth noting. In the mere preparation for their work, the Commissioners had delivered to them upwards of 10,000 books, 80,000 sheets and 3,000,000 card tickets; the gross weight of all not being less than fourteen tons!

The determination of the authorities to supply, as far as possible, the starving people with cooked food, especially soup, made the question of preparing it for millions one of vast importance. To produce the greatest quantity of cooked food in a palatable form, at the minimum of cost and with the maximum of nutrition, might save the country half a million pounds, and many thousands of lives besides. With that object the Government fixed upon Monsieur Soyer of the Reform Club, and appointed him Head Cook to the people of Ireland. His elevation to this unique office was announced with considerable flourish.

'We learn', said one of the London journals, 'that the Government have resolved forthwith to despatch M. Soyer, the *chef de cuisine* of the Reform Club, to Ireland with ample instructions to provide his soups for the starving millions of Irish people.' This journal further informed us that artisans were busy day and night constructing kitchens, apparatus, etc., with which M. Soyer was to start for Dublin. His plans had been examined and approved of. The soup had been served to several of the best judges 'of the noble art of gastronomy in the Reform Club, not as soup for the poor, but as soup furnished for the day, in the *carte'*. It was declared excellent.

He undertook to supply the whole poor of Ireland, at one meal for each person each day. This meal with a biscuit, he assured the Executive, would be more than sufficient to sustain the strength of a strong and healthy man. One hundred gallons of the soup was to be produced for £1. And M. Soyer had satisfied the Government that he would furnish enough and to spare of most nourishing food 'for the poor of these realms'; and it was confidently anticipated that there would be no more deaths from starvation in Ireland.[1]

M. Soyer arrived in Dublin on 1 March, bringing with him his model kitchen and apparatus, and a building to receive them was erected on the ground in front of the Royal Barracks, not far from the principal entrance to the Phoenix Park. Before leaving London he had published some of the recipes according to which he intended to make various kinds of soups for the starving Irish. Objections were raised in the columns of the *Times* against the small quantity of meat he used in making some of those soups.

'A brother *artiste*', as M. Soyer called him, maintained that a quarter of a pound of meat, allowed in making two gallons in his soup No.1, was not at all enough. M. Soyer rather jauntily replied that he had made two gallons of excellent soup without any meat and that he had, at the moment, three soups 'on taste', two with meat and one without and he defied the 'scientific palate' of his brother *artiste* 'to tell which was which'.

'The meat', said M. Soyer, 'I consider of no more value than the other ingredients, but to give a flavour by properly blending the gelatine and the osmazome, for', he added with complacent self-reliance, 'in compounding the richest soup, the balance of it is the great art.'

His brother *artiste*, M. Jaquet, of Johnson's tavern, Clare Court, rejoined that he never questioned M. Soyer's ability to make a palatable and pleasing soup with little or no meat, but that he himself had not acquired the valuable art of making nutritious and useful soup without meat and that he would not like to make the experiment of doing so, 'for the use of the destitute poor'. He expressed the hope that recipe no. 1 might be analysed, and if it had all things necessary for nourishment, he, of course, was silenced.

M. Jaquet had his wish. Scientific people took up M. Soyer's receipts, and dealt with them, correctly and justly, no doubt, but in a manner that must have been anything but agreeable to the great *artiste* of the Reform Club, who seems to have had very exalted ideas of the importance of the mission on which he was sent to Ireland.

Thus wrote the *Lancet* on the subject: 'The mass of the poor population of Ireland is in a state of starvation. Gaunt famine, with raging fever at her heels, are marching through the length and breadth of the sister island and they threaten to extend their fury to this country. The British public, under the form of clubs, committees and relief associations, are actively engaged in sending food to the famine districts. All this is done without boasting or ostentation. But parliament and the executive, in the midst of the best intentions, seems to be agitated by a spasmodic feeling of benevolence; at one time adopting public works, at another preaching a poor law — now considering the propriety of granting sixteen millions for railways, and then descending to M. Soyer, the chief cook of the Reform Club, with his ubiquitous kitchens and soups, at some three farthings the quart, which is to feed all hungry Ireland.

'As this soup quackery (for it is no less) seems to be taken by the rich as a salve for their consciences, and with a belief that famine and fever may be kept at bay by M. Soyer and his kettles, it is right to look at the constitution of this soup of pretence, and the estimate formed of it by the talented but eccentric self-deceived originator.

'M. Soyer proposes to make soup of the following portions: — Leg of beef, four ounces; dripping fat, two ounces; flour, eight ounces; brown sugar, half an ounce; water, *two gallons*.

'These items are exclusive of the onions, a few turnip parings, celery tops and a little salt, which can hardly be considered under the head of food. The above proportions give less than three ounces of solid nutriment to each quart of soup à la Soyer'. Of this its inventor is reported to have said to the Government "that a bellyful once a day, with a biscuit (we quote from the *Observer*), will be more than sufficient to maintain the strength of a strong healthy man."

'To bring this to the test. Organic chemistry proves to us that the excretae from the body of a healthy subject by the eliminatory organs must at least amount to twelve or fourteen ounces; and organic chemistry will not, we fear, bend to the most inspired receipts of the most miraculous cookery book, to supply the number of ounces without which the organic chemistry of the human body will no more go on than will the steam-engine without fuel. M. Soyer, supposing each meal of his soup for the poor to amount to a quart, supplies less than three ounces, or less than a quarter the required amount, and of that only one solitary half ounce of animal aliment, diluted, or rather dissolved in a bellyful of water. Bulk of water, the gastronomic may depend, will not make up for the deficiency of solid convertible aliment.

No culinary digesting, or stewing, or boiling, can convert four ounces into twelve, unless, indeed, the laws of animal physiology can be unwritten, and some magical power be made to reside in the cap and apron of the cook for substituting fluids in the place of solids, and *aqua pura* in place of solids in the animal economy. 'It seems necessary to bring forward these facts, as M. Soyer's soup had inspired the public mind with much satisfaction — a satisfaction which, we venture to say, will never reach the public stomach.

'Marquises and lords and ladies may taste the meagre liquid, and pronounce it agreeable to their gustative inclinations; but something more than an agreeable titillation of the palate is required to keep up that manufactory of blood, bone and muscle which constitutes the ''strong healthy man''.'

During M. Soyer's visit to Ireland, a Dublin chemist read, before the Royal Dublin Society, a paper upon the nutritive and pecuniary value of various kinds of cooked food. He had previously put himself in communication with M. Soyer, who showed him over his model kitchen, and allowed him to analyse his soups. The result of this analysis was remarkable, for they found that M. Soyer's dearest soup was the least nutritive, whilst his cheapest soup was the most so: a proportion which held through all the soups analysed; their nutritive qualities being in an inverse ratio to their prices.'[2] So the famous cook of the Reform Club did not know the comparative nutritive qualities of his own soups.

But a still greater came on the scene in the person of Sir Henry Marsh, the Queen's physician and long at the head of his profession in this country. He published a pamphlet of some ten pages, not for the purpose of finding fault with M. Soyer or his soups, but evidently to set the public right on the question of food, as they seemed to have taken up the idea that there resided some hidden power in the cook's recipe, distinct from the ingredients he used.

Sir Henry thus dealt with soup food: 'A soft semi-liquid diet will maintain the life and health of children, and in times of scarcity will be sufficient for those adults whose occupations are sedentary, and is best suited to those who are reduced by and recovering from a wasting disease. For the labourer the food must be in part solid, requiring mastication and insalivation, and not rapid of digestion. Food, however nutritious, which is too quickly digested is soon followed by a sense of hunger and emptiness and consequent sinking and debility. Food of this description is unsuited to the labourer. It will not maintain strength nor will it maintain health and, if long persevered in, it will be followed

by some one or other of the prevailing diseases which result immediately from deficient, imperfect and impoverished blood.'
Sir Henry Marsh, said one of the morning journals, did not attack M. Soyer, but he demolished the soup kitchens as effectively as if he did.

As soon as M. Soyer's model soup depot was completed, he resolved to open it for public inspection with a good deal of ceremony. On 5 April, therefore, the opening day, the space in front of the Royal Barracks presented a very animated scene; flags floated gaily in the breeze; the rich dresses of ladies of birth and fashion contrasted pleasingly with the costly and superb military uniforms among which they moved; and M. Soyer was all politeness in explaining to his distinguished visitors the arrangements and perfections of his soup kitchens. In a famine-stricken land, the good taste of this exhibition was doubtful enough: at any rate it was criticised with no sparing hand.

'When I got a card of invitation', wrote one, 'I thought I was to see M. Soyer's peculiar appliances for making soup for the poor; but no — it was a ''gala day'': drums beating, flags flying.' Then the writer grew political, and said bitterly that he 'envied not the Union flag the position it occupied as it flaunted in triumph from the chimney top of the soup kitchen; it was its natural and most meet position; the rule of which it is the emblem has brought our country to require soup kitchens — and no more fitting ornament could adorn their tops'. All the parade he could have borne, he added, but what he considered indefensible was the exhibition of some hundreds of Irish beggars 'to demonstrate what ravening hunger will make the image of God submit to'.[3]

'His Excellency the Lord Lieutenant was there', wrote the *Evening Packet* (a conservative journal); 'the ladies Ponsonby and many other fair and delicate creatures assembled; there were earls and countesses and lords and generals and colonels and commissioners and clergymen and doctors; for, reader, it was a *gala day — a grand gala.*' The provincial press dealt with the proceedings in the same spirit.

Like many other great men, M. Soyer, in a short time, found that Ireland was his 'difficulty'; so he resolved, somewhat suddenly, it would appear, to return to the more congenial atmosphere of the Reform Club. His resolution was thus announced in one of the Dublin morning journals: 'SOYER'S MODEL KITCHEN — By the special desire of several charitable ladies, who have visited and paid particular attention to the working of the model kitchen, it will be opened again on Saturday next, from two to six, on which day those ladies, under the direction of Mrs L -, will attend and serve the poor. The admission for the view on that day will be five shillings each, to be distributed by the Lord Mayor in charity; after which the kitchen will be closed, M. Soyer being obliged to leave for the Reform Club, London.'

This smacked very much of a 'positively last appearance'. Referring to it, a Dublin journal exclaimed: — 'Five shillings each to see paupers feed! Five shillings each to watch the burning blush of shame chasing pallidness from poverty's wan cheek! Five shillings each! When the animals in the Zoological Gardens can be inspected at feeding time for sixpence!'[4]

A few gentlemen gave M. Soyer a dinner and a snuff box before he left, and so his Irish mission was brought to a close; but his name was not forgotten, for *Sawyer's soup* was long a standing joke with a certain class of the Dublin people. Had the word come into popular use at the time, there is little doubt that M. Soyer's undertaking to feed the starving Irish would have been called a *fiasco*.[5]

Philanthropists of a stamp different from M. Soyer brought forward schemes for the good of Ireland at this time. They related chiefly to the reclamation of her waste lands. At the opening of Parliament in 1847, Lord John Russell, as we have seen, proposed to introduce a Bill on this subject, one million being the first grant to be made for the purpose. The plan on which the reclamation was to be carried out is given in the resumè of Lord John's speech at the opening of the session. It was the very best of the Premier's measures for the permanent improvement of Ireland; but, according to Mr Disraeli, it was faintly proposed and finally abandoned in deference to the expressed opinion of Sir Robert Peel who, at the time, governed from the Opposition benches.

The area of Ireland is 20,808,271 statute acres. Of these it is commonly admitted that 18,000,000, or thereabouts, are susceptible of cultivation. In 1845, somewhat over 13,000,000 of acres were in cultivation, whilst nearly 5,000,000, which could be brought under culture, lay barren. Referring to the estimate of those writers who held that Ireland contained 4,600,000 acres of waste, which could be made arable, Dr Robert Kane, author of *Industrial Resources of Ireland*, said he did not think the estimate too high; and this opinion was quoted approvingly by Lord John Russell.[6]

But the question might still remain, — could those 4,600,000 acres be profitably cultivated? Would their cultivation give remunerative interest on the capital expended? That is the purely commercial view of the matter; but there is another which should not be overlooked: Would it not be wise policy to increase the resources of a country — to increase its area of cultivation — to extend the means of employing and feeding its population, even though the work did not actually make a very remunerative commercial return? English capital has gone to make canals and railroads and harbours, and open mines for the antipodes, often with little or no return; not unfrequently with total loss; surely as much risk ought to be taken for home improvements, in which patriotism should come to the aid of commercial enterprise.

It would seem to be a question well worth the consideration of statesmen, whether or not, in the reclamation of wastes, it would be the true and enlightened policy to act upon the commercial idea alone.

From whatever cause, Irish landowners did not, to any considerable extent, take up in earnest the question of the reclamation of waste lands. Roused by the pressure of the times and the impending poor-rate, the majority of them looked 'for salvation' to other means — to the eviction of their numerous tenantry — the clearing of their estates from the seemingly superfluous population by emigration or ejectment.

The readers of these pages cannot forget that Mayo suffered as much as, if not more than any other county during the Famine; yet here was the state of its surface at the time of that dreadful visitation: entire area of the County Mayo 1,300,000 acres; of these only 500,000 acres were under cultivation, 800,000 acres being unreclaimed; of which 800,000 acres, Griffith says, nearly 500,000 could be reclaimed with profit — that is, just half the county was cultivated.

The Dean of Killala gave the following evidence about the same county before the Devon Commission:

Quest.73. 'Is there sufficient employment for the people in the cultivation of the arable land?'

Answer. 'No; it does not employ them half the year.'

Quest.74: 'But there would be employment for them in reclaiming the waste?'

Answer: 'Yes; more than ample, if there was encouragement given. Where I reside there are many thousands of acres waste, because it would not be let at a moderate rent.'

Quest.75: 'Is the land with you termed waste, capable of being made productive?'

Answer: 'Yes, every acre of it.'

On this same question of the reclamation of Irish waste lands and redundant population, Commissary-General Hewetson, one of the principal assistants of Sir Randolph Routh, wrote in the height of the Famine: 'The transition from potatoes to grain requires tillage in the proportion of *three to one*. It is useless, then, to talk of emigration, *when so much extra labour* is indispensable

225

to supply the extra food. Let that labour be first applied, and it will be seen whether there is any surplus population. *If the waste lands are taken into cultivation* and industrious habits established, it is very doubtful whether there will be any surplus population, or even whether it would be equal to the demand.'

'Providence', he added, 'has given everything needful, and nothing is wanting but industry to apply it.'

From causes which can be only guessed at, there seems to have been always a passive but most influential opposition to the reclamation of the waste lands of Ireland. Its opponents never met the question in the field of logical argument, yet, somehow, they had power enough to prevent its being carried into effect.

When Lord John Russell proposed the million-pound grant to begin the work, Sir Robert Peel said he thought some more useful employment could be found for that sum, but he did not even hint at what it was.

On the other hand those who were favourable to the reclamation of our waste lands were rich in facts and arguments. In the Parliamentary Session of 1835, a Committee of the House of Commons on public works reported that 'no experiment was necessary to persuade any scientific man of the possibility of carrying into effect the reclamation of bogs.' Nor is this strongly expressed opinion to be wondered at, founded, as it was, upon such evidence as the following:

Mr Richard Griffith deposed that:

'The mountain bog of the south of Ireland — the moory bog — varies in depth from nine inches to three feet, below which there is a clayey or sandy subsoil. On the average, about £4 per statute acre is required to bring it from a state of nature to one of cultivation and then it will fetch a rent of from 5s. to 10s. per English acre.'

Again: '£1 4s. an acre is the highest estimate for the draining of this land in covered drains; the remainder of the expense consists in the trenching up the surface, turning up the subsoil, and mixing it with the bog; no manure is wanted, a portion of the bog being burned for that purpose.'

With regard to deep bogs, his testimony was as follows: 'The expense of reclaiming deep bogs per acre may be estimated thus: Drainage of an English acre, in the most perfect way, about £1 4s., which is about 40s. the Irish acre; that includes the under drain: the levelling and digging comes to about £1 10s; and afterwards the claying comes to about £6 12s. per statute acre.'

Finally, he said: 'The reclamation of mountain land is very profitable, and easily effected; but the reclamation of deep bog land is attended with a much greater expense and requires both care and judgment. But both are certainly reclaimable, and would give a successful return when judiciously treated.'

What grave mysterious reasons of State, then, have prevented the Irish wastes from being reclaimed? In the Famine, our roads were torn up and made impassable to apply a labour test to destitution; food was next served out without any such test; M. Soyer was sent over to make cheap soup for the millions; the bone and sinew of the country were shipped off to spend themselves in trying to subdue the wildernesses of another hemisphere, or die in transit, or on Grosse Isle and such charnel-houses, whilst nearly five millions of reclaimable acres in their own fertile land were still left as nature had left them.

The second report of the Relief Commissioners bears the date 15 May. For practical purposes it may be looked upon as the first report, the one called the first being merely preliminary. We learn from it that only 1,248 electoral divisions had come under the operation of the Act up to that date, a state of things with which the Commissioners expressed themselves dissatisfied, for they say the Act should have been, at the time of their report, in full operation over the whole country. They found a difficulty in establishing soup kitchens, because dry meal was universally preferred; and they further say that relief by food instead of by public works was extremely unpopular with every class. All works, they announce, had been stopped on 1 May.

The second report of the Relief Commissioners, embracing a most trying period of over two months, is very curt and unsatisfactory. The dismissal, within six weeks, of nearly three quarters of a million of workmen, representing more than three millions of people, could scarcely be effected without the infliction of considerable suffering. The Government were right in compelling labour to apply itself to the production of food by the cultivation of the land, and they began this movement in the spring, the proper time for it, but they began too late. The twentieth of March was far too late for the first dismissal of twenty per cent for much of the spring work ought to have been done then. They should have begun a month earlier at least, which arrangement would have had the further advantage of enabling them to make the dismissals more gradually, and therefore with less inconvenience to the people.[7]

It was either great negligence or a very grave error on the part of the Government that they began to close the public works against the people before any other means of getting food was open to them. The Relief Act, 10 Vic. c.7, was intended to take the place of the public works, *and that immediately on their cessation;* but this was far from being the case, — a point upon which this second report is not at all satisfactory. In it the Commissioners express their regret that on 15 May there were only 1,248 electoral divisions under the operation of the Act, whilst all relief works had ceased on 1 May. That was bad enough; but what the report makes no mention of is that the Act was not in operation in any part of Ireland on 20 March, the day on which twenty per cent — 146,000 individuals — of those who were employed on the public works were dismissed.

On introducing that Act in Parliament, both the Prime Minister and the Irish Secretary promised that employment on the public works should be continued until the new system of relief would be in full operation, whilst this report tells us that on 15 May, a full fortnight after all public works had been stopped, out of 2,049 electoral divisions only 1,248 were under the operation of the Act.

On 23 March, three days after the twenty per cent were dismissed, a Dublin newspaper said, with regard to the new Relief Act: 'It is not in operation in any district in Ireland. Even in Dublin — the headquarters of the Relief Commissioners — the residence of the official printer — the requisite forms for arranging the preliminaries could not be supplied to the relief committees yesterday, they not having been as yet printed'.[8]

On 25 March some of the Irish members appealed, in the House of Commons, to the Irish Secretary not to allow the labourers on the public works to be dismissed until provision could be made for their support under the new Act.

Mr Labouchere said in reply that the greatest caution was necessary in removing the labourers from the works, and that although twenty per cent of them were ordered to be struck off on the 20th instant, that did not mean that twenty per cent of the people employed in every district on public works should be dismissed, but that in the aggregate twenty per cent of those employed should be put off, leaving to the Irish Government to decide upon the proportion to be removed from each district. It would be necessary and proper to make a general reduction, but the Irish government was left to the exercise of its discretion in making the several reductions by districts, as the executive in Ireland could best decide where it might be dangerous or improper to make any change, and where a change might be made with propriety and safety.

Four days later, on the question that the Irish Poor Relief Bill should be re-committed, Mr Smith O'Brien adverted to the discharge of the labourers from the public works. He repeated that the House and others had been led to believe that the dismissal would not take place until new measures for temporary relief should come into operation; that, nevertheless, in various parts of Ireland labourers had been dismissed before any other relief had been provided; and he had, he said, received from a part of the county he represented a letter from a Protestant clergyman, stating that not only twenty per cent but many more labourers had been dismissed and were, therefore, on the verge of starvation.

To Smith O'Brien's remarks, Mr Labouchere gave the following reply, a more formal and elaborate one than the above. He said: 'Her Majesty's Government were satisfied, after the best inquiry they were able to make upon the subject, that it was expedient and proper that on a certain day the number of persons employed on the public works throughout Ireland should be reduced by twenty per cent. They thought that was a step which, upon their responsibility, they were bound to adopt, and in that respect they left no discretion whatever with any one connected with the Irish Government; but the rule laid down was this — they required that twenty per cent should be reduced on the aggregate number of the persons employed throughout the whole of Ireland, leaving to the Board of Works in Ireland a discretion as to whether, in each particular instance, that precise number should be the proportion to be reduced or not. The Board of Works in Ireland thought they should best meet the views of the Government, by striking off twenty per cent from the number of persons employed in each district, but it was not the case that the rule had been applied strictly and invariably on every public work in Ireland.

He also read a letter that had been received that day, addressed from Colonel Jones, the chairman of the Board of Works, to Mr Trevelyan: 'Upon reading the Dublin journals,' wrote Colonel Jones, 'it would be supposed that the men discharged from the works had been deprived in an instant of their daily food; the fact is, that they were not entitled to be paid until the Tuesday or Wednesday following, and the payments so made were to be the means of procuring subsistence for another week, so that with the time between the publishing of the order and the moment when the money would be expended, ample time was afforded for procuring other employment, or for the electoral division committees to have made the necessary preparations for supplying the destitute with food.'

'He [Mr Labouchere] trusted the House would be satisfied that as much consideration had been shown for the people as it was in their power to bestow, and he had the satisfaction to think that on the whole this great reduction had been carried into effect with as little temporary suffering and embarrassment as possible.'

The first thing that strikes one with regard to the above reply is that the Board of Works used the discretion given to them with reference to the dismissals, in opposition to what Mr Labouchere said was the intention of the Government. Government wished the dismissals to be twenty per cent in the aggregate, which means ten or fifteen per cent of a reduction in one district and twenty-five or thirty per cent in another, according to circumstances. But the Secretary *naively* added that the Board of Works thought they should best meet the views of the Government by striking off twenty per cent of those employed in each district.

The Secretary next told us that employment on the public works was far more popular with the people than the new system of relief. This he asserted in the House of Commons on 29 March. We know the official printed forms of putting the new Relief Act into operation were not ready for delivery, even in Dublin, on 22 March, just one week before. How, in that one week, they were got ready and sent by tons and hundredweights to all parts of the country; how the new committees were organised; how the boilers were set up, the fires lighted, and the soup made and distributed to three quarters of a million of people; how those people discussed its flavour and qualities, and how they had had time to give expression to their views, and how those views reached the Irish Secretary in London before 29 March, are things which could be explained by only the Irish Secretary himself. This fact, however, was known to the general public, that on 23 March there was not a quart of the new relief-system soup yet made in Ireland; and that on the 29th, at the moment the Secretary was answering Smith O'Brien, it is more than probable that the fact was still the same.

The most curious part of Mr Labouchere's explanation is the extract from Colonel Jones' letter. In the Colonel's opinion it was a great mistake of the Dublin press to assume that the men discharged from the works had been deprived, in an instant, of their daily food. No such thing: It was gross ignorance or wilful calumny to assert it. The dismissed labourers, Colonel Jones told us, had no right to claim their wages till Tuesday or Wednesday, yet he generously paid them on the Saturday — two or three days before! But did he pay them for the Monday and the Tuesday? — not a word about that. Then where was the generosity? The order was that the men were to be dismissed on Saturday, 20 March, and Colonel Jones's vast bounty consisted in paying them the day he dismissed them, instead of compelling them to loiter about two or three days waiting to be paid. It well became Colonel Jones, indeed, to brag of such an act, in fact of the many inquests at which such verdicts as this were returned: 'Died of hunger, in consequence of not being paid by the Board of Works, a fortnight's wages being due at the time of death.'

The effect of the dismissals soon began to manifest itself in complaints and remonstrances.

Of Balla, in the county of Mayo, we read that the order was rigidly enforced there, that the people had no seed to sow their land, and that there was no provision for supplying them with food. All remonstrance with the inspecting officer, wrote a correspondent from Ballyglass, in the same county, was useless; he said the Government orders were peremptory. No seed, no food.

Ballinagh, Co. Cavan: Twenty per cent dismissed, no provision whatever having been made for their support.

Enniscorthy, Co. Wexford: No provision made to supply food to the dismissed labourers.

Clones, Co. Monaghan: No provision.

Maryborough, Queen's County: No means of support.

Clonmel, Co. Tipperary: No provision. The relief committee under the new Act is in course of organisation, but some time must elapse before it can afford relief.

From persons who were in possession of some land, the first twenty per cent, as we have seen, were to be selected for dismissal, but in Kilnaleck, in County Cavan, all those employed on the public works were about equally destitute, so that the twenty per cent with land could not be furnished: lots had to be cast, and those on whom the lot for dismissal fell received it like a sentence of death. Of course the Board of Works felt they were best carrying out the intentions of Government by dismissing the full twenty per cent at Kilnaleck.

The state of things in Cashel was this: the twenty per cent were dismissed before the committee had any preparation made, or was, in fact, appointed. The old committee had emphatically protested against the dismissal, and published a resolution condemnatory of it, as an inexcusable cruelty. Although twenty per cent of the labouring population were turned adrift in that locality, not one supernumerary was disemployed. No pay-clerk lost his salary, though his labour was diminished by one-fifth; no check-clerk was dismissed, though there were twenty per cent fewer to check; no steward or under-steward was displaced. Such are specimens of the accounts from nearly every part of the country.

Threatening meetings of the disemployed began to be held. Towards the end of April we read of vast crowds assembling in the neighbourhood of Drone, County Tipperary, crying aloud for food and employment. They consisted chiefly of the dismissed

231

labourers. Their wretched emaciated children were clinging to them for sustenance, but they had not wherewith to satisfy their hunger. Large numbers also assembled near Thurles, crying out for bread and employment; they proceeded to that town, and had an interview with the head officer under the Board of Works.

The news from Galway was that the funds of the old relief committee were completely exhausted and, although it was 5 May, the new one had not completed the lists, so as to procure food for distribution to the unemployed destitute. Some of the public works were stopped for want of money; the labourers on the others were dismissed, with very few exceptions. The labourers paraded the streets with a white flag bearing the inscription, 'We are starving'; 'Bread or employment'. They conducted themselves with the utmost order.

About 400 men who had been employed on the public works near Ballygarvan assembled and marched in procession into Cork. Having drawn up before the door of the Board of Works' office, they sent a deputation to confer with Captain Broughton, to state the distress they were suffering in consequence of being suddenly dismissed off the works. He assured them he could do nothing for them.

The *Limerick Reporter* says: 'On Monday morning the people of Meelick and its neighbourhood, who had been lately discharged from the public works, assembled at Ahernan Cross, to the number of 200, and afterwards proceeded to the residence of Mr Delmege, JP, of Castle Park, with whom they had an interview, declaring that they should get work; that they were ready and willing to work, but that they would not put up with nor endure the use of soup or porridge; that they could not, nor would they live upon one pound of meal in the twenty-four hours.'

They proceeded to the soup-kitchens of the parish, broke the boiler and all utensils belonging to the kitchen, and tore the books which contained the names of those to be relieved. Their numbers increased to about 600, when they proceeded to demolish the soup-kitchen at Ardnacrusha, quite close to the police barrack. The police succeeded in taking a man named Pat Griffin in the act of breaking the boiler with a large stone hammer, and succeeded in getting him to the barracks. The crowd attempted to rescue him. They broke the windows, and were demolishing the doors, when the police began to fire from within. Two men were severely wounded. The police discharged forty rounds before the people dispersed. Griffin stated that neither himself, nor many of the people assembled, had eaten any food for two or three days.

In several other places the soup-kitchens were attacked and the boilers broken or attempted to be broken. At Kilfenora, the people carried off the boiler and threw it into a lough. So that in the matter of the new relief system, the Government were not only very slow in getting it into operation, but when they did so, it was distasteful to the people in various places.

Although the spring work must have absorbed a very considerable portion of the dismissed labourers, it did not absorb them all, nor anything near it; whilst those who failed to get employment, or were unfit for it, had not the new relief to turn to. The poorhouses became dangerously crowded. The Poor Law statistics of 1847 show this in a striking manner: in the beginning of the year — that is in mid-winter, a time when there is scarcely any employment — the total number receiving relief in the Irish workhouses was 52,626. One month after the dismissals of 20 March — namely, on 17 April, perhaps the very busiest period in the farmer's year — the number in the workhouses had doubled; the figure standing on that day at 104,200; being about 11,000 more than they were built to accommodate; nor did this suffer any notable diminution until the harvest came in.

The Relief Commissioners published their third report on 17 June, at which time 1,677 electoral divisions were under the operation of the Relief Act; being 429 more than at the date of the second report, 15 May. They were then distributing 1,923,361 rations per day gratuitously, at an average cost of 2½d. per ration; and 92,326 rations were sold, making in all 2,015,687 rations. Of the 1,677 electoral divisions under the Act, 1,479 had received loans or grants, 198 had not applied for any advances, and 312 had not sent in any return up to the time the report was published. The Commissioners made this calculation: If, they said, the number of rations necessary for the returns still to be received shall be in proportion to those of which we have already cognisance, the entire number of rations will be 2,388,475; and if the ordinary proportion for children at half rations be added the number of persons to receive relief will be 2,729,684, of whom 2,622,684 will receive relief gratuitously.

The springing up of abuses under such an extensive system of relief was unavoidable, some of which the Commissioners mentioned in their third report. Cases occurred in which more rations were demanded than there were individuals in the whole district. Hundreds of names were struck off by the inspecting officers, including servants and men in the constant employ of persons of station and property; these latter were frequently themselves members of the committees; and in some cases the very chairmen, being magistrates, had sanctioned the issue of rations to tenants of their own of considerable holdings, possessed of live stock, and who, it was found, had paid up their last half year's rent. The intimidation attempted in various places, said the Commissioners, was generally successfully resisted, although to this there were exceptions deserving of notice. It was reported to them that the introduction of cooked food had produced the best effects on the health and appearance of the people.

An inspector asked this question: 'Is a man who owns a horse, or a cow, or such things, destitute?' The Commissioners answered: 'No, in the abstract; but better give him relief than to drive him to permanent destitution.' On 27 May an inspector, who appeared to have been in a state of worry and excitement, wrote to headquarters: 'Entirely deserted by the landlords and their representatives; the working of the Committee (he names a particular committee) has fallen into the hands of a class who insist on *'Universal Relief'*! who will not think of scrutinising lists to prevent fraud, and who are eager to have brothers, cousins and dependants employed in the distribution.'

Alluding to the violence on the part of the people, another inspector wrote: 'I have spoken to the Roman Catholic clergymen on this subject, and take this opportunity of stating that I have received great assistance from those gentlemen.' Another said: 'The people who ought to have an interest in checking abuses are mostly absentees, and the few who are living in the country try all they can to provide for their own tenants.' Another: 'All jobbing and intrigue here.' Another: 'A day or two since I found the wife of a coachman of a magistrate of £2,000 a year on the relief list.' The Commissioners, however, were strongly of opinion that the introduction of cooked food was a great means of checking fraud.

Up to 17 June there were 570 electoral divisions which had received neither grant nor loan; some of these were the richest, and some were the poorest in the county. Perhaps, said the Report, the rich ones had other means, and the poor ones could not get the loan, and may have had the remains of subscriptions. The Commissioners had much difficulty in getting the accounts from committees; the clerks in rural districts were, for the most part, totally inefficient, and the weekly stipend of twenty-one shillings was not sufficient to induce any person accustomed to keep accounts to quit the towns and undertake such duties.

Ireland, it would seem, was destined at this time to have sorrow upon sorrow; her great Liberator, O'Connell, died in May 1847. For some time his powers had been evidently failing, and no wonder, after the life of hard work he had gone through.

In the last days of March 1847, O'Connell left Dublin for London to attend his parliamentary duties. He presented some petitions on 1 February and spoke at some length about the Famine on the eighth, his speech, the last he ever made, occupying about 100 lines of a newspaper column. He was imperfectly heard. One report said: 'Mr O'Connell rose, but spoke very indistinctly, and directed his voice very much to the lower part of the house.'

His last words were an appeal to their charity; they also contained a prophecy, which was, alas! but too strictly verified. 'She is in your hands,' he said, 'she is in your power. If you don't save her, she can't save herself; and I solemnly call upon you to recollect that I predict, with the sincerest conviction, that one-fourth of her population will perish, unless you come to her relief. (cheers from both sides)'

So ended the public career of the great leader of the Irish nation, to be followed in two short months by his death. Two days after he had spoken in the House of Commons, the rumour reached the Clubs that he was dangerously ill. This was contradicted, and a letter from himself to the Repeal Association, which was read at their next meeting, reassured the public. Next, the news came that writing fatigued him and that his physicians forbade it; so, for the future his son John wrote, in his own name, to the Association, always, as might be expected, taking the sanguine view of his father's health.

A month passed. His physicians ordered him to Hastings and after spending a fortnight there, he sailed to France. His intention was to go to Rome. At Lyons, he felt so poorly that he was obliged to refuse audiences to the various deputations of that Catholic city which crowded to his hotel to do him honour. He arrived at Genoa, his final stage, on 6 May and breathed his last in that city on the evening of the fifteenth, with the tranquillity of a child. His faithful friend, the Rev. Dr Miley, and several of the principal clergy of the place were kneeling in prayer around his bed when he expired.

The remaining reports of the Relief Commissioners do not call for any very lengthened notice. The fourth of the series was published on 19 July, at which time 1,823 electoral divisions were receiving relief under the Act. They said: 'By an arrangement with the Commissary General we are clearing out the Government depots of provisions, by orders on them in lieu of so much money. These depots were established at an anxious period of a prospect of great deficiency of supplies, which no longer exists.' It is needless to repeat here what has been abundantly proved before, that the people died of starvation within the shadow of those sealed-up depots and they would not be opened; they were opened when the supplies they contained were not required, there being plenty in the market.

From the accountant's department we learn that 2,643,128 rations were being daily issued, which it was hoped would be the maximum relief that the Commissioners would be called on to administer; 79,636 of these were sold. This shows an increase of daily rations from last report of 291,028. The fall in provisions had reduced the price of each ration from 2½d. to 2d. The amount given in loans and grants was now reduced by about £3,000 a day, the expenditure in that way being then about £20,000 a day. The aggregate amount of money issued up to 19 July was £1,010,184 7s 10d. to 1,803 electoral divisions. The cost of the Government staff for superintending the issuing of relief, is set down at two and a half per cent — 6d. in the pound, — a low figure, indeed, but it must be taken into account that they only superintended; the committee did the actual work of giving out the relief.

The issue of cooked food was opposed by the people in some places, and this opposition was punished, by a reduction being made in the quantity of rations issued in such places. In a fortnight, about 8,000 tons of the food in the Government depots were given in lieu of money, the money value of which was £98,723, the daily market price being that charged by the Commissary General. The arrangement was carried out in this way: There was issued on 1 June a circular to the inspecting officer of each Union, by virtue of which an order on the Government depot was given to the Finance Committee of the Union, instead of the amount (in cash) of the fortnightly estimate sent in of the sum required for each electoral division of that Union; but the whole fortnightly estimate was not usually supplied in meal only, to any one electoral division; it was given partly in meal and partly in money. At this time there were thirty-three Commissariat depots, and sixteen British Association depots.

By circular No. 58 it was announced that after 15 August the support of destitute persons was to be provided for under the new Poor Law, 10 Vic., c.31. All relief committees were warned to be prepared to close their arrangements for the issue of rations, when the funds provided for the estimates, ending on 13 August, would be expended.

The hope expressed in the fourth report, that the Commissioners had arrived at the maximum daily relief which the country required, was not verified by fact. The fifth report was published on 17 August. At that date there were 1,826 electoral divisions under the Act. The maximum relief within the period embraced in the report was: gratuitous rations per day, 2,920,792; sold, 99,920; total, 3,020,712 rations daily![9] Thus, considerably more than one third of the whole population was living on what may be termed outdoor relief. This, the highest point, was reached on 3 July; the daily rations had, on 1 August, come down to 2,467,989 gratuitous, and 52,387 sold rations, being a total of 2,520,376 rations.

The absolute termination of advances on account of temporary relief was fixed by the Act of Parliament for the end of September. The number of temporary fever hospitals established under the Act 10 Vic., c. 22, amounted at the date of the fifth report to 326.

The Relief Commissioners published their sixth report on 11 September. It was a helpful one. The crops were abundant and a rapid decrease in the number of rations issued was the result, more especially from the middle of August. Out of 127 Unions, which were under the Act, fifty-five had had no advances made to them, on estimate, for any period after 15 August; twenty-six more ceased to call for advances on 29 August; and the remainder were to cease on 12 September, with the exception of the advances to the fever hospitals, which were continued to 30 September.

The Commissioners expressed the opinion that the discontinuance of relief had not been attended by the suffering which might have been apprehended. They said the relief 'was made a system of bonus rather than of necessity, which increased the expenditure in an enormous degree'.

We learn from this sixth report that the Commissioners had expended a sum approaching £2,000,000 within a period of eight months, through the agency of upwards of 2,000 committees, constituted by general regulation, and subject only to a very general control. Such being the case, the testimony borne by the inspecting officers to those committees, is highly creditable to them; the inspecting officers, said the report, 'express their belief that there has been almost a total absence of misappropriation of money by committee'.

On 28 August the number of daily rations issued was down to 967,575.

The seventh and last report of the Commissioners under the Relief Act, bears the date 15 October. In it they said they had the satisfaction of believing that the Act was thoroughly successful in its primary object; and they did not consider the expenditure excessive in proportion to the object. The entire outlay under the Act was £1,676,268 11s. 7d.,[10] a part of which was a free gift from the State, the remainder a charge to be repaid by the Unions, by a percentage on the rateable property, which, in the opinion of the Commissioners, should in no case exceed three shillings in the pound. The summary of the accounts department informs us that the rations issued on 11 September, the day previous to

237

the final stoppage of relief under the Act, were 442,739, being
a decrease from 28 August of 599,816 daily rations.
The expenditure under the Act is thus detailed:

	£	s	d
To Sir Randolph Routh for provisions from depots	136,795	0	8
Money advanced fortnightly to the several electoral divisions for relief	1,420,417	14	11
To fever hospitals	119,055	16	0

The advances at one time exceeded £60,000 a day, distributed
over nearly 2,000 accounts.

The sum given to Sir Randolph Routh for the food in the depots
shows there were about 12,000 tons of provisions in them.

The sum set down to the fever hospitals included the erection
and furnishing of the fever sheds. In addition to this amount,
£4,479 was expended in providing proper medical inspection and
superintendence in localities in which great sickness prevailed
and £60,000 was advanced for the enlargement of the Workhouse,
principally by the erection of fever wards.[11]

In the appendix to this, their last report, the Commissioners
bore honourable testimony to the manner in which the people
behaved. They said: 'The order and good conduct of the
peasantry, and of the people generally, notwithstanding the great
influx of paupers into the towns, is highly to be commended. All
admit that the resignation and forbearance of the labouring classes
was astonishing, when it is remembered with what rapidity the
real famine encompassed them.'

14

Fever — and emigration

In anticipation of fever and other epidemics resulting from the Famine, a Fever Act was passed for Ireland in the early part of the Session of 1846, by which the Lord Lieutenant was empowered to appoint Commissioners of Health, not exceeding five in number, who were to act without salaries. They constituted what was called the Central Board of Health. He was further empowered to appoint medical officers for the Poor Law Unions, with salaries to be paid by the Treasury; such medical officers to be under the control of the guardians. The Board of Health was authorised to direct guardians to provide fever hospitals and dispensaries, together with medicines and all other necessaries for those hospitals. This Act was to cease in September 1847, but in April of that year an Act to amend and extend it to November 1847 was passed. Eventually, it remained in its amended form in force until the end of the Parliamentary Session of 1850.

The changes made by this second or amended Fever Act were of a very extensive kind. By the previous one medical relief was to be given through the guardians of the poor; by the Act as amended, the Board of Health was empowered to certify to the Relief Commissioners the necessity of medical relief being afforded, in *any electoral* division in which there was a Relief Committee. It was also to direct such Committees to provide few hospitals, and every other thing necessary for the treatment of patients. And further: the Relief Commissioners, on the certificate of the Board of Health, were to issue their order to Relief Committees, to provide medical attendance, medicines and nutriment, if necessary, for such patients as were not received into hospital, either because there was not accommodation for them, or because it might endanger their lives to remove them.

The Board of Health acted as little as possible upon this clause; holding that, under existing circumstances, it was impossible to treat patients with advantage in their own houses. Those hospitals and dispensaries were managed by the Relief Committees, under the control of the Relief Commissioners, appointed to carry out

239

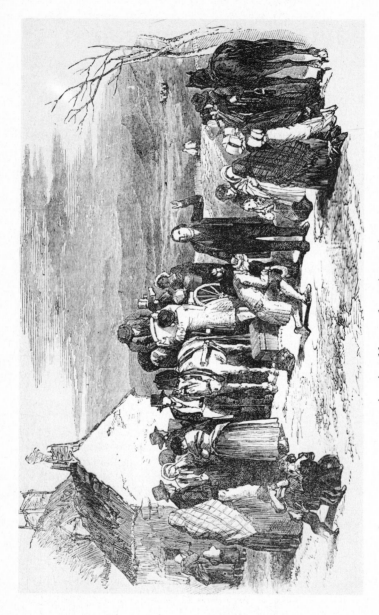

A priest blesses departing emigrants.

the Act 10 Vic., cap. 7. By the sixteenth clause of the amended Fever Act, provision was made 'for the proper and decent interment of the deceased destitute persons who shall die of fever or any other epidemic disease in any electoral division or district, for which any Relief Committee shall have been constituted'.

Whilst this very extensive system of medical relief was established and carried out under the second Bill, the guardians of the poor continued to use the powers granted to them in the former Bill, of giving medical relief. The returns from these two sources give, respectively, the number of fever cases received into their hospitals, but we have no authentic means of determining the number of persons who died of fever in their own houses, or on the highways and byways, as they wandered about in search of food. Such cases must have been very numerous.

Although fever or other epidemics did not arise to an alarming extent in 1846, still, that year showed a decided increase of them over previous years. The following summary, derived from circulars issued, shows the origin and progress of fever in 1846:

'Fever began in Mitchelstown, County Cork. It attacked equally those in good and bad health; but in some instances, as in Innishannon and in Cove, many , in the best health; while in Mitchelstown, the majority had previously suffered from privation. Young persons appear to have been the subject of the epidemic more than those of more advanced life. The pressure from without upon the city (of Cork) began to be felt in October; and in November and December, the influx of paupers from all parts of this vast county was so overwhelming that, to prevent them from dying in the streets, the doors of the Workhouse were thrown open and in one week, 500 persons were admitted without any provision, either of space or clothing, to meet so fearful an emergency. All these were suffering from famine, and most of them from malignant dysentery or fever.

The fever was, in the first instance, undoubtedly confined to persons badly fed or crowded into unwholesome habitations; and, as it originated with the vast migratory hordes of labourers and their families congregated upon the public roads, it commonly was termed 'the road fever'. In Cloughjordan, Co. Tipperary, the fever cases doubled in 1846 what they had been in the previous year. The disease commenced in Clonmel in November. The accounts from Counties Limerick and Kerry do not record any increased sickness during this year. The epidemic commenced in Co. Tyrone in December 1846. Young persons were those chiefly attacked there. The fever commenced at Loughgall, Co. Armagh, in the end of this year.

The lower classes were chiefly attacked, the majority of those

241

affected having been previously in bad health. The epidemic materially declined as the poor were better fed. The fever was frequently preceded by scurvy. Individuals at the age of puberty were chiefly attacked — females more generally than males.

In Newry, dysentery existed as an epidemic during the autumn of 1846, being fatal among the old and infirm who, if not carried off, were so debilitated by its effects as to render them an easy prey to the fever which followed. In Dublin, although the great outbreak of the fever was in 1847, yet, cases were noticed to have occurred in the latter end of 1846 in a greater proportion than usual. Those first attacked were individuals who had been reduced by bad diet or insufficiency of food, and throughout the continuance of the epidemic, the lower classes were chiefly affected. In many cases, the fever set in immediately after recovering from the effects of starvation and, although scurvy preceded the disease, neither it nor purpura was noticed to have occurred as a concomitant symptom.

In the Province of Connaught the epidemic commenced in many places during 1846, especially in Counties Sligo and Leitrim; in the former locality the young were chiefly attacked; in the latter fever broke out as early as June when upwards of 200 cases were at one time in the workhouse of Carrick-on-Shannon; while in the remote northern hilly districts of the county, it did not appear until December 1847; those attacked were, for the most part, reduced from want of food. In some parts, the fever was preceded by aphthous ulcers on the tongue and gums; young persons were those chiefly attacked, and females more than males.

In County Roscommon the previous health of the population was much impaired; bowel complaints were frequent; the fever commenced in the end of 1846 or beginning of 1847 and was very prevalent.

The workhouse at Castlerea was one of the most severely afflicted during the epidemic, of any similar class of institution in Ireland — as many as fifty persons a week having died at one period subsequent to this — and for a long time all attempt at separate burial was found impossible. In Co. Galway the epidemic of both dysentery and fever appeared at Ahascragh and Clifden, separate ends of the district, at the end of this year.[1]

As was anticipated, fever rose to a fearful height in 1847. And, said the Commissioners of Health, 'the state of the medical institutions of Ireland was, unfortunately, such as peculiarly unfitted them to afford the required medical aid on the breaking out of the epidemic. The county infirmaries had not provision for the accommodation of fever patients. The county fever hospitals were destitute of sufficient funds; and dispensaries, established for the purpose of affording only ordinary outdoor medical relief, could, of course, afford no efficient attendance on the numbers of destitute persons, suffering from acute contagious diseases in their own miserable abodes, often scattered over districts several miles in extent.'

In January fever complicated with dysentery and smallpox became very rife in Belfast and accounts from various other places soon showed that it had seized upon the whole country. The week ending 3 April, the total number of inmates in Irish workhouses was 104,455, of whom 9,000 were fever patients. The deaths in that week were 2,706, and the average of deaths in each week during the month was twenty-five per 1,000 of the entire inmates — a death rate which would have hurried to the grave, every man, woman and child in the workhouses of Ireland in about nine months! But it gradually decreased, until in October it stood at five per 1,000 in the week.

On 19 January we read that 'the number suffering from fever in Swinford is beyond calculation'. Some idea of the dreadful mortality then prevalent in Cork may be found from the fact that in one day thirty-six bodies were interred in the same grave; the deaths in the workhouse there from 27 December 1846, until the middle of April — less than four months — amounted to 2,130. At this period, dropsy, the result of starvation, became almost universal. On 16 April there were upwards of 300 cases of fever in the Carrick-on-Shannon workhouse and the weekly deaths amounted to fifty. Again: every avenue leading to the plague-stricken town of Macroom had a fever hospital; persons of all ages were dropping dead in the streets.

In May it was announced that fever continued to rage with unabated fury at Castlebar. 'Sligo is a plague spot; disease in every street, and of the worst kind.' 'Fever is committing fearful ravages in Ballindine, Ballinrobe, Claremorris, Westport, Ballina and Belmullet, all in the county of Mayo.' From Roscommon the news came that the increase of fever was truly awful; the hospitals were full and applicants were daily refused admission. 'No one can tell', said the writer, 'what becomes of these unfortunate beings; they are brought away by their pauper friends, and no more is heard of them.'

'Seven bodies were found inside a hedge', in the parish of Kilglass; the dogs had the flesh almost eaten off. Under date of 18 May, I find this entry: 'Smallpox, added to fever and dysentery, is prevalent at Middleton, Co. Cork; and, near Bantry Abbey, 900 bodies were interred in a plot of ground forty feet square. From the autumn of 1846 to May 1847, 10,000 persons were interred in Father Mathew's cemetery at Cork — he was obliged to close it. On 12 June, the number of fever patients in the hospitals of Belfast was 1,840. 'Awful fever', 'Fearful increase of fever', were the ordinary phases in which the spread of the disease was announced from every part of Ireland.[2]

'Of the extent of the epidemic in Dublin, it would not be easy to give any very correct idea. The hospital accommodation of the city amounted to about 2,500 beds, a greater amount by 1,000, I believe, than were opened in any previous epidemic. It may give some idea of the vast amount of sickness to state that, at the Cork Street hospital, nearly 12,000 cases applied during a period of about ten months. At one period there were upwards of 400 outstanding tickets; and as many as eighty applications for admission have been made in one day. Still it may be safely stated that all this would give a very imperfect idea of the real amount; for all who had to go amongst the poor at their own houses were well aware that vast numbers remained there, who either could not be accommodated in hospital or who never thought of applying. It was quite common to find three, four and even five ill in a house, where application had been made but for one. I think the very lowest estimate which could be arrived at cannot make the numbers who sickened in Dublin short of 40,000. The greatest pressure on the hospital took place in the month of June, from which time the fever gradually declined, till the month of February 1848, when the epidemic may be said to have ceased'.[3]

In February 1847 fourteen applications were made to the Board of Health for providing temporary hospital accommodation; in March they received fifty-one such applications; in April, fifty-three, in May, fifty-two; in June, twenty-two; in July, sixty; in August, forty-eight; in September the number was ten, and in October only eight. The applications to the Board of Health for temporary fever hospitals in 1847 were 343; the entire number of such applications up to 1850, when the Board closed its labours, were 576, of which 203 were refused.

Relapse was a remarkable feature of this famine-fever. 'Relapses were so common', wrote Dr Freke from a western county, 'as to appear characteristic of the epidemic; in several cases they have occurred so frequently as three or even four times in the same individual.' At Nohaval, Kinsale Union, out of 250 cases 240 relapsed.

The cases received into the permanent and temporary fever hospitals of Ireland, in the year 1845, were 37,604; in 1846 they increased to 40,620; and in 1847 they rose to the enormous amount of 156,824 cases[4] of which, according to the Report of the Board of Health, 95,890 were admitted into temporary hospitals,[5] in which the percentage of deaths was ten and two-fifths; more males dying than females, the percentage of deaths among males being eleven and one-fifth and among females nine and six-tenths.

But the mortality in the fever sheds sometimes rose to fifteen, twenty, twenty-five, and in a few instances to twenty-eight and twenty-nine per cent; the cause being previous dysentery (on which cholera sometimes supervened) and starvation. In Eyrecourt, Ballinrobe Union, the death-rate rose to twenty-nine and one-third per cent; in West Schull to twenty; and in Parsonstown to twenty-nine and five-eights. The principal complications of this famine-fever, according to the Commissioners of Health, were dysentery, purpura, diarrhoea and smallpox; and they further said of it that it was, perhaps, unparalleled for duration and severity.[6]

The average weekly cost of each patient in the temporary hospitals, including the salary of the medical officer, was four shillings and one halfpenny.

'Some approximation to the amount of the immense mortality that prevailed may be gleaned from the published tables which show that, within that calamitous period between the end of 1845 and the conclusion of the first quarter of 1851, as many as 61,260 persons died in the hospitals and sanitary institutions, exclusive of those who died in the workhouses and auxiliary workhouses. Taking the recorded deaths from fever alone, between the beginning of 1846 and the end of 1849 and assuming the mortality at one in ten, which is the very lowest calculation, and far below what we believe really did occur, 1,595,040 persons, being about one in four of the population in 1851, must have suffered from fever during that period.

'But no pen has recorded the numbers of the forlorn and starving who perished by the wayside or in the ditches, or of the mournful groups, sometimes of whole families, who lay down and died, one after another, upon the floor of their miserable cabins and so remained uncoffined and unburied till chance unveiled the appalling scene. No such amount of suffering and misery has been chronicled in Irish history since the days of Edward Bruce and yet, through all, the forbearance of the Irish peasantry and the calm submission with which they bore the deadliest ills that can fall on man, can scarcely be paralleled in the annals of any people'.[7]

An unusual disease on land, scurvy, appeared during the Famine. The Commissioners of Health attributed its appearance

1. to the want of variety of food: the potato being gone, they said, the people did not understand the necessity for variety and men, such as railway porters, who had wages enough to buy

food, took scurvy for want of this variety, coffee and white bread being their common dietary.

2. Another cause was the eating of what was called 'potato flour', got from rotten potatoes; it was not flour at all and did not contain the elements of the potato but consisted wholly of starch as foecula.

3. The use of raw or badly cooked food also brought on scurvy; and the Commissioners of Health, therefore, strongly recommended the giving of food in a cooked form.[8]

Emigration played a very leading part in the terrible drama of the Irish Famine of 1847; indeed it was the potato failure of 1822, and the consequent famine of 1823, which first gave emigration official importance in this country.

A Parliamentary Committee was appointed in the latter year, before which Mr Wilmot Horton, the Under Secretary of State, explained in detail a plan of emigration from Ireland then under the consideration of Government and which was afterwards carried into effect. The emigrants were sent to Canada, and Peterborough, at the time a very insignificant place, was fixed upon as their headquarters.

On two subsequent occasions, Mr Horton stated this emigration to have been eminently successful, which was fully corroborated by the evidence of Captain Rubidge, before the Lords' Committee of 1847, on 'Colonisation from Ireland'. But this emigration, as well as that of 1825, both of which were superintended by the Hon. Peter Robinson, was on a very limited scale. The number taken out to Canada in the first emigration was only 568 persons, men, women and children. The Government supported them for eighteen months after their landing, which very much increased the expense; each of those emigrants having cost the country £22 before they were finally settled.

In 1825 Mr Robinson took out 2,024 emigrants under the same conditions, but in this instance the expense was slightly diminished, the cost of each person being £21 10s. These emigrants also prospered, but the money outlay in each case was so considerable that the experiment could not be extended, nor, in fact, repeated.[9]

From this period, committees continued to sit on the subject of emigration, almost year after year, emigration from Ireland, even in the absence of famine, being considered of the highest importance — and why? Chiefly because Irish labourers were lowering the rate of wages in the English labour market — so it is stated in the report of the Select Committee of 1826, in the following words:

'The question of emigration from Ireland is decided by the

population itself; and that which remains for the legislature to decide is, whether it shall be turned to the improvement of the British North American colonies, or whether it shall be suffered and encouraged, *to deluge Great Britain with poverty and wretchedness*, and gradually, but certainly, to equalise the state of the English and Irish peasantry. Two different rates of wages, and two different conditions of the labouring classes, cannot permanently co-exist. One of two results appears to be inevitable; the Irish population must be raised towards the standard of the English or the English depressed towards that of the Irish. The question whether an extensive plan of emigration shall or shall not be adopted appears to your Committee to resolve itself into the simple point whether the wheat-fed population of Great Britain shall or shall not be supplanted by the potato-fed population of Ireland?'[10]

The same reasons are given by the same Committee in 1827 and they are again repeated in 1830, by another Committee, whose duty it was to inquire into the state of the Irish poor.

The famous Devon Land Commission, which was called into existence in 1842, presented its voluminous report to Parliament in 1845, which was founded on the examination of 1,100 witnesses whose evidence was taken on the spot in every county in Ireland, the Commissioners having visited more than ninety towns for the purpose; that Commission recommended emigration from Ireland but in a cautious and modified way.

The Commissioners said: 'After considering the recommendations, thus repeatedly made by Committees of Parliament upon this subject, and the evidence of Mr Godley, in which the different views of the subject are well given, we desire to express our own conviction that a well-organised system of emigration may be of very great service, as one among the measures which the situation of the occupiers of land in Ireland at present calls for. We cannot think that either emigration or the extension of Public Works or the reclamation or improvement of land can, singly, remove the existing evil. All these remedies must be provided concurrently, according to the circumstances of each case. In this view, and to this extent only, we wish to direct attention to the subject of emigration.'[11]

A Select Committee of the House of Lords, on the operation of the Poor Law in Ireland, spoke approvingly of emigration as a relief to the labour market at home and it therefore recommended 'that increased facilities for the emigration of poor persons should be afforded, with the co-operation of the Government'.[12]

Previous to the Famine there was a large and steady emigration from Ireland for many years, independent of Government aid. The total colonial and foreign emigration between 1831 and 1841 amounted to 403,459, to which the returns add 25,012, for probable births, that item being calculated at one-and-a-half per cent per annum; making a total of 428,471. These figures give a year average of nearly 43,000.[13] Of these, 214,047 embarked from Irish ports, 152,738 from Liverpool; and ten per cent was added for imperfect returns. The largest number of those who went from Ireland *direct* to the colonies or foreign countries, from any one port, embarked at Belfast, viz., twenty per cent of the whole. From Cork nearly the same. From the ports of Ulster there went 76,905. From the ports of Munster 70,046. From Leinster 34,977 and from Connaught only 32,119. Those emigrants who embarked from Irish ports proceeded as follows: 189,225 to British America, namely 107,792 males and 81,233 females; to the United States of America 19,775, namely 10,725 males and 2,950 females; to the Australian colonies, there went 4,553, in the proportion of 2,300 males and 2,253 females; and 494 persons embarked for the West Indies — 300 males and 194 females.[14]

Within the decade from 1831 to 1841, emigration was at its minimum in 1838, the number that left our shores in that year being only 14,700; it rose to its maximum in 1841, namely 71,392. It rose still higher in 1842, the emigrants of that year being set down at 89,686. The year 1843 was named by O'Connell the Repeal year; the people were filled with the hope of soon seeing a parliament in College Green and to this fact may probably be attributed the great falling-off in emigration, the number for that year being only 37,509. It increased in 1844 to 54,289; and in 1845, the eve of the Famine, to 74,969 persons.

In the year 1846, as might be expected, emigration from Ireland reached a height which it had never attained before in a single year; the number, as estimated by the Emigration Commissioners, being 105,955. Besides which between 13 January and 1 November 278,005 immigrants arrived at Liverpool from Ireland; but the Irish labourers who at that time annually visited England and who were variously estimated at from 10,000 to 30,000 are included in the number. For the protection of the emigrants, additional agents were appointed by the Government at Liverpool and some Irish ports; and the annual vote in aid of colonial funds for the relief of sick and destitute emigrants from the United Kingdom was increased from £1,000 to £10,000.[15]

In the spring of 1847, a gigantic emigration scheme was launched. It was said to have emanated from and was certainly patronised by members of the so-called Irish party which, with so few elements of cohesion, was inaugurated at the Rotunda meeting; but the father of the scheme seems to have been Mr J.R. Godley. By it, 2,000,000 Irish Catholics were to be transferred to Canada in three years, it being a leading feature in the scheme to send none but Catholics. It was, the promoters said, to be an Irish Catholic colony, with a distinct and well-marked Irish nationality — in fact, a New Ireland! There was a memorial on the subject which extended over fifty-one pages of a pamphlet and which was prepared by Mr Godley with much ability. It went very fully into the whole scheme. This, accompanied by a short explanatory letter, was presented to the Prime Minister on the last day of March.

How was this vast scheme to be carried to a successful issue? A joint-stock company, to be called 'The Irish Canadian Company', was to undertake the entire management of it. This company was to be legalised by Act of Parliament and recognised by the Canadian Government. It was to transmit to Canada and settle there 1,500,000 Irish people in three years, being at the rate of 500,000 a year.

To do this, £9,000,000 was to be lent by the Government, at the rate of £3,000,000 each year, on the security of Irish property and an Irish income tax. This tax was to be one per cent the first year, two per cent the second year, three per cent the third year, and to stand at three per cent until the first instalment of the loan could be paid and was, of course, to cease altogether when the last instalment was paid. Repayment was to be made at the rate of six-and-a-half per cent per annum, which would extinguish principal and interest in twenty-two years.

The £9,000,000 so lent and to be so repaid was to be expended in this manner: the passage money of each individual was computed at £3; of this the Government was to advance one pound, the emigrants themselves finding the other two in some way — to be given by friends — saved from wages — obtained from their landlords — however the £2 was to be found, that sum was to be provided by the emigrant. One pound to each of 1,500,000 emigrants would absorb £1,500,000 of the £9,000,000.

The joint-stock company that was to work the concern must, of course, have profits, and be paid for its labours; it was, therefore, to have a bonus of £5, or a sum of about that amount, for each emigrant it would prove to the satisfaction of Government that it had located in Canada. It was to have other profits. It was to be empowered to lend money to the district councils in Canada to effect local improvements, and the interest of this money was to be a portion of its profits. All the emigrants were to be settled on the land in Canada; this would be bought in its rude state by the company, and resold at a profit, when it had improved it, and established upon it those 'aids to location' enumerated further on. This bonus of £5 on each emigrant would amount to £7,500,00 which, together with the £1,500,000 mentioned above, would absorb the £9,000,000.

As already stated, it was a marked characteristic of this systematic emigration, or colonisation, that it was to be exclusively Catholic and that a number of priests, proportioned to the number of emigrants, should be appointed to accompany them and settle down with them. This Mr Godley held to be absolutely necessary.

The memorial to Lord John Russell, praying that the Government would give its sanction and support to Mr Godley's scheme of colonisation, was signed by one archbishop, four marquises, seven earls, three viscounts, thirteen barons, nine baronets, eighteen members of parliament, some honourables and several deputy-lieutenants. The memorialists were, in all, eighty — that is eighty of the leading peers, members of parliament and landowners approached the First Minister, to beg that he would aid them in sending 2,000,000 Irish Catholics to Canada to reclaim the land in that colony.

Everybody knew that the statement of Sir Robert Kane was accepted as a truth, that there were in Ireland 4,500,000 barren acres, the greater portion of which would richly, and promptly, repay for their reclamation. Yet the Government Bill for beginning that reclamation was withdrawn by the Prime Minister and no single voice was raised in favour of going on with it; moreover, he said his reason for withdrawing it was the opposition which the House of Lords offered to it. Yes; they would have no reclamation of Irish lands but they would submit to bear increased taxation in order to send the Celtic race by the million to delve in Canada! Yet, even for that it became the Irish people to be duly grateful, inasmuch as it was a decided improvement upon the older colonisation scheme of 'To hell or Connaught'.[16]

The colonisation scheme met with little or no support in Ireland. It was suspected. It was regarded as a plan for getting rid of the Celt by wholesale. A Protestant gentleman, Mr Thomas Mulock, thus commented on the memorial: 'And is it come to this, O ye lords and gentlemen! representatives of the Irish party, with prospective adhesions after the Easter holidays from the vast majority of Irish Protestant proprietors? Do you avow yourselves to be in the position of landowners, who stand in no relation of aristocracy or leadership, government or guidance, succour or solace to millions of the people, who famish on the territorial possessions from which you derive your titles, your importance, your influence, your wealth? Has confiscation been mellowed into the legal semblance of undisputed succession, only to bring about a state of things which the most ruthless ravagers of nations never permanently perpetrated?'[17]

The memorial was extensively circulated. Amongst many others, one was sent to the Right Rev. Dr Maginn, Coadjutor Bishop of Derry. He replied in terms scathing as they were indignant. The following is an extract from his letter: 'In sober earnestness, gentlemen, why send your circular to a Catholic bishop? Why have the barefaced impudence to ask me to consent to the expatriation of millions of my co-religionists and fellow-countrymen? You, the hereditary oppressors of my race and my religion; you, who reduced one of the noblest peoples under heaven to live in the most fertile island on earth on the worst species of a miserable exotic, which no humane man, having anything better, would constantly give to his swine or his horses; you, who have made the most beautiful island under the sun a land of skulls or of ghastly spectres; you are anxious, I presume, to get a Catholic bishop to abet your wholesale system of extermination — to head in pontificals the convoy of your exiles, and thereby give the sanction of religion to your atrocious scheme. You never, gentlemen, laboured under a more egregious mistake than by imagining that we could give in our adhesion to your principles, or could have any, the least confidence, in anything proceeding from you. Is not the *ex-officio* clause in the Poor-law Bill your bantling, or that of your leader, Lord Stanley? Is not the quarter of an acre clause test for relief your creation? Were not the most conspicuous names on your committee the abettors of an amendment as iniquitous as it was selfish — viz., to remove the poor-rates from their own shoulders to that of their pauper tenantry? Are not they the same members who recently advocated, in the House of Commons, the continuation of the fag-end of the bloody penal code of the English statute book, by which our English brethren could be transported or hanged for professing the creed of their conscience, the most forward in this Catholic emigration plan? What good could we expect from such a Nazareth?'[18]

The Prime Minister did not take up the great colonisation scheme. He said in the House of Commons, on 29 April, that he declined, on the part of the Government, assuming the responsibility of providing for the absorption of the great excess of labour then existing in Ireland. 'I deny,' said Lord John, 'on the part of the Government the responsibility of completely, still less suddenly, resolving that question. What we can do and what we, the Government, have endeavoured to do is to mitigate present suffering.'

The Government was of opinion that emigration, left to itself, would transfer the starving people to the United States and British America, as quickly as they could be provided for in those countries. This calculation turned out to be correct enough, as the following figures will show: Emigration from Ireland in the year 1845 is set down at 74,969; it increased in 1846 to 105,955, although the Famine had not to the full extent turned the minds of the people to seek homes in the New World. The emigration of 1847 more than doubled that of 1846, being 215,444; it fell in 1848 to 178,159, but in 1849 the emigration of 1847 was repeated, the emigrants of that year being 214,425, of which 2,219 were orphan girls from the workhouses. The magnitude of the exodus was maintained in 1850, that year giving 209,054 voluntary exiles; but the emigration in 1851, which year closed the decade, quite outstripped that of any previous year, the figure in that year standing at 257,372.[19]

The census of 1841 shows the population of Ireland to have been in that year 8,175,124. Taking the usual ratio of births over deaths, it should have increased in 1851 to 9,018,799, instead of which it fell to 6,552,385; thus, being nearly 2,500,00 less than it should have been. These 2,500,000 disappeared in the Famine. They disappeared by death and emigration. The emigration during the ten years from 1842 to 1851, both inclusive, was 1,436,862. Subtracting this from the amount of decrease in the population, namely, 2,476,414, the remainder will be 1,039,552; which number of persons must have died of starvation and its concomitant epidemics; but even this number, great as it is, must be supplemented by the deaths which occurred among Famine emigrants, in excess of the percentage of deaths among ordinary emigrants.

During the Famine-emigration period this excess became most remarkable and alarming. The deaths on the voyage to Canada rose from five in 1,000 (the ordinary rate) to about sixty in 1,000; and the deaths whilst the ships were in quarantine rose from one to forty in 1,000. So that instead of six emigrants in 1,000 dying on the voyage and during quarantine, 100 died. Subtracting six from 100, we have ninety-four emigrants in 1,000 dying of the Famine as certainly as if they had died at home. Furthermore, great numbers of those who were able to reach the interior died off almost immediately. Sir Charles Trevelyan, the Government official, from whose *Irish Crisis* I take the above figures, adds these remarkable words: 'besides *still larger* numbers who died at Quebec, Montreal, and elsewhere in the interior'.[20]

Some 89,738 emigrants embarked for Canada in 1847. One in every three of those who arrived were received into hospital and the deaths on the passage or soon after arriving were 15,330, or

Waiting to board ship at Cork.

more than *seventeen* per cent. As the deaths amongst emigrants, in ordinary times, were about three-and-three-quarters per cent, at least sixteen per cent of those deaths may be set down as being occasioned by the Famine. But seventeen per cent, high as it seems, does not fully represent the mortality amongst the Famine emigrants. Speaking of those who went to Canada in 1847, Dr Stratten says: 'Up to November, one emigrant in every seven had died; and during November and December there have been many deaths in the different emigrant hospitals; so that it is understating the mortality to say that one person in every five was dead by the end of the year'.[21]

This would give us twenty per cent of deaths up to the end of 1847; but the mortality consequent upon the Famine-emigration did not stop short at the end of December; it must have gone on through the remainder of the winter and spring, so that, everything considered, twenty-five per cent does not seem too high a rate at which to fix it for that year. It is, however, to be taken into account that the mortality amongst Irish emigrants in 1847 was exceptionally great, so, in an average for the six years from 1846 to 1851, we must strike below it. Seventeen per cent does not seem too high an average for those six years.

We have not such full information about those who emigrated to the United States as we have of those who went to Canada; the Canadian emigrants had certainly some advantages on their side; for until the year 1847 there was no protection for emigrants who landed at New York. In that year the legislature of the State of New York passed a law establishing a permanent Commission for the relief and protection of emigrants which, in due time, when it got into working order, did a world of good.

Previous to this, private hospitals were established by the shipbrokers (the creatures of the shipowners), in the neighbourhood of New York. A committee appointed by the Aldermen of New York in 1846 visited one of those institutions, and thus reported upon it: 'The committee discovered in one apartment fifty feet square, 100 sick and dying emigrants lying on straw; and among them, in their midst, the bodies of two who had died four or five days before but who had been left for that time without burial! They found in the course of their inquiry that decayed vegetables, bad flour and putrid meat were specially purchased and provided for the use of strangers! Such as had strength to escape from these slaughter-houses fled from them as from a plague and roamed through the city, exciting the compassion — perhaps the horror — of the passers by. Those who were too ill to escape had to take their chance — such chance as poisonous food, infected air and bad treatment afforded them of ultimate recovery.'[22]

It may be fairly assumed that the mortality amongst the emigrants who went to the United States was at least as great as amongst those who went to British America. The emigration from Ireland for the above six years was, as already stated, 1,180,409, seventeen per cent of whom will give us 200,668, which, being added to 1,039,552, the calculated number of deaths at home, we have 1,240,000 deaths resulting directly from the Irish Famine and the pestilence which followed in its track.

The mortality on board some of the emigrant ships was terrible; and, whatever the cause, the deaths in *British ships* enormously exceeded those in the ships of any other country.[23] The *Erin Queen* sailed with 493 passengers, of whom 136 died on the voyage. The scenes of misery on board this vessel could hardly have been surpassed in a crowded and sickly slaver on the African coast. It appears, wrote Dr Stratten, that the *Avon*, among 552 passengers, had 246 deaths; and the *Virginius*, in 476, had 267 deaths.[24] An English gentlemen, referring to a portion of Connaught in which he was stationed at the time, wrote thus: 'Hundreds, it is said, had been compelled to emigrate by ill-usage, and in one vessel containing 600 not 100 survived!'[25]

Much sympathy was shown in Canada for the poor emigrants and their orphans were, to a great extent, adopted by charitable families. The legislature of the State of New York and many of its leading citizens showed a laudable desire to aid and protect emigrants, in spite of which the most cruel and heartless villainies were practised upon the inexperienced strangers the moment they landed; in fact, before they landed the ship was surrounded by harpies, who seized their luggage and partly by violence, partly by wheedling and misrepresentation, led them where they pleased and plundered then at will.

The legislature of the State of New York, in 1847, appointed a committee to inquire into the frauds practised upon emigrants. It made its report in January 1848. In the fourth page of that report these words occur: 'Your committee must confess that they had no conception of, nor would they have believed the extent to which these frauds and outrages have been practised, until they came to investigate them.' The first set of robbers into whose hands the emigrants fell were called 'runners'. They are described in the report as a class who boarded the emigrant ship and brought the emigrants to their special lodging-houses in spite of them and in spite of the authorities. They took charge of their luggage, pretending that nothing would be demanded for the storage of it, the price claimed for which afterwards was exorbitant and the luggage was held until it was paid.

The frauds committed with regard to passage tickets were if possible more grievous than those practised by the runners. 'The emigrant', said the report, 'buys a ticket at an exorbitant price, with a picture on it representing a steam-boat, railway cars and a canal packet drawn by three prancing horses, to bring him to some place beyond Albany. *He gets a steam-boat ticket to Albany.* Here his great ticket, with the pictures, is protested; he has to pay once more and, instead of railroad cars and a packet-boat, he is thrust into the steerage or hold of a line boat, which amongst other conveniences is furnished with false scales for weighing his luggage.'

A few extracts from the testimony of some of the witnesses examined before the Committee show how unexaggerated was the report.

Henry Vail was examined: he testified that he was employed by E. Matthews. His practice was to get all he could for tickets; he retained whatever was over the proper price and got his monthly pay besides. The only exception to his getting all he could was, he declared upon his oath, that he *'never shaves a lady that is travelling alone'*. It was bad enough, in his opinion, 'to shave a man'.[26]

Charles Cooke said, in his examination, that he had been employed by many offices. He heard Rieschmüller tell passengers to go to the d—-l, they could not get less than twelve dollars as deck passengers on the lake, and he made them believe they must get their tickets from him, which they did.

'Rieschmüller told me', said Cooke, 'that all he was compelled to pay for a passenger to any port on the lakes was from two dollars to two and a-half. Wolfe told me that two dollars was the price, and all luggage free'.[27] Mervyn L. Ray swore that he knew Mr Adams to take twelve dollars for a passenger to Buffalo, when he (Ray) would have given him the same fare at two dollars.

One of the witnesses, T.R. Schoger, entered into some details. 1. 'The first fraud practised on emigrants is this: the moment the vessel arrives it is boarded by runners whose first object appears to be to get emigrants to their respective public houses. Once there they are considered sure prey. There are, of course, rival establishments; each has agents (runners) and bullies. There is often bloodshed between them. The emigrant is bewildered. He is told he will get meals for sixpence apiece — he never gets one less than two shillings and he is often charged a dollar a meal. 2. The next ordeal is called booking; that is, he is taken to the forwarding office and told it is the *only office*, the proprietors being owners of boats, railways, &c. The runner gets one dollar for everyone booked. 3. The next imposition is at Albany; it is there the great fraud is perpetrated. If they find the emigrant has plenty of money they make him pay the whole passage over again — repudiating all that was done at New York. 4. The next is the luggage. It is falsely weighed and the emigrant is often made to pay five or six times more than the proper charge'.

'The emigrant', added Mr Schoger, 'now thinks himself out of his difficulty, but finds himself greatly mistaken. The passengers are crowded like beasts into the canal boat, and are frequently compelled to pay their passage over again or be thrown overboard by the captain.'[28] The mates of the ships often took the property of emigrants; their locks were picked and their chests robbed; for none of which outrages was there the slightest redress.[29]

Before the legislature took any effective action in protecting the emigrants who landed at New York, many philanthropic and benevolent societies were formed for that purpose. Of those societies one Hiram Huested gave the following testimony on oath: 'I am sure there is as much iniquity amongst the emigrant societies as there is amongst the runners.'[30]

What with shipwrecks, deaths from famine, fever, overcrowding; what with wholesale robbery committed upon them at almost every step of their journey, it is matter for great surprise indeed that even a remnant of the Famine-emigrants survived to locate themselves in that far West to which they fled in terror and dismay from their humble but loved and cherished homes in the land of their fathers.

The Irish race get but little credit for industry or perseverance; but in this they are most unjustly maligned, as many testimonies already cited from friend and foe clearly demonstrate. If one be wanting I would point to a fact in the history of the worn-out remnant of our Famine-emigrants, who had tenacity of life enough to survive their endless hardships and journeyings. That fact is the large sums of money which, year after year, they sent to their friends — every penny of which they earned by the sweat of their brow, by their industry and perseverance.

Thus wrote the Commissioners of Emigration, in their thirty-first General Report: 'In 1870, as in former years, the amount sent home was large, being £727,408 from North America and £12,804 from Australia and New Zealand. Of this sum there was remitted in prepaid passages to Liverpool, Glasgow and Londonderry, £332,638; more than was sufficient to pay the passage money for all who emigrated that year! Imperfect as our accounts are they show that, in the twenty-three years from 1848 to 1870 inclusive, there has been sent home from North America, through banks and commercial houses, upwards of £16,334,000. Of what has been sent home through private channels we have no account.'[31]

A public writer, reviewing the Commissioners' Report, said: 'Even this vast sum does not represent more than the one half of the total sent home. Much was brought over by captains of ships, by relatives, friends or by returning emigrants.' No doubt a great deal of money came through private channels, but it is hardly credible that another £16,000,000 or £17,000,000 reached Ireland in that way. It is only guess-work, to be sure, but if we add one-fourth to the sum named in the report, as the amount transmitted by private hand, it will probably bring us much nearer the truth. This addition gives us, in all, £20,417,500.

There, then, is the one more testimony that the Irish race lack neither industry nor perseverance. For the lengthened period of twenty-three years, something like £1,000,000 a year have been transmitted to their relatives and friends by the Irish in America. In twenty-three years, they have sent home over £20,000,000. Examine it; weigh it; study it; in whatever way we look at this astounding fact — whether we regard the magnitude of the sum, or the intense, undying, all-pervading affection which it represents — it stands alone in the history of the world.

15

The good — and bad — donors

The Temporary Relief Act, popularly known as the Soup-kitchen Act, was limited to 1 October 1847. The Government determined that, after its expiration, relief should be given through the poor law system only. In preparation for this arrangement, an Act (the 10th and 11th Vic. cap. 31) was passed in June, sanctioning outdoor relief.

The harvest of 1847 was a good one but, so utterly prostrate was every interest in the country, that the outdoor relief system soon expanded into alarming proportions. In February 1848, the cost of outdoor relief was £72,039, and in March it rose to £81,339. The numbers and cost were then both at their maximum and, according to the best estimate which can be formed, the number of outdoor poor relieved was 703,762 and of indoor 140,536, making an aggregate of 844,298 persons, irrespective of more than 200,000 school children who were, as stated above, fed and in part clothed by 'The British Association'. So that the total number receiving relief in March 1848 exceeded 1,000,000; being about one in every seven of the population.

In the short statement I am about to give, I follow Sir Charles Trevelyan's figures; being Secretary to the Treasury, he must have known the sums actually advanced by the Treasury, and the sums returned to it in payment of the loans granted.

Amount advanced from the Treasury				Amount finally charged under the Consolidated Annuities Act		
	£	s	d	£	s	d
Under 9th Vict., cap. 1..............	476,000	0	0	238,000	0	0
Under 9th and 10th Vict., cap 107, 'The Labour-rate Act'	4,766,789	0	0	2,231,000	0	0
Under 10th Vict., cap. 7 'The Temporary Relief Act'...............	1,724,631	0	0	953,355	0	0
Loans for building workhouses	1,420,780	0	0	122,707	0	0
Loans to pay debts of distressed unions	300,000	0	0	300,000	0	0

Grants by Parliament at various times:
1845, 1846, 1847, 1848 and 1849......   844,521 0 0

                          Total   9,532,721 0 0   4,845,062 0 0

During the years 1846, 1847 and 1848,
the following sums were also
expended by the Board of Works: £   s   d
For arterial drainage.................   470,617 10 3
Works under the Labouchere letter...   199,870   9 2
For land improvement...............   520,700   0 0

                          Total   10,723,908 19 5

In the above £10,700,000, it may be fairly assumed, we have all the moneys advanced by Government to mitigate the effects of the potato failure. Our next duty is to inquire how much of this sum was paid back by Ireland, and how much of it was a free gift from the Treasury.

The money advanced under the Labouchere letter for land improvement and for arterial drainage cannot, of course, be regarded as a free gift towards staying the Famine; arterial drainage and land improvement go on still, through money advanced by Government. The works under the Labouchere letter were, no doubt, intended to give reproductive employment during the Famine, but the cost of them was a charge upon the land and not a free gift.

The money spent on arterial drainage and land improvement, under the Labouchere letter and various drainage Acts, during the years 1846, 1847 and 1848, was, as given above, £1,191,187 19s. 5d. which, being deducted from £10,723,908 19s. 5d. leaves the sum of £9,532,721, of which there was finally charged to this country £4,845,062. Deducting this from the £9,532,721 we have £4,687,659 as the amount of money given by the Government as a free gift to Ireland to sustain the people through the Great Famine. To this, however, there is to be added a sum of about £70,000 paid for freights.

The American people, when they had collected those generous contributions of theirs and when they had resolved to send them in the form of food to Ireland, began to make arrangements for paying the freights of their vessels, but all trouble and anxiety on this head was removed by the action of the English Government which undertook to pay the freights of all vessels carrying to Ireland food purchased by charitable contributions. Those freights finally reached about £70,000. The addition of this sum brings the whole of the Government's free gift towards the Irish Famine to £4,757,659.

The amount collected and disbursed by charitable associations can be only approximated to. There is a list of those subscriptions, as far as they could be ascertained, given in the report of the Society of Friends. They amount to £1,107,466 13s., but the compiler of the report was of the opinion that the sums so collected and distributed could not have fallen far short of £1,500,000.

No effective means were taken to ascertain the moneys sent to Ireland by emigrants until the year 1848; however, Mr Jacob Harvey, a member of the Society of Friends, from inquiries made by him in New York, Baltimore and Philadelphia, computed the remittances from emigrants in 1847 at £200,000, but it is highly probable that the actual amount was far in excess of that; for we find in the next year, 1848, there came to Ireland through the banks and commercial houses alone, £460,180; which sum may also be regarded as a contribution towards the Irish Famine. I think we are justified in naming £300,000 for 1847, instead of £200,000, Mr Harvey's estimate. These two sums make £760,180, which being added to the acknowledged amount of public subscriptions, we have a total of £1,867,646, 13s. as the amount voluntarily and charitably contributed to our Famine-stricken people. But if we take £1,500,000 to represent *the actual charitable subscriptions*, as assumed by the report of the Society of Friends, and add to it the money sent by emigrants in 1847 and 1848, we will have the enormous sum of £2,260,180.

The most important of all the associations called into existence by the Famine was 'The British Association for the Relief of Extreme Distress in Ireland and Scotland'. There are about 5,550 distinct subscriptions printed in the appendix to its report but the number of individual subscriptions was far beyond this for many of the sums set down are the result of local subscriptions sent to the Association from various parts. This Association established about forty food depots in various districts. They were, of course, most numerous in the South and West — most numerous of all in Cork, the wild and difficult coast of which county was marked by a line of them, from Kinsale Head to Dingle Bay.

Noblemen and gentlemen of high position volunteered their services to the Association and laboured earnestly among the starving people. Amongst them may be named the Count Strezelecki, Lord R. Clinton, Lord James Butler and Mr M. J. Higgins, so well known in the London press by his *nom de plume* of 'Jacob Omnium'.

Besides the sums contributed directly to the Association, the Government gave it the distribution of the proceeds of two Queen's letters, amounting in the aggregate to £200,738 15s.1d.[1]

In August 1847 when the Association was about to enter upon what it called the second relief period, it found itself in possession of a clear cash balance of £160,000. It had to consider how this sum could be most beneficially applied during the ensuing winter.

In that month the Secretary of the Treasury, Mr Trevelyan, wrote to the chairman, recommending the Association to select, through the Poor Law Commissioners, a certain number of Unions in which there was reason to believe the ratepayers would not be able to meet their liabilities, and that the Association should appropriate, from time to time, such sums as the Poor Law Commissioners might recommend for the purpose of assisting to given outdoor relief in certain districts of such Unions.

After much deliberation the Association accepted this advice and asked for the names of the most distressed union. A list of twenty-two was supplied to it in September. Some others were added later on. The grants of the Association were issued in food and the Assistant Poor Law Commissioners aided in the distribution of it. Under this arrangement the advances made by the Association from October to July amounted to £150,000.

A peculiar feature of this relief system, adopted and carried into effect by the advice of Count Strezelecki, was the giving of clothing and daily rations to children attending school. This was done in twenty-seven of the poorest Unions, and with the best results. By the first of January 1848 the system was in full operation in thirteen Unions and 58,000 children were on the relief roll of the Association. The numbers went on increasing until, in March, there were upwards of 200,000 children attending schools of all denominations, in twenty-seven western Unions, participating in this relief. The total sum expended on food for the children amounted to £80,854, in addition to which £12,000 was expended on clothing for them.

On 1 November 1848, £12,000 was still to the credit of the Association. By a resolution, it was handed over to the Poor Law Commissioners for Ireland; and so closed the labours of the British Relief Association, so vast in its operations, so well managed, so creditable to all engaged in it and such a lasting testimony to the generous charity of the subscribers.

Such frequent reference has been made in these pages to the 'Transactions' of the Relief Committee of the Society of Friends during the Famine, and so much use has been made of the information contained in that carefully compiled book that I will only here repeat the amount of the charitable offerings confided to them for distribution. It was £198,326 15s. 5d.

The General Central Relief Committee for all Ireland, which met in College Green, received in contributions £83,934 17s. 11d., but of this, £20,000 was given by the British Association. The Marquis of Abercorn, the Most Rev. Dr Murray, Archbishop of Dublin, the Lord Mayor, the Provost of Trinity College, Lord Charlemont, O'Connell, the Dean of St Patrick's and several other noblemen and gentlemen were members of this Committee. The president was the Duke of Leinster, then Marquis of Kildare. It remained in existence just one year, from December 1846 to December 1847.

'The chief source', said the 'Transactions' of the Society of Friends, 'whence the means at our disposal were derived, was the munificent bounty of the citizens of the United States. The supplies sent from America to Ireland were on a scale unparalleled in history.'

When authentic intelligence regarding the Irish Famine reached America a general feeling of sympathy was at once excited. Beginning with Philadelphia, in all the great cities and towns throughout the Union, meetings were almost immediately held to devise the best and speediest means of relieving the starving people of this country.

'All through the States an intense interest and a noble generosity were shown. The railroads carried, free of charge, all packages marked "Ireland". Public carriers undertook the gratuitous delivery of any package intended for the relief of the destitute Irish. Storage to any extent was offered on the same terms. Ships of war approached our shores, eagerly seeking not to destroy life but to preserve it, their guns being taken out in order to afford more room for stowage'.[2]

The total contributions received from America by the Central Relief Committee of the Society of Friends, were: Money, £15,976 18s. 2d.; Provisions 9,911 tons, valued at £133,847 7s. 7d. Some 642 packages of clothing were also received, the precise value of which could not be exactly ascertained. The provisions were carried in ninety-one vessels, the united freights of which amounted to £33,017 5s. 7d.[3]

The total number of ships which carried provisions, the result of charitable contributions, to Ireland and Scotland in 1847, is set down at 118; but as only four of these went to Scotland, 114 of them must have come here. The total freightage paid to those ships by Government was £41,725 8s. 5.5d; but as I find in another part of the Blue Book that between £60,000 and £70,000 was paid by Government for freights on the cargoes of provisions consigned to the Society of Friends and to the British Association, and which I have above assumed to be £70,000, we may take it for granted that something like 20,000 tons of provisions were consigned to both Societies, the money value of which was about £280,000.

Two American ships of war, the *Jamestown* and *Macedonian*, carried cargoes of provisions to Ireland, for which no freight was charged. The *Jamestown*, a sloop of war lent by the government for the voyage, was freighted by the people of Massachusetts with 8,000 barrels of flour. She sailed from Boston on 28 March 1847 and arrived at the Cove of Cork on 12 April, after a most prosperous voyage. The people of Cove immediately held a public meeting and adopted an address to her Commander, Captain Forbes, which they presented to him on board. The citizens of Cork addressed him a few days later; and the members of the Temperance Institute gave him a soirée, at which the Rev. Theobald Mathew assisted.

The *Macedonian*, another ship of war, arrived later on, conveying about 550 tons of provisions, a portion of which was landed in Scotland. Both ships were manned by volunteers.

On the appearance of the potato blight scientific men earnestly applied themselves to discover its cause, in the hope that a remedy might be found for it. Various theories were the result. There was the Insect Theory; the Weather Theory; the Parasitical Theory; the Electrical Theory; the Fungus Theory; the Fog Theory. But whilst philosophers were maintaining their different views; whilst Sir James Murray charged electricity with being the agent of destruction, and Mr Cooper cast the blame upon the fogs; whilst Professors Lindley, Playfair and Kane were busy with their tests and retorts and alembics; and whilst others again — microscope in hand — were in active pursuit of the *Aphis vastator*, or *Thrips minutissima*, a not inconsiderable class of persons, departing widely from all such speculations, discovered, beyond all doubt, that *Popery* was the true cause of the potato blight.

'As this predicted system' (popery), said a pamphleteer, 'is an idolatrous one, any treaty with it must be opposed to God's will, and call down his wrath upon those nations who have commerce with it: more particularly upon nations wherein its hideous deformities are most signally manifested. Now, how have we seen in the first part of this work, that He has repeatedly punished? By famine and pestilence! Oh, beloved countrymen of every diversity of creed, in the heart-rending scenes around us do we witness punishment for national idolatry, systematic assassinations, performed occasionally with a refinement of cruelty worthy of incarnate devils.'[4]

'This much is certain', wrote a public journalist, 'that our country is scourged with famine.' Three causes were then given for the scourge; the second of which was 'idolatry in the professing people of God, especially when sanctioned by the rulers of the country'. After quoting examples from the Old

Testament of the manner in which God punished idolatry, he proceeded: 'It [idolatry] is just as true of the millions of Ireland as it was of the millions of Judah: "They worship the work of their own hands, that which their own fingers have made." And to complete the resemblance to apostate Israel, and fill the measure of our national guilt, the prevalent idolatry is countenanced and supported by our government. The Protestant members of the Houses of Lords and Commons have sworn before God and the country that Popery is idolatrous; our Queen, at her coronation, solemnly made a similar declaration, yet, all have concurred in passing a Bill to endow a college for training priests to defend, and practise, and perpetuate, this corrupt and damnable worship in this realm. The ink wherewith the signification of royal assent was given to that iniquitous measure was hardly dry when *the fatal rot* commenced its work of destruction; and as the stroke was unheeded, and there was no repentant effort to retrace the daring step of the first iniquity, but rather a disposition to multiply transgression, we are now visited with a second and severer stroke of judgment.'[5]

The Rev. Hugh McNeill preached a 'Famine' sermon in St Jude's, Liverpool, and published it under the title of 'The Famine, a rod'; a rod that was meant to scourge England for tolerating Popery, of which he said: 'That it is a sin against God's holy law to encourage the fables, deceits, false doctrines, and idolatrous worship of Romanism, no enlightened Christian — no consistent member of the Church of England can deny.'[6] 'She [England] is fondly anticipating, as the result of generous concession, that she shall witness Roman Cooperation in general Liberty! Alas, for the Romans! With equal reason might she expect the Ethiopian to change his skin, or the leopard his spots. With the rich and responsible inheritance of an open Bible before her, and with free access to the illustrations of authentic history, this absurdity is England's sin, England's very great sin. There can be little doubt, that except repentance *and amendment* avert the stroke, this will prove England's plague, England's great plague, England's very great plague.'[7]

Let us hear another and a very different stamp of man. 'I don't know whether I have mentioned before', wrote Charles Dickens, 'that in the valley of the Simplon, hard by here, where (at the Bridge of St Maurice over the Rhone), this Protestant canton ends and a Catholic canton begins, you might separate two perfectly distinct and different conditions of humanity, by drawing a line with your stick in the dust on the ground. On the Protestant side, neatness; cheerfulness; industry; education; continual aspiration, at least, after better things. On the Catholic side, dirt; disease;

ignorance; squalor; and misery. I have so constantly observed the like of this, since I first came abroad, that *I have a sad misgiving, that the religion of Ireland lies as deep at the root of all her sorrows even as English misgovernment and Tory villainy.'*[8]

Charles Dickens is looked upon not only as the strenuous denouncer of vice but as the happy exponent of the higher and purer feelings of human nature also. For three-fourths of his life he wrote like a man who felt he had a mission to preach toleration, philanthropy, universal benevolence. He had travelled much. He had been over Belgium and France; he was through the Rhenish Provinces; in all which places the people are Catholics; they have received the highest praise from travellers and writers for their industry; their thrift; their cleanliness; Charles Dickens saw all this, but it never occurred to him to credit their religion with it. When the contrary occurs, and when fault is to be found, Popery, like a hack-block kept for such purposes, is made responsible and receives a blow.

He had, indeed, a sad misgiving that the religion of Ireland lay deep at the root of her sorrows. Surely this is enough to try one's patience. We have passed through and outlived the terrible codes of Elizabeth and James and Anne and the first two Georges, under which gallows-trees were erected on the hillside for our conversion or extinction; we have even survived the iron heels and ruthless sabres of Cromwell's sanctimonious troopers; and we can go back upon the history of those times calmly enough now. But this 'sad misgiving' of Mr Dickens; this patronising condescension; this contemptuous pity, is more than provoking.

It is probable he had not the time or inclination to read deeply into Irish history but he must have had a general knowledge of it more than sufficient to inform him that there were causes in superabundance to account for the poverty and degradation of our people, without going to their religion for them. Instead of doing so, he should have confessed with shame and humiliation that his own countrymen, for a long series of years, did everything in their power to destroy the image of God in the native Irish, by driving them like beasts of chase into the mountains, and bogs and fastnesses and over the Shannon. Our people suffered these things and much more for conscience sake; inflicted, as they were, by Mr Dickens' countrymen, in the name of religion; in the name of conscience; in advancing, as they pretended, the sacred cause of the right of private judgment. *He* makes Popery responsible for the results.

Those who held that Popery was the real cause of the potato-rot were influential, if not by their numbers, at least by their wealth; so they set about removing the fatal evil energetically.

Large sums of money were collected, and a very active agency was established throughout the West of Ireland for this purpose; with, it would seem, very considerable success. But whilst those engaged in the work maintained that the conversions were the result of instruction and enlightened investigation, others believed that most of the converts were like the poor woman mentioned by the late Dr Whately, in a conversation with Mr Senior.

In 1852, Mr Nassau Wm. Senior was on a visit with the Archbishop, at his country house, near Stillorgan, five miles from Dublin. Mr Senior asked him to what cause the conversions made during the Famine were attributable. The Archbishop replied that the causes must be numerous. Some, he said, believed or professed to believe that the conversions were purchased; this of course was the Catholic view. He then related the following anecdote on the subject:

'An old woman went to one of my clergy, and said, "I'm come to surrender to your Reverence — and I want the leg of mutton and the blanket". "What mutton and blanket?" said the clergyman. "I have scarcely enough of either for myself and my family, and certainly none to give. Who could have put such nonsense into your head?" "Why, Sir", she said, "Father Sullivan told us that the converts got each a leg of mutton and a blanket; and as I am famished and starving with cold, I thought that *God would forgive* me for getting them"'.[9]

Dr Whately was president of the 'Society for Protecting the Rights of Conscience', and he indignantly denied that any reward or indemnity had been held out, directly or indirectly, by that Society to persons to induce them to profess themselves converts; and he added: 'not only has no case been substantiated — no case has been brought forward'. This may be true of that particular society, but to deny that neither money nor food were given, to induce persons to attend the Scripture classes and proselytising schools, is to deny the very best proven facts.

In the *Tralee Chronicle* of 19 November 1852, Archdeacon O'Sullivan of Kenmare published an abstract of a report of one of those Missionary Societies which fell into his hands. The expenditure of a single Committee was £3,557 1s. 9d. The salaries of clerical and lay agents are set down at £382 0s. 11d. What became of the remainder of the money?

But here is testimony that Dr Whately himself would scarcely impugn: Dr Forbes, in his *Memorandums made in Ireland* in 1852, visited Connaught and examined many of the proselytising schools. He spoke without any doubt at all of the children who attended those schools receiving food and clothing. It did not seem to be denied on any side. Here is an extract; 'I visited two of the Protestant Mission Schools at Clifden, one in the town and the other leading to the mouth of the bay. In the former, at the time of my visit, there were about 120 boys and 100 girls on the books, the average attendance being about 80. Out of the 80 girls there were no less than 56 orphans, *all of whom are fed and clothed out of the school funds, and a large proportion provided with lodgings also.* Only two of these girls were children of Protestant parents; and in the boy's school there was only one born of parents originally Protestant .... At the probationary girl's school there were 76 on the books, at the time of my visit, their ages varying from eight to eighteen years. They are all Catholics, or children of Catholic parents; and out of the number no fewer that 40 *were orphans.* All the children at this school receive daily rations of Indian meal; 45 of them one pound, and the remainder half that quantity. *Whether this is exclusive of the stirabout breakfast I saw preparing for them in the school,* I forgot to ask. All the children of these schools read the Scriptures and go to the Protestant Church, Catholic and Protestant alike.'[10]

But I turn with pleasure from this uninviting and uncongenial subject to one more elevating — to the all but unlimited private charity which was called forth by the Irish Famine. I have already endeavoured to give some idea of it but of course an imperfect one. The feelings evoked and the almost unasked alms bestowed with a noble Christian generosity, during that awful time, can be fully known only to Almighty God, the Great Rewarder. The Merciful Rewarder has recorded them and that is enough, at least for the givers.

However, there were some amongst them who should not be passed over in silence. Baring Brothers & Co.; Rothschild & Co.; Smith, Payne & Smith; Overend, Gurney & Co.; Truman, Hanbury & Co.; The Duke of Devonshire; Jones, Lloyd & Co.; an English friend (in two donations); and an Irish landlord (for Skibbereen) subscribed £1,000 each.

Irish landlords did not contribute very munificently to the Famine-fund; but here is £1,000 from one, and for a special locality. Who was the retiring but generous donor? The following extract of a letter will answer the question; and throw light upon another remarkable offering sent every month to Skibbereen for more than a year.

'The first case of death clearly established as arising from starvation', wrote Mr McCarthy Downing, 'occurred at South Reen, five miles from the town of Skibbereen. The case having been reported to me, as a member of the Relief Committee, I procured the attendance of Dr Dore, and proceeded to the house where the body lay; the scene which presented itself will never be forgotten by me.

'The body was resting on a basket which had been turned up, the head on an old chair, the legs on the ground. All was wretchedness around. The wife, emaciated, was unable to move; and four children, more like spectres than living beings, were lying near the fire-place, in which apparently there had not been fire for some time. The doctor opened the stomach and, repugnant as it was to my feelings, I, at his solicitation, viewed its contents, which consisted solely of a few pieces of raw cabbage undigested.

'Having visited several other houses on the same townland and finding the condition of the inmates therein little better than that of the wretched family whom I had just left, I summoned the Committee and had a quantity of provisions sent there for distribution by one of the relieving officers; and then published in the Cork and Dublin papers a statement of what I had witnessed.

'Many subscriptions were sent to the Committee in consequence, and I received from an anonymous correspondent a monthly sum varying from £6, to £8, for a period of more than twelve months.

'One subscription of £1,000 came from another anonymous donor and for years the Committee knew not who those generous and really charitable parties were; but I had always a suspicion that the giver of the £1,000 was Lord Dufferin. The grounds for my supposition were that, during the height of the sufferings of the people, I heard that two noblemen had been in the neighbourhood, visiting some of the localities. One was Lord Dufferin, then a very young man, who alluded subsequently in feeling terms to the wretchedness and suffering which he had witnessed; the other, I heard, was Lord John Manners.

'In some years after, I met at the house of Mr Joshua Clarke, QC, in Dublin, Mr Dowse, then a rising barrister, now a Baron of the Court of Exchequer, who addressed me, saying, "We are old acquaintances"; to which I replied that I thought he was mistaken, as I had never the pleasure of meeting him before. He said: "That is quite true, but do you remember having received monthly remittances during the severe pressure of the Famine in Skibbereen?" I answered in the affirmative; and thereupon he said, "I was your correspondent, I remitted the moneys to you, they were the offers of a number of the students of Trinity College".

'I need scarcely say that the incident created in me a feeling

Irish emigrants embarking at Liverpool for the fearful Atlantic crossing.

of esteem and regard for Mr Dowse, which has continued to the present moment.

'During the passing of the Land Bill through the House of Commons, in the year 1870, I proposed several amendments, in consequence of which I received a letter from Lord Dufferin, asking for an interview, which subsequently took place at his house and lasted more than three hours. When about to leave, I said that I had a question to put to his Lordship which I hoped he would not refuse to answer; and having received his assent, I said: "Lord Dufferin, are you the anonymous donor of a subscription of £1,000 to the Relief Committee at Skibbereen twenty-three years ago?" And with a smile, he simply replied "I am".

'I left with feelings of high admiration for the man.'[11]

To conclude. Every reader will, doubtless, form his own views upon the facts given in this volume; upon the conduct of the people; the action of the landlords; the measures of the Government; those views may be widely different; but of the bright and copious fountains of living charity which gushed forth over the Christian world during the Great Irish Famine history has but one record to make — posterity can hold but one opinion.

Notes

Chapter 1: How the potato came to Europe

1. Raleigh earned this property by some terrible services. He was an officer in the expedition of the Lord Deputy Gray, when he attacked the Italian camp on Dún an Óir, at Smerwick harbour in Kerry. After some time the Italians yielded, but on what precise terms it is now impossible to say, the accounts of the transaction are so various and conflicting. Indeed, O'Daly says the English were the first to send a flag of truce. Anyhow, the Italian garrison, which had come to aid the Irish, fell into the power of the English, and here is Dr Leland's account of what followed: 'Wingfield was commissioned to disarm them, and when this service was performed an English company was sent into the fort. The Irish rebels found they were reserved for execution by martial law. The Italian general and some of the officers were made prisoners of war, but the garrison was butchered in cold blood; *nor is it without pain that we find a service so horrid and detestable committed to Sir Walter Raleigh.'*
2. The people of Quito said *papas*. The Spaniards corrupted this to *battata*, and the Portuguese to the softer *batata*.
3. Edwards *(Life of Sir W. Raleigh,* McMillan, 1868) says that Hooker is the only contemporary writer who asserts that Raleigh sailed with this expedition, and Edwards adds: 'It is by no means certain that he did so.' But from the following entry in the State Papers of Elizabeth's reign it appears quite certain that he did sail with it: 'The names of all the ships, officers, and gentlemen, with the pieces of ordnance, &c., gone in the voyage with Sir Humfrey Gylberte, — Capt. Walter Rauley, commanding the Falcon' *(State Papers [Domestic],* Vol. 126, No. 149, November 18 & 19 1578). Mr Edwards may not have met this entry, as he does not refer to it.

   In spite of his many failures, Raleigh was, to the last, confident in the final success of his scheme for colonising America. After the failure of nine expeditions, and on the eve of his fall, he said: 'I shall yet live to see it [America] an English nation' (Edwards).
4. Perhaps *Kartoffel,* one of the German names for potato, is a corruption of this.
5. Mr Edwards says, I know not on what authority, that the land given to Raleigh was about 12,000 acres. The grants are set forth plainly enough in the following entries: 'The Queen, desirous to have the Province of Munster, in the realm of Ireland, re-peopled and inhabited with civil, loyal and dutiful subjects, in consideration of the great charge and trouble which Sir Walter Raleigh sustained in transporting and planting English people into the province, and in recompense of his good service rendered in Ireland, pursuant to her royal letters dated the last of February 1586 to the Lord Deputy and Lord Chancellor directed, and intending to bestow upon him three seignories

273

and a half of land ... ''lying as near to the town of Youghall as they may be conveniently'', *each seignory containing 12,000 acres of tenantable land, not accounting mountains, bogs, or barren heath.'* And again: 'And as Sir Walter made humble suit, to enable him the better to perform the enterprise for the habitation and repeopling of the land, to grant him and his heirs, in fee-farm for ever, the possessions of the late dissolved abbey or monastery called Molanassa, otherwise Molana, and the late dissolved priory of the Observant Friars, or the Black Friars, near Youghall ... and, as they lie adjoining the lands already granted to him, her Majesty is pleased to comply with his request, and by her letters, dated at Greenwich the 2nd of July, 1587, directed to the Lord Deputy, expressed his intention to that effect' (*Patent and Close Rolls, Chancery, Ireland, reg. Elizabeth,* Mem. 5, 41, 1595, p. 323). As the lands at first granted did not measure the 42,000 acres, the Lord Deputy was instructed to issue a commission to measure off so much of other escheated lands adjoining 'as shall be requisite to make up the full number and quantity of three seignories and a half of tenantable land, without mountains, bogs, or barren heath; To hold for ever in fee-farm, as of the Castle of Carregroghan, in the Co. of Cork, in free soccage and not in capite' (Ibid, p. 327). Alas! how soon he tired of that great and coveted prize.

6. Hooker supplement to Hollinshed's *Chronicle,* p. 183.
7. 'Some Considerations for the Promoting of Agriculture and Employing the Poor', addressed to members of the House of Commons, by R.L. V.M. Halliday, collection of pamphlets in the library of the Royal Irish Academy, Vol. 54.
8. Page 18.
9. Page 35.
10. *Short View of the State of Ireland,* Halliday pamphlets, Vol. 74.
11. An answer to a paper called *A Memorial of the Poor Inhabitants of the Kingdom of Ireland,* same vol.
12. Answer to *Memorial,* signed A.B., 25 March 1728.
13. Ibid.
14. *Letter to the Duke of Newcastle.*
15. Vol. I, p. 166.
16. 'The famine of 1741 was not regarded with any active interest in England or in any foreign country, and the subject is scarcely alluded to in the literature of the day. No measures were adopted, either by the Executive or the Legislature, for the purpose of relieving the distress caused by this famine' (*Irish Crisis* by Sir C.E. Trevelyan, Bart., p. 13).
17. Probably the origin of the potato pit, as we now have it in Ireland, was the following advice given in *Pue's Occurrences* of 20 November 1740:
    'Method of securing potatoes from the severest frost. Dig up your potatoes in the beginning of December, or sooner, and, in proportion to your quantity of potatoes, dig a large hole about ten foot deep in such place as your garden or near your house where the ground is sandy or dry, and not subject to water; then put your potatoes into the hole, with all their dirt about them, to within three feet of the surface of the ground. If you have sand near you, throw some of it among the potatoes and on top of them. When you have thus lodged your potatoes, then fill up the rest of the hole with the earth first thrown out, and, with some stuff, raise upon the hole a large heap of earth in the form of a large haycock, which you may cover with some litter or heath. By the covering of earth of five or six feet deep, your potatoes will be secured against the severest frosts, which are not known to enter over two feet into the ground. The same pit will serve you year after year, and when the frosts are over you may take out your potatoes.'
18. *O'Halloran on the Air.*

19. *Exshaw's Magazine.*
20. *Pue's Occurrences,* 11 March 1740.
21. Sir John Rogerson's Quay, of course.
22. *Pue's Occurrences,* 1 January 1740.
23. This storm visited other parts of the coast. The news from Dundalk under the same date is that the *Jane and Andrew* of Nantes was wrecked there, 'the weather continuing very stormy, with a very great frost.' Accounts from Nenagh under date of 5 January say: 'The Shannon is frozen over, and a hurling match had taken place upon it; and Mr Parker had a sheep roast whole on the ice, with which he regaled the company who had assembled to witness the hurling match.' Under 29 January we have a ludicrous accident recorded, namely, 'that the Drogheda postboy's horse fell at Santry, near Dublin, and broke his neck. One of the postboy's legs being caught under the horse *got so frozen that he could not pull it out!'* At length some gentlemen who were passing released him (Ibid).
24. I find by the newspapers of the time that Primate Boulter acted with much generosity, especially in the second year of the famine, feeding many thousands at the workhouse at his own expense. He also appealed to his friends to subscribe for the same purpose. The Right Honourable William Conolly, then living at Leixlip Castle, distributed £20 worth of meal in Leixlip, and ordered his steward to attend to the wants of the people there during the frost. Lords Mountjoy and Tullamore, Sir Thomas Prendergast and other influential persons commenced a general collection in Dublin, but it was only for the starving artisans of Dublin. The co-heirs of Lord Ranelagh ordered £110 to be distributed in Roscommon; Lady Betty Brownlow, then abroad, sent home £440 for her tenants in the north; Chief Justice Singleton gave twenty tons of meal to be sold in Drogheda at one shilling and a penny a stone; the Right Honourable William Graham did the same — it was then selling from one shilling and sixpence to one shilling and eightpence a stone; Lord Blundell gave £50 to his tenants; Dean Swift gave £10 to the weavers of the Liberty.

An obelisk 140 feet in height, supported upon open arches and surrounded by a grove of full-grown trees, stands on a hill near Maynooth, and can be seen to advantage both from the Midland and the Great Southern Railway. It is usually known as 'Lady Conolly's Monument'. From its being built without any apparent utility, ill-natured people sometimes call it 'Lady Conolly's Folly'. It is said to have been designed by Castelli (anglicised Castells), the architect of Carton, Castletown House and Leinster House, Kildare Street, now the Royal Dublin Society House. It bears on the keystones of its three principal arches the suggestive date '1740'. It was erected to give employment to the starving people in that year, not by Lady Louisa Conolly, as is generally supposed, but by a Mrs Conolly, as the following information, kindly supplied by the Marquis of Kildare, will show:

'I find in my notes,' says the Marquis, 'that the obelisk was built by Mrs Conolly, widow of the Right Honourable William Conolly, Speaker of the Irish House of Commons. She had Castletown for her life, and died in 1752, in her ninetieth year. Mrs Delany, in her autobiography, Vol. III, p. 158, mentions that her table was open to her friends of all ranks, and her purse to the poor.... A plain and vulgar woman in her manners, but had very valuable qualities. 1740 was a year of great scarcity, and farmers were ploughing their wheat in May to sow summer barley. In March Mrs Conolly's sister, Mrs Jones, wrote to another sister, Mrs Bound, that Mrs Conolly was building an obelisk opposite a vista at the back of Castletown House, and that it would cost £300 or £400 at least, and she wondered how she could afford it. The nephew of the Speaker, also the Right Honourable William

Conolly, lived at Leixlip Castle till he succeeded to Castletown in 1752. He married Lady Anne Wentworth, daughter of an Earl of Strafford. His son was the Right Honourable Thomas Conolly, who married Lady Louisa Lennox, daughter of the Duke of Richmond. From her Castletown passed to the father of the present Mr Conolly, after the death of Lady Louisa.'

Mrs Jones must have made a very erroneous guess at the expense of building the obelisk, even at that time; now, instead of £300 or £400, double as many thousands would scarcely build it. Although erected by Mrs Conolly, it stands on the Duke of Leinster's property. The site is the finest in the neighbourhood, and she obtained it from the Earl of Kildare, by giving him a portion of the Castletown estate instead. Lately those two pieces of ground have been re-exchanged, and when they came to be measured, they were found to be of exactly the same extent.

25. The coming of the thaw was indicated by some accidents on the ice. On 10 February, it was reported from Derry that the ice gave way there and several persons were drowned. In Dublin, at the same date, a man was also drowned who attempted to cross the river on the ice near the Old Bridge. But a boy was more fortunate. He, too, was on the ice on the Liffey, and the part on which he stood becoming detached was driven by the current through Ormond and Essex Bridges; he kept his position, however, on the floating ice until he was taken off in a boat.

26. The following story is told in *Pue's Occurrences*, in May 1740: A broguemaker had been committed to Dungannon jail for some offence, but managed to make his escape. He was pursued and searched for in vain. The jailer gave him up as lost when, one day, after being at large during five weeks, he presented himself at the jail to the astonishment of the jailer, who questioned him as to the cause of his return. He replied that he had travelled to Dublin and had gone through a great part of Munster but, finding nowhere such good quarters as he had in Dungannon jail, he came back.

27. On the passing of this bill Sir Charles E. Trevelyan remarked with quiet severity: 'There is no mention of grants or loans; but an Act was passed by the Irish Parliament, 1741 (15 George II, cap. 8), for the more effectual securing the payment of rents and preventing frauds by tenants' (*Irish Crisis*, p. 13).

28. Matthew O'Connor's *History of the Irish Catholics*, p. 222.

29. 'The judges held the assizes in Tuam instead of Galway this year, on account of the fever in the latter place, *(Dutton's Galway)*.

30. *The Groans of Ireland*, in *Letter to an MP*, 1741. The estimated population in 1731 was 2,010,212. Rutty says it was computed, perhaps with some exaggeration, that one-fifth of the people died of famine and pestilence. This agrees with the higher estimate.

31. *Philo-Ierne*, London, 20 May 1755. Reprinted in Cork with the author's name, Richard Bocklesly, Esq., MD. It is hardly necessary to say that the 'people' referred to in the above extract mean merely the English colony in Ireland.

32. Ibid, pp. 5 & 6. He seems to use the word 'dairy' here in a sense somewhat different from its present application.

33. The Bristol barrel contained twenty-two stone — one stone more than the Irish barrel.

34. A disease called the curl appeared in the potato in Lancashire in 1764. It was in that shire the potato was first planted in England; and we are told the curl appeared in those districts of it in which it was first planted. The nature of the disease is indicated by its name. The stalk became discoloured and stunted almost from the beginning of its growth; it changed its natural healthy green for a sickly greenish brown, the leaves literally curling like those of that species of ornamental holly known as the 'screw-leaved'. The plant continued to grow and even to produce tubers, but they never attained any

considerable size, and from their inferior quality could not be used for food. The curl appeared in Ireland about the year 1770, where it caused much loss, as we find a large quantity of grain was imported for food about that period. Isolated cases of the curl were not unfrequent in this country long after it ceased to cause alarm to the farmer. I have seen many such cases, especially where potatoes were planted on lea. On examining the set beneath a plant affected with curl, I invariably found it had not rotted away as was usual with those sets that produced healthy plants. There were as many remedies propounded for the curl as for the blight of 1846-7 with a like result — none of them was of any use.

35. Report of the Committee for the Relief of the Distressed Districts in Ireland, appointed at a general meeting held at the City of London Tavern, on 7 May 1822.

36. *Impartial Review*, Miliken, Dublin, 1822.

37. Report of Parliamentary Committee.

38. Amongst the means resorted to at this time to raise funds for the starving Irish was a ball at the Opera House in London, at which the King was present, and which realised the large sum of £6,000. This piece of information the Irish Census Commissioners for 1851, curiously enough, insert in that column of their Report set apart for 'Contemporaneous Epidemics'.

39. The chief part of this £60,000 is still under the management of the Society for Bettering the Condition of the Poor of Ireland.

40. The following extract from a letter of Mr Secretary Legge, dated London, 4 May 1740, and addressed to Dublin Castle, expresses very naively an English official's feelings about the terrible frost and famine of that year: 'I hope the weather, which seems mending at last, will be of service to Ireland, *and comfort our Treasury, which, I am afraid, has been greatly chilled with the long frost and embargo.'* (*Records*, Birmingham Tower, Chief Secretary's Department, Box 10).

41. Speech, p. 26; quoted by Plowden, Vol. I, p. 253, note.

42. Answer to Address of Commons, 2 July 1698.

43. Arthur Young's *Tour in Ireland*, App., p. 149.

44. *Groans of Ireland*, p. 20.

45. Mr Prior's pamphlet was dedicated to the Viceroy, Lord Carteret, and both Houses of Parliament, which proves how certain he was of his facts and statements.

46. 'The present miserable state of Ireland'. How like the Ireland of the other day!

47. Arthur Young's *Tour in Ireland*, App., p. 40.

48. *Impartial Review*, p. 3.

49. *History of the Penal Laws*.

50. 13 & 14 Geo. II, cap. 35.

51. 11 & 12 Geo. II, cap. 21.

52. Plowden.

53. *History of the Penal Laws*.

54. By 1 Geo. II, cap. 9, sec 7, it was enacted that no Papist could vote at an election without taking the oath of supremacy — an oath which no Catholic could take. Primate Boulter thought he saw a disposition on the part of the English colony to make common cause with the natives in favour of Irish interests and, taking alarm at the prospect of such a dreadful calamity, he got the Ministers to pass this law. It is said it was carried through Parliament under a false title, being called a Bill for Regulating, etc.; but it would have passed under any title.

55. The feelings of the Irish Catholics for these concessions are curiously illustrated by an inscription on the Carmelite Church in Clarendon Street, Dublin, in which the year 1793 is called, 'the first year of restored liberty', and George III is proclaimed as the 'best of kings'. Here is the full inscription:

D.O.M.
Sub invocatione B.V. Mariae.
C.

Primum hujus Ecclesiae lapidem
posuit Johannes Sweetman, Armiger.
Memoriale hoc grati animi restitutae
Catholicae Libertatis Georgio
tertio Regum optimo, annuente Parlia-
mento ac toto populo
acclamante, Dedicat Patriae Pietas. Anno
supradictae Libertatis primo.
Regni vigesimo tertio, ab Incarnatione
1793, die Octobris tertio.

T. Beahan,
Arch.

56. Forty-shilling freeholders in Ireland and forty-shilling freeholders in England
were quite different classes. The latter, by the statute, 8 Henry VI, cap. 7,
passed in 1429, must be 'people dwelling and resident in the counties, who
should have free land or tenement to the value of forty shillings by the year
at least, above all charges'; whilst in Ireland, every tenant having a lease
for a life was entitled to a Parliamentary vote, provided he swore that his
farm was worth forty shillings annual rent, more than the rent reserved in
his lease. Mr Pim writes: 'A numerous tenantry having the right to vote,
and practically obliged to exercise that right at the dictation of their landlord,
was highly prized.... When the Emancipation Act was passed in 1829, the
forty-shilling freeholders were disfranchised, and, being no longer of use
to their landlords, every means has since been employed to get rid of them.'
The Condition and Prospects of Ireland, by Jonathan Pim, late MP for Dublin city.
'It is in vain to deny or to conceal the truth in respect to that franchise
(the forty-shilling franchise). It was, until a late period, the instrument through
which the landed aristocracy — the resident and the absentee proprietor —
maintained their local influence through which property had its weight, its
legitimate weight, in the national representation. The landlord has been
disarmed by the priest.... That weapon which (the landlord) has forged with
so much care, and has heretofore wielded with such success, has broken
short in his hand.' — Mr Peel's speech in the House of Commons, 5 March
1829, introducing the Catholic Relief Bill.
    Leaving out the 'legitimate weight' of landed proprietors, as exercised
through the forty-shilling freeholders, the above statement, besides being
a remarkable one from such a cautious Minister, is not far from being correct.

Chapter 2: The blight arrives

1. *Morning Post*, 11 September.
2. *Ipswich Gazette*, 9 September.
3. *Cambridge Chronicle* for September.
4. *Freeman's Journal*, 4 November.
5. The letter is dated Cork, 22 November 1845.
6. All the emphases in the quotations are Mr Foster's own.
7. The last short sentence about the 'low estimate' was not quoted by Sir Robert,
   although it immediately follows the previous one in the portion of the

communication given in the *Memoirs*, part 3, page 171.

8. *Memoirs*, part 3, p. 143.
9. The remedies which Dean Hoare said the people were 'slow' to adopt were proved to be worthless and in some instances even pernicious. The steward on Mr Leslie's estate in Monaghan wrote that 'The potatoes dug and arranged according to the advice of the Government Commissioners had become diseased and useless.' On the very day the Dean's letter was written, there was a meeting of the landlords of Cavan held; and in a report emanating from that meeting, signed by Lord Farnham, the following passage occurs: 'With reference to the potatoes stored with solid substance, or packing stuff, intervening in any form, in pit, on floors, or lofts, the use of packing stuff appears to be highly prejudicial. In the words of an extensive contractor the heap becomes "a mass of mortar".' The report adds: 'This description includes the plan of pitting recommended by her Majesty's Commissioners, which we strongly deprecate.'
10. *Memoirs*, part 3, p. 123.

Chapter 3: Government reaction

1. Letter of 17 October: Robert Peel's *Memoirs*, part 3.
2. Writer of the article Sir Robert Peel, in *Encycl. Brit.*
3. *Memoirs*, part 3, p. 100.
4. Ibid.
5. Ibid., p. 98.
6. Ibid., p. 113.
7. Ibid., p. 119.
8. Ibid.
9. Ibid., p. 121.
10. *Quarterly Review*, September 1846.
11. *Memoirs*, part 3, p. 131.
12. Ibid., p. 132.
13. Ibid. p. 134.
14. Ibid., p. 158.
15. It is a great pity we have not this Mem. before us. It was returned to Lord Stanley, at his request, and Sir Robert says he kept no copy of it.
16. *Memoirs*, part 3, p. 181.
17. Ibid., p. 185.
18. 'You will have heard the termination of our attempt to form a government. All our plans were frustrated by Lord Grey.' T.B. (Lord) Macaulay's letter to J.F M'Farlane, 23 December 1845.
19. *Memoirs*, part 3, p. 259.

Chapter 4: More talk in the Commons

1. Smith O'Brien occupied far more of the time and attention of the House of Commons, during the session, by his refusal to serve on a railway committee than by his speeches. This refusal gave rise to some delicate questions of constitutional law, and consigned the honourable gentleman to prison for twenty-five days.
2. *Lord George Bentinck: a political biography*, fifth edition, revised, p. 158.
3. Ibid.
4. *The Irish Crisis*, by Sir Charles E. Trevelyan.
5. This observation was, in all probability, levelled at the *Dublin Evening Mail*,

a newspaper which Sir Lucius would be sure to read, being one of the organs of his party, and which had, some time before, with a heartless attempt at humour, called the blight 'the potato mirage'.

6. *The Freeman's Journal.*

7. Ibid. This correspondent tells an anecdote of a peasant whose heroic generosity contrasts strongly with the conduct of the above noble proprietors. He (the correspondent) stood by a pit of potatoes whilst the owner, a small farmer, was turning them for the purpose of picking out and rejecting the bad ones. The man informed him it was the fourth picking within a fortnight. At the first picking, he said the pit contained about sixty barrels, but they were now reduced to about ten. Whilst this conversation was going on, a beggar came up and asked an alms for God's sake. The farmer told his wife to give the poor woman some of the potatoes, adding 'Mary, give her no bad ones, God is good, and I may get work to support us'. The correspondent concluded: 'I am warranted in saying that by 10 May there will not be a single potato for twenty miles around Clonmel.'

8. There were twenty principal Government Food Depots established in various parts of Ireland in 1846, at which the following quantities were issued:

	Tons	cwts	qrs	lbs
Indian corn.................	30	00	00	00
Indian corn meal............	11,593	11	00	19
Oat meal....................	528	00	3	24
Biscuit	6	3	00	7
Total	12,157	15	0	22

R.J. Routh, Commissary General.

— *Famine Reports. Commissariat Series.* Vol. 1, p. 2.
The number of Relief Committees in this, the first year of famine, was 600. In 1847, they numbered nearly 2,000.

Chapter 5: Irish ranks split

1. *Times* of 31 July 1846.
2. The emphases are the author's.
3. Mr Mitchell evidently alludes to the passage so often found in O'Connell's speeches, commencing -
   O Erin, shall it e'er be mine
   To wreak thy wrongs in battle line, &c.

It is a curious fact that the Liberator, in the lapse of years, forgot where he had originally found the passage, as the following extract from the proceedings of the Repeal Association, on 12 April 1844 will show: 'Mr O'Connell — As Mr Steele began by correcting some errors which had crept into a published report of some of his observations, there is quite enough in that fact to justify me in following his example. The errors to which I allude appear in a book recently published by a Frenchman, the Viscount D'Arlingcourt, whom I met accidentally at Tara, and who felt somewhat surprised and mortified, on being informed that I had not heard of him before. In his work he speaks of the meeting, and he makes me state to him that six lines, which I wrote in an album he presented to me for the purpose, were my own composition. Now, I am a plain prose writer, and I neither wrote, nor said I wrote, the lines in question. You may recollect them; they are as follows:

> O Erin shall it e'er be mine,
> To wreak thy wrongs in battle line;
> To raise my victorhead and see
> Thy hills, thy dales, thy people free, -
> That glance of bliss is all I crave,
> Betwixt my labours and my grave! (Cheers)

The rhythm is perfect, the versification excellent, and my disinclination to take the parentage is not because of any defect in them; but it is a matter of fact, there is only one word which I inserted, and which I claim as my own composition — that word is "Erin". In the original lines the word was "Scotland"; they are from a poem of Miss Mitford, called "Wallace" — a poem not as well known as it ought to be.'

Mr Maurice O'Connell — 'The lines are by Miss Holcroft.'

Mr O'Connell — 'My son differs with me as to the authorship, but I cannot help that; but there is one thing we cannot dispute about, and that is, the lines are not mine.'

Although Mr Maurice O'Connell undertook to set his father right, he was equally at fault himself, for the lines are Scott's.

In *Lord of the Isles,* canto 4, stanza 30, King Robert says:

> O Scotland! shall it e'er be mine
> To wreak thy wrongs in battle line;
> To raise my victorhead and see
> Thy hills, thy dales, thy people free, -
> That glance of bliss is all I crave,
> Betwixt my labours and my grave.
> Then down the hill he slowly went, etc.

4. The author was present at the two days' discussion. As Smith O'Brien, on leaving, went towards the door, several persons, seizing him by the hands and arms, said to him, in a spirit of earnest but friendly appeal: 'Sure you are not going away, Mr O'Brien?' He only answered by a determined shake of his head and moved on. For some time after the departure of Smith O'Brien and his supporters silent depression reigned in the hall. John Augustus O'Neill, in an eloquent speech, endeavoured to put the meeting in good spirits again, but with very limited success. Every one seemed to feel that a great calamity had occurred. O'Brien and Mitchel spoke with cool, collected determination — more especially the latter. John O'Connell took his stand on the Rules of the Association, as embodied in the Peace Resolutions. I was near him during his speech on each day; and, although evidently labouring under the gravity of the occasion, he never ceased to be master of himself. His style was clear, but his voice being neither powerful nor resonant, he failed to make that impression upon his hearers which was warranted by his reasoning. Meagher's delivery of the sword speech had more of ostentation than grace in it. A common gesture of his (if it can be called such) was to place his arms akimbo, and turn his head a little to one side, suggesting the idea that this attitudinising was meant to attract admiration to himself rather than to his argument. His voice was good, but his intonation unmusical, and he invariably ended his sentences on too high a note; but his fiery rhetoric carried the audience almost completely with him and he was cheered again and again to the echo.

5. Many a fine, stalwart peasant said to me, during the great era of the Monster Meetings, 'I'm afraid, sir, we'll never get the union without fighting for it.' I know for a fact that wives and daughters and sisters endeavoured to

dissuade fathers and husbands and brothers from going to the great Tara meeting — suspecting, as they said, that 'bad work would come out of it', ie. fighting.

6. *Daily and Weekly Press. Census of Ireland, 1851.*
7. *Correspondence relating to the measures adopted for the relief of the distress in Ireland (Commissariat Series),* p. 3.
8. This estimate is said to have been compiled from the best available sources for *Thom's Almanac and Directory* for 1847. The quantity of potatoes in each of the four Provinces, and their probable value were:

Ulster,	352,665 acres, valued at	....	£4,457,562
Munster,	460,630 ,,	,, ...	6,030,739 10s
Leinster,	217,854 ,,	,, ...	2,814,150
Connaught,	206,292 ''	''	2,645,468
	1,237,441		£15,947,919 10s

9. Letters on the state of Ireland, by the Earl of Rosse: London, 1847. *Halliday Pamphlets,* Vol. 1993. These letters were originally sent to the *Times,* but that journal having refused them insertion, the noble author published them in a pamphlet. The Rev. Theobald Mathew said: 'I do not know on what authority that two millions of acres of potatoes were irrevocably lost, being worth to those who raised them £20 an acre. This estimate would make the loss £40,000,000.'

10. *Mayne on the Potato Failure.* The potato crop, for the most part, continued to look well up to the end of July, but the blight had appeared, in the most decided way, during the first half of that month, although not then very apparent to a casual observer. Mr Mayne, like many persons at the time, attributed the blight to an insect which some called *Aphis vastator,* others *Thrips minutissima.* There was a glass case in the Dublin Exhibition of 1853, showing this insect feeding on the leaves and stalks of the potato plant. Mr Mayne and those who agreed with him, seem, in this instance, to have mistaken cause for effect. Indeed the insect, it would appear, was a natural parasite of the potato, and some observers have gone so far as to assert that the *Aphis Vastator* abounded more on healthy plants than upon those affected with the blight.

11. Letter to the Duke of Leinster quoted in *Irish Census* for 1851. M. Zander, of Boitzenberg, in Prussia, published, about this time, a method by which full-sized potatoes could be produced in one year from the seed, and he further stated that the seedlings so produced had resisted the blight. The old idea was that it took three years to produce full-sized potatoes from the seed. M. Zander's method was tried in various parts of Ireland and England, its chief peculiarity being that the seed was sown on a light hot bed and the plants so produced were transferred to the ground in which they were to produce the crop. Full-sized potatoes were the result, each plant producing, on an average, 1½ lb of potatoes, or rather more than 29 tons to the Irish acre. This method appeared satisfactory to those who interested themselves about it, but it does to seem to have been followed up.

12. *Proceedings of the Royal Dublin Society.* This opinion as to fogs preceding or accompanying the potato blight was corroborated from various parts of the United Kingdom. A correspondent of the *Gardener's Chronicle,* wrote on 14 November 1846: 'In the early part of August 1846 there was not a diseased potato in the North Riding of Yorkshire. Late in August, I think the 25th, a very thick dense fog prevailed. The air was not, however, at all chill. The heat and closeness was most oppressive. This continued all night, and

anything similar to it I never before saw, with so high a temperature. It occurred also on the following night. On the morning after the fog, the whole of the potato fields have precisely the disorganised appearance they have after a night's frost. They soon became black, and the disease followed in a very few days.'

In the *Gardener's Chronicle* of 5 September, it is mentioned that shortly before, and about the time the disease appeared at Aberdeen, 'there was a succession of unusually dense fogs, followed by great warmth.'

In one of the Orkney Islands it was remarked by a farmer that 'a very dense fog rested in patches on certain parts of the island; at times it was so defined, that the observer could point out the exact measure of ground over which it rested. It hung low, and had the appearance of a light powdering of snow. In passing, it fell down on his small farm, and he smelt it very unpleasant, exactly like, he says, the bilge water of a ship — a sulphurous sort of stench. After the wind rose and cleared off those clouds or lumps of fog, there remained on the grass over which they had hung, as well as on the potato shaws [stalks], an appearance of grey dew or hoar frost. The next morning he noticed the leaves of his potatoes slightly spotted.... Before ten days, not a shaw was in his potato patch more than if it had been a bare fallow . . . . Everywhere through the island, the disease, after the fog, began in spots and corners of fields, and spread more slowly over all.' *Observations on the probable cause of the Failure of the Potato Crop*, by David Milne, Esq., p. 37. *Halliday Pamphlets*, Vol. 1,994.

13. Public letter of 26 August.

14. In the debate on the 'Fever (Ireland) Bill,' on 18 March, Mr Scrope said he must observe that he held to the opinion that the first resource for the people of Ireland which should have been looked to, on the failure of the potato crop, should have been the oats which they themselves had grown by the side of their potatoes, and that the burden should have been thrown upon the Unions of taking care that a sufficient stock of those oats should have been stored to provide against necessity.

In replying to Mr Scrope, Sir James Graham called this 'a forced purchase of oats' which would be most injurious, by increasing the demand for the article. Mr Wakley, addressing himself to that observation, said he would ask, 'was not England open to the same or similar effects? Did not the guardians of the poor in this country make purchases upon the spot? Surely, meat, flour and other provisions for the workhouses were purchased in the immediate neighbourhood of such workhouses — in short, was not everything given in the workhouses obtained in the immediate vicinity of them?' *Hansard*, Vol. 150. Columns 1168 and 1191.

15. 'Gentlemen, when I reflect that as much as £30,000,000 of money have been expended in one year in contending with foreign countries for objects of infinitely less importance to us.'

Sir H.W. Barron (interrupting) '£30,000,000 per annum.'

Lord Stuart — 'I stated so — infinitely of less importance than assisting to relieve an immensity of our fellow-countrymen from starvation. I have not, nor can I feel, any distrust in those to whom her Majesty has entrusted the government of the country so as to believe they could hesitate ... in granting a sixth of that sum for rendering Ireland prosperous and contented.' — Speech of Lord Stuart de Decies at Dungarvan, recommending the Government to reclaim the waste lands, 13 November 1846.

16. 'I have visited the wasted remnants of the once noble red man, on his reservation grounds in North America, and explored the ''negro quarter'' of the degraded and enslaved African, but never have I seen misery so intense, or physical degradation so complete, as among the dwellers in the

bog-holes of Erris.' *Visit to Connaught in the Autumn of 1847,* by James H. Tuke of York.
17. Ante, p. 158.

Chapter 6: Government 'aid'

1. This rule gave great dissatisfaction, the wages in many places being already far too low, in proportion to the price of provisions. When the Cork deputation waited on Lord John Russell, the Chancellor of the Exchequer said, in reply to Rev. Mr Gibson, that the Minute of the Lords of the Treasury requiring that wages should be twopence under the standard of the country was not the law, and if necessary could be modified.
2. The emphases are their lordships'.
3. Letter to Mr Trevelyan, *Commissariat Series,* Part 1, p. 439, who did not like it all, and sent in reply, on the part of the Treasury, an elaborate defence of high prices and large profits; although the people in many districts could only purchase one meal a day with the wages they received on the public works, as is testified by Commissary-General Dobree's letter (p. 444); and by numberless other letters from almost every part of the country; hence men in full employment on the Government works died of starvation, or of dysentery produced by it. And why should they not? They were earning 8¼d. a day at task work, whilst meal was 3s. a stone; and the next shop in which it was sold for that sum was often a great distance from them — in some cases twenty, and even twenty-five miles!
   The following paragraph went the round of the newspapers at the close of December: 'A fact for Lord John Russell. Mr Bianconi, ex Mayor of Clonmel, had shipped to him on 14 December, at New York, a small lot of best Indian corn, at twenty-three shillings per quarter of 480 lbs.; and the same post which brought the invoice brought a letter stating the price at Liverpool was seventy-two shillings. What will Lord John Russell say to this?'
4. *Board of Works' Series,* Vol. L., p. 97.
5. The Case of Ireland, &c., contained in two letters to the Right Hon. Henry Labouchere, Chief Secretary of Ireland, by the Rev. William Prior Moore, A.M., Cavan, p. 6. *Halliday Pamphlets,* Vol. 1991.
6. The Case of Ireland, &c., p. 11.
7. Ibid. p. 11,12. The emphases in the quotations are Mr Moore's.

Chapter 7: Relief — of sorts!

1. Letter in *Commissariat Series of Blue Books,* Vol. I., p. 360.
2. Ibid. p. 349.
3. Mr Brett, County Surveyor of Mayo to the Board of Works. *Board of Works Series of Blue Books,* Vol. L, p. 125.
4. 'Employment, with wages in cash is the general outcry.'- Commissary – Gen. Hewetson to Mr Trevelyan; *Commissariat Series,* p. 12.
5. 'Those at taskwork had fivepence, and in some cases as low as threepence per diem. In other cases, again, an opposite extreme existed, and as much as two shillings and twopence per diem was found in two instances to have been paid.... I fear there was not, in all cases, sufficient sympathy for the present sufferings of the poor — a feeling quite compatible with a firm and honest discharge of duty. This inflames the minds of the people against the system generally, and they become victims alike to their own intemperance, and the mismanagement of those placed over them. Throughout the country,

in the majority of cases, disturbances are attributable wholly, or in a great degree, to such errors, overseers acting more as slave-drivers than as the messengers of benevolence to an afflicted but warm-hearted people.' *A Twelvemonth's Residence in Ireland during the Famine and the Public Works, with suggestions to meet the coming crisis.* By William Henry Smith, C.E., late conducting Engineer of Public Works. London, 1848, p. 94.

Again: 'I much regretted leaving, and but for the circumstance of some imperative engagements recalling me to London, my intended sojourn of two or three months, which I originally named to the Commissioners, would probably have been prolonged even beyond what it eventually was, amongst a people whom I saw no reason to fear, even when using necessary severity, but on the contrary every reason to admire, from their strongly affectionate dispositions and resignation in deep suffering: they treated it as the will of God, and murmured, ''Thy will be done.''' Ibid, p. 18.

6. 'In cases where disturbances arose in any one district, the works of the whole barony were suspended, inflicting injury upon all, the guilty and innocent indiscriminately.' Ibid, p. 93.
7. See Note from Mr Smith's valuable book, *A Twelvemonth's Residence in Ireland.*
8. He thus complains in italics: 'None of the gentry will take our part except one.' *Board of Works Blue Books,* Vol. L, p. 352, Appendix.
9. 'The works under 9 and 10 Vic., c. 107, are sanctioned for sake of the relief and not for sake of the works themselves.' Mr Trevelyan to Lieut-Colonel Jones, 5 October 1846.
10. Memorial to Lord John Russell, 14 December 1846.
11. *Board of Works Blue Books,* Vol. L (50), p. 352.
12. Another account makes it only 376,133. It is easy to see that perfect accuracy with regard to the number of persons employed on the works at any given time was, for obvious reasons, not to be attained. The figures given above from the official returns are, therefore, only an approximation to the truth, but they may be accepted as substantially correct.

Chapter 8: The Famine worsens

1. *Commissariat Series,* p. 6.
2. Ibid. p. 15
3. Ibid. p. 16.
4. Treasury Minute, 29 September. *Commissariat Series,* p. 63.
5. Letter to Mr Trevelyan, dated 19 September. *Commissariat Series* p. 80.
6. *Commissariat Series,* p. 208.
7. *Cork Examiner.*
8. MS. Memoir of his experience during the Famine, kindly written for the author by Daniel Donovan, Esq., MD, Skibbereen.
9. *Commissariat Series,* part I, p. 46.
10. *Commissariat Series,* part I, p. 55.
11. Ibid. p. 50.
12. *Commissariat Series,* p. 122.
13. Mr Trevelyan gave the following caution to the Commissary-General at Malta: 'I am told that the Egyptian wheat is mixed with the mud of the Nile; and if such be the case, it will, of course, be washed before it is ground.' *Commissariat Series,* p. 156.
    Salm was the word used at Malta for 'quarter', being, probably, a corruption of the Spanish *salma,* a ton.
14. In some parts of Ireland there existed a custom of boiling new wheat in this manner, but without steeping. It was merely intended as a mess for children,

in order to give them the first of the wheat at reaping time, but was not continued as a mode of cooking it. This mess was called in Irish *grán brúite*, boiled or cooked grain.

Chapter 9: What did the landlords do?

1. 'It cannot be too strongly lamented, the opportunity which has been lost for the present, of adopting reproductive employment; but it is not now a question of productive or non-productive employment, it is a question of life or death to those famishing and destitute, anxiously waiting for the means of procuring food.... A general and well-digested Drainage Bill, applicable to Ireland, cannot be hastily prepared; if so it may be again a nugatory one, and it is some great measure, and great expenditure for some years to come, under a Drainage and reclaiming of waste lands Bill, that is to be of permanent and effectual relief to this impoverished country.' Mr Lambert of Brookhill's letter to the Lord Lieutenant, 4 October.
2. *Irish Crisis,* p. 68.
3. See inquest on Jeremiah Hegarty, p. 149.
4. This view differs considerably from that put forward in the Memorial of the twenty-fifth of the previous month, in which the Society tell his Excellency, 'that, from their experience as the Royal Agriculture Improvement Society of Ireland, they are confident that every part of this country affords the opportunity of at once employing the rural population in the improvement of the soil, and of returning to the ratepayers a large interest for the capital expended, and thus providing an increased quantity of food and certain employment for the working classes in future years.'
5. Letter to Edward Bullen, Esq., Secretary to the Royal Agricultural Society.
6. A weight of potatoes in the South of Ireland varied from 21 to 23lb.
7. A driver or bailiff is a man employed by Irish landlords to warn tenants of the rent day, serve notices upon them, watch their movements, see how they manage their farms, play the detective in a general way and supply useful information to the landlord and his agent. They are regarded with pretty much the same feelings as tithe-proctors were, until that historic class became extinct. They are called drivers by the people, because one of their duties is to drive tenants' cattle off their lands, that they may be sold for the rent. When a peasant wishes to speak politely of this functionary he calls him 'a kind of under agent'. 'There are many parts in Ireland in which a driver and a process-server — the former a man whose profession it is to seize the cattle of a tenant whose rent is in arrear, the latter an agent for the purpose of ejecting him — form regular parts of the landlord's establishment. There are some in which the driver, whether employed or not, receives an annual payment from every tenant'. *Journals, Conversations and Essays relating to Ireland,* Nassau William Senior, Second Edition, Vol. 1, p.33.
8. An Irish word, so given in the report, but more correctly *creacan* or *criocan*. It is used to express anything diminutive. When applied to potatoes, it means they are small and bad.
9. Letter of Rev. B. Durcan, PP, Swinford, 16 November 1846.
10. The Windmill is a bare rock, or collection of rocks, which was used as a fair field. It overlooks the town. It derives its name from the fact that a windmill had been formerly in use there. Hence, several lanes leading to it are called Windmill Lane. *Letter* from Rev. C. Davis, Administrator of Skibbereen.
11. Letter of Rev. R. Henry, PP, Islandeady.

12. Special Correspondent of *The Cork Examiner,* writing from Skibbereen, 14 December 1846.
13. 'The first case of death, clearly established, as arising from starvation, occurred at South Reen, five miles from the town of Skibbereen. The case having been reported to me, as a member of the Relief Committee, I procured the attendance of Dr Dore and proceeded to the house where the body lay. The body was resting on a basket which had been turned up; the head reclined on an old chair; the legs were on the ground. All was wretchedness around. The wife, miserable and emaciated, was unable to move and four children, more like spectres than living beings, were lying near the fire place, in which, apparently, there had not been a fire for some time. The doctor, of course, at once communicated with the Committee.' *Letter* of Mr McCarthy Downing MP, to the author.
14. MS. Memoir of his famine experiences, by Dr Donovan. 'Up to this morning, I, like a large portion, I fear, of the community, looked on the diaries of Dr Donovan, as published in *The Cork Southern Reporter,* to be highly coloured pictures, doubtless intended for a good and humane purpose; but I can now, with perfect confidence, say that neither pen nor pencil ever could portray the misery and horror, at this moment, to be witnessed in Skibbereen.' Mr Mahony, the artist of the *Illustrated London News,* in his letter from Skibbereen to that journal, 13 February 1847, p.100.

Chapter 10: Committees and resolutions

1. *The Morning Chronicle.*
2. In some reports of the speech the words are 'beggars enough for all Europe'.

Chapter 11: The railway scheme

1. *Lord Bentinck, a political biography,* Fifth Edition, p. 340.
2. Speech of Dr (later Sir John) Gray, at the Tuam Banquet, 24 January 1854.

Chapter 12: Black '47

1. Letter from Captain Wynne, Government District Inspector to Lieutenant-Colonel Jones. *Commissariat Series,* part 1, p. 438. (The emphases are Captain Wynne's.)
2. *Report of Central Relief Committee of the Society of Friends,* pp. 180-2.
3. *Census of Ireland* for the year 1851. Report on tables of deaths.
4. The circumlocutions used by relief committees and Government officials to avoid using the word Famine were so many and so remarkable that at one time I was inclined to attempt making a complete list of them. Here are a few: 'Distress', 'Destitution', 'Dearth of provisions', 'Severe destitution', 'Severe suffering', 'Extreme distress', as above; 'Extreme misery', 'Extreme destitution', etc. The Society of Friends, with honest plain speaking, almost invariably used the word 'Famine'; and they named their report *Transactions during the Famine in Ireland.'*
5. *Appendix to Report of British Association,* p.181.
6. *Report of Central Relief Committee of Society of Friends,* p. 168.
7. This Workhouse was built to accommodate 900 persons. The Fever Hospital and sheds had room for only 250.
8. *A Visit to Connaught in the Autumn of 1847,* by James H. Tuke, in a letter to the Central Committee of the Society of Friends, Dublin, p.8. At the end

of February there was a meeting of coroners in Cork, at which they came to the determination of holding no more starvation inquests.

9. Letters from Mayo to the Dublin *Freeman's Journal* signed W.G.

10. The emphases in the quotation are W.G.'s.

11. It is not to be inferred from this that evictions were rare in Ireland immediately preceding the Famine. A writer has taken the trouble of recording in a pamphlet Irish evictions, from 1840 to 3 March 1846; a period of about five years. Up to March 1846 evictions arising from the Famine had not really begun, although preparations were being made for them; so that those recorded in the pamphlet were carried out under no special pressure of circumstances whatever. The writer promises that he regards his list as far from complete, inasmuch as it was compiled chiefly from the public journals, and every evicting landlord uses all his power and precaution to keep his evictions as secret as possible. Still, it was found on record that there were over 8,000 individuals evicted in Ireland during those five years, many of the evictions being attended with much hardship and suffering, such as the removal of sick and dying persons in order to take possession. In one case a dead body was actually carried out. In two instances, comprising the dispossession of 385 individuals, the evictions took place avowedly for the purpose of bringing in Protestant tenants; in a third, 1,175 persons were evicted by a noble lord and although he did not give his reason, his name and his whole career abundantly justify the conclusion that this vast clearance was effected to make way for a Protestant colony.

12. Letter of Mr Joseph McKenna to Lord John Russell. Mr McKenna gives the names of all the parties. Yet still more dreadful is the case we read of as having occurred in Galway. A man having been sentenced for sheep-stealing in that city, it was stated to the bench by the resident magistrate 'that the prisoner and his family were starving; one of his children died and he was, he said, credibly informed that the mother ate part of its legs and feet. After its death he had the body exhumed and found that nothing but the bones remained of the legs and feet.' *Freeman's Journal*, April 1848.

13. Letter dated from Killybegs, 18 December 1846. *Report*, p. 151.

14. Count Strezelecki's report to the British Association, p. 97. 'In addition to the Government aid, large sums were distributed by the British Association, through the agency of the generous and never-to-be-forgotten Count Strezelecki.' *MS. letter* from a Mayo gentleman, in author's possession.

15. *Report*, p. 97.

16. MS notes taken down from Mr Egan.

17. Joseph Crosfield's report to the Society of Friends, p. 145.

18. James H. Tuke's report to the same Committee, p. 147.

19. In Irish *corrac*, pronounced *corrach* or *currach*. This primitive boat was made of a slight framework of timber and covered with skins, whence its name. In early times *corrachs* were used in all the British islands. They are mentioned by many Latin authors, especially by Caesar, who had several of them made after the British model.

20. Mr Tuke's report, p.148.

21. *Letter* dated from Killybegs, 18 December 1846. *Report*, p. 151.

22. *Letter* of Commander J. Cruford Caffin, RN, of Her Majesty's steam sloop *Scourge*, dated 15 February 1847 written to Captain Hamilton.

23. Assistant-Commissary Bishop's letter of 14 February 1847.

24. So he always signed himself, although Captain Caffin calls him Dr Traill.

25. Letter to Mr Trevelyan of 14 February 1847.

26. Correspondent of Dublin *Freeman's Journal*.

27. *Report: Colonisation from Ireland*. Brought from House of Lords 23 July 1847; ordered by the House of Commons to be printed 23 July 1847; pp. 243 and 244.

28. This physician had three large crosses made from the timber of a sliding or hinged coffin. One of these he kindly presented to the author, which is now in his possession. It bears the following inscription: 'During the frightful famine-plague, which devastated a large proportion of Ireland in the years 1846-47, that monstrous and unchristian machine, a 'sliding coffin', was, from necessity, used in Bantry Union for the conveyance of the victims to one common grave. The material of this cross, the symbol of our Redemption, is a portion of one of the machines, which enclosed the remains of several hundreds of our countrymen, during their passage from the wretched huts or waysides, where they died, to the pit into which their remains were thrown. T.W'.

29. *The Winter of 1846-7 in Antrim, with Remarks on Out-door Relief Colonisation.* By A. Shafto Adair, FRS London: Ridgway, 1847. *Halliday Pamphlets*, Royal Irish Academy, Vol. 1,992. Mr Adair was landlord of large possessions in County Antrim, and he exerted himself very much to alleviate the sufferings of the people during the Famine. He was raised to the Peerage in 1873 as Baron Weaveney.

Chapter 13: Expansion of public works

1. *Sunday Observer;* which journal should, for the information of posterity, have placed upon record what, if any, were the other courses in the *carte* at the Reform Club, the day on which M. Soyer's Irish Soup No.1 was so highly approved of.

2. *The comparative nutritive and pecuniary value of various kinds of cooked food,* by John Aldridge, MD, MRIA, read at a meeting of the Royal Dublin Society on 6 April 1847.

3. *Freeman's Journal,* 6 April.

4. *Evening Packet.*

5. He did not even escape the shafts of ridicule. A writer in the Dublin *Nation,* imitating the witches' scene in *Macbeth,* thus attacked him:

   1st Cook — Round about the boiler go,
   In twice fifty gallons throw
   Water that in noisome tank
   Mossed with verdure rich and rank.

   2nd Cook — Shin of beef from skinny cow
   In the boiler then you'll throw;
   Onion sliced and turnip top,
   Crumb of bread and cabbage chop.

   3rd Cook — Scale of cod fish, spiders' tongues,
   Tomtits' gizzards, head and lungs
   Of a famished, French-fed frog,
   Root of phaytee digged in bog, etc.

6. The Commission of 1809 on the reclamation of the bogs of Ireland returned as improvable:

   1,576,000 acres of flat bog
   1,254,000 acres of mountain top bog
   2,070,000 acres of convertible mountain bog
   _____
   4,900,000 acres in all.

7. The number of persons employed on the public works reached its highest point in March 1847, viz., 734,000. But this was the average for the whole month. Before the Committee of the House of Lords on 'Colonisation from Ireland', Captain Larcom, one of the Commissioners of Public Works, said that the Commissioners expected the number employed on those works to rise to 900,000 in June and July, having risen to 740,000 when the first stoppage took place on 20 March, at which time they were increasing at the rate of 20,000 weekly. — *Answer to Question 2,547*, p.265.
8. *Freeman's Journal.*
9. At length, in the seventh month, this system of relief reached its height. In that month, 3,020,712 persons received daily rations. Even under this gigantic system of relief, we found that our distribution could not be discontinued. There were several classes of persons whose claims we were bound to recognise, and in these cases relief was still afforded, though on a reduced scale, and with considerable caution.' *Transactions during the Famine in Ireland*, the Society of Friends.
10. This was up to 15 October only, but on 31 December, when the account was finally closed, Mr Bromley, the head accountant, said: Total expended to this day, £1,724,631 17s. 3d.
11. *Irish Crisis.*

Chapter 14: Fever — and emigration

1. *Census of Ireland* for the decade of years ending 1851. Tables of deaths. Vol. 1, p. 277. quotation from *Dublin Quarterly Medical Journal.*
2. See *Census of Ireland*, from 1841 to 1851, Tables of deaths, Vol. 1, p. 296.
3. Dr H. Kennedy, in *Dublin Quarterly Journal.*
4. Census returns.
5. Those admissions increased to 110,381 in 1848.
6. The percentage of deaths of the cholera, which succeeded to this fever in 1849, was forty-two one-fifth.
7. *Census of Ireland* for the year 1851. Report on tables of deaths.
8. Report of Commissioners of Health.
9. It is pleasant to know that the settlement at Peterborough continued to flourish, as the following extract from the late John F. Maguire's *The Irish in America* will show: 'The shanty, and the wigwam, and the log-hut have long since given place to the mansion of brick and stone; and the hand-sleigh and the rude cart to the strong wagon and the well-appointed carriage. Where there was but one miserable grist mill, there are now mills and factories of various kinds. And not only are there spacious schools under the control of those who erected and made use of them for their children, but the 'heavy grievance' which existed in 1825 has long since been a thing of the past. The little chapel of logs and shingle — 18 feet by 20 in which the settlers of that day knelt in gratitude to God, has for many years been replaced by a noble stone church, through whose painted windows the Canadian sunlight streams gloriously, and in which two thousand worshippers listen with the old Irish reverence to the words of their pastor. The tones of the pealing organs swell in solemn harmony, where the simple chaunt of the first settlers was raised in the midst of the wilderness; and for miles round may the voice of the great bell, swinging in its lofty tower, be heard in the calm of the Lord's day, summoning the children of Saint Patrick to worship in the faith of their fathers.' — *The Irish in America*, by John F. Maguire, MP London, 1868, p. 110.
10. Quoted in *Report of Committee of the House of Lords on Colonisation from Ireland in 1847*, p. 7.

11. Quoted in *Report of Committee of the House of Lords on Colonisation from Ireland in 1847*, p. 10.
12. Sessional Papers, 1846, No. 24.
13. The Census Commissioners, whose Emigration Statistics are used, do not add the one-and-a-half per cent for probable births; hence they state the number of emigrants between 1831 and 1841 at 403,459 only.
14. *Census Returns* for 1851 — Tables of deaths, p. 227-8.
15. *Census of Ireland* for the year 1851 — Report on table of deaths, p. 278. *Thom's Directory* for 1848, p. 126.
16. One-and-a-half million emigrants was the number contemplated by Mr Godley's scheme, but his opinion was that there would be 'a parallel stream of half a million, drawn out by the attraction of the new Irish colony, which would make the whole emigration two millions'.
17. Public letter.
18. Reply to M.J. O'Connell, MP, W.H. Gregory, MP, and John R. Godley, Secretaries to the Canadian Colonisation Scheme; 9 April 1847.
19. Taken from *Thom's Almanack* for 1853, p.252. The census of 1851 gives only the emigration for the first three months of that year. The number of emigrants in 1852 was largely in excess of those of 1851.
20. 'At Quebec in particular, we read that "the mortality is appalling"; it was denominated the ship fever'. *British American Journal*. 'Upwards of £100,000 was expended in relieving the sick and destitute emigrants landed in Canada in 1847.' Nicholls' *History of the Irish Poor Law*, p. 327 — *note*.
21. Dr Stratten, in *Edinburgh Medical and Surgical Journal*, quoted by Census Commissioners for 1851 in p.305 of their Report on tables of deaths.
22. *The Irish in America*, by John Francis Maguire, p. 186.
23. *Report of Commissioners of Emigration for the State of New York*, quoted by Mr Maguire.
24. Dr Stratten in *Edinburgh Medical and Surgical Journal*.
25. *Twelve months' residence in Ireland during the Famine and the Public Works*, by William Henry Smith, CE, late conducting engineer of Public Works, p. 92.
26. *Report* p. 27. *Halliday Pamphlets*, Vol. 1990.
27. *Report*, pp. 29, 30.
28. Ibid., pp. 33, 34.
29. Ibid., pp. 54, 55.
30. Ibid., p. 73
31. The report of the Emigration Commissioners for 1873 (issued 28 October 1874) gives the following facts. In the course of last year 310,612 emigrants sailed from the ports of the United Kingdom, being a larger number than in any year since 1854. Of these, 123,343 were English, 83,692 Irish, 21,310 Scotch, 72,198 foreigners, who had merely touched at British ports, and 10,929 whose nationality was not ascertained. The remittances of Irish emigrants to their friends at home were as usual very large, the total sum being, according to the information within reach of the Commissioners, £724,040. This includes the remittances of both the United States and Canada. Of this sum £341,722 came in the shape of prepaid passages, more than sufficient, says the Report, to defray the cost of steerage passages at £6.6s. each for the 83,692 Irish who emigrated within the year. *Thirty-first General Report of the Emigration Commissioners*, p.4.

Chapter 15: The good — and bad — donors

1. The first Queen's letter produced £170,571 0s. 10d.; the second only £30,167 14s. 4d.

2. *Transactions of Society of Friends during the Famine in Ireland*, p. 49.
3. Ibid., Appendix VII, p. 334.
4. *The connection between Famine and Pestilence, and the Great Apostasy*, Nagnatus, p. 49, P.D. Hardy, Dublin, 1847. *Halliday Pamphlets*, Vol. 1990.
5. The *Achill Missionary Herald* for August 1846, p. 88.
6. *The Famine, a rod*. By the Rev. Hugh McNeill, p. 23.
7. Ibid., pp. 25,26. The emphases are Mr McNeill's.
8. Letter quoted in *Forster's Life of Dickens*, written in the Autumn of 1846. Vol. II, p. 233.
9. *'Journals, Conversations, and Essays relating to Ireland*, Nassau William Senior, Vol. II, Second Edition, p. 60.
10. *'Memorandums made in Ireland in the Autumn of 1852.'* John Forbes, MD, FRS, Hon. DCL Oxon., Physician to Her Majesty's Household, Vol. 1, pp. 246 and 247. Dr Forbes was afterwards knighted.
11. Letter of McCarthy Downing, Esq., MP, to the author, dated Prospect House, Co. Cork, 31 August 1874.

Index

(References to Notes in italics)